Conundrums for the Long Week-End

Conundrums
for the
Long Week-End

England, Dorothy L. Sayers,
and Lord Peter Wimsey

Robert Kuhn McGregor, with Ethan Lewis

The Kent State University Press
KENT, OHIO, & LONDON

© 2000 by The Kent State University Press, Kent, Ohio 44242
All rights reserved
Library of Congress Catalog Card Number 00-036876
ISBN 0-87338-665-5
Manufactured in the United States of America

07 06 05 04 03 02 01 00   5 4 3 2 1

Library of Congress Cataloging-in-Publication Data
McGregor, Robert Kuhn, 1952–
Conundrums for the long week-end: England, Dorothy L. Sayers,
and Lord Peter Wimsey / Robert Kuhn McGregor, with Ethan Lewis.
p. cm.
Includes bibliographical references and index.
ISBN 0-87338-665-5 (alk. paper) ∞
1. Sayers, Dorothy L. (Dorothy Leigh), 1893–1957—Characters—Lord Peter Wimsey.
2. Detective and mystery stories, English—History and criticism.
3. Wimsey, Peter, Lord (Fictitious character)
I. Lewis, Ethan, 1964–   II. Title.

PR6037.A95 Z78 2000
823'.912–dc21   00-036876

British Library Cataloging-in-Publication data are available.

Contents

Acknowledgments

WE HAVE ARGUED MUCH OVER THE MAIN TITLE OF THIS BOOK, while reaching common ground on the subtitle very easily. This is a book about England, Dorothy L. Sayers, and Lord Peter Wimsey. The ordering of the three subjects is arbitrary; the choices are not. We have endeavored to treat each theme equally: England in its history, Sayers in her artistry, and Lord Peter in his development as a fictional character. We are most interested in exploring the mutual influences of these themes — how each affected and shaped the others. Our claim to originality is in this treatment; certainly any number of authors have treated these topics separately and well. We seek to weave them together, to make a whole and coherent story of Sayers's development of Wimsey as a reflection of English history. In doing so, we have carefully contemplated Dorothy L. Sayers's fictional work in all its nuances. We have also relied heavily on the foundations laid by generations of excellent scholars.

If we have employed an interpretive model, it is that of Modris Ecksteins, presented in his thoughtful and provocative *Rights of Spring: The Great War and the Birth of the Modern Age*. Ecksteins argues that the first years of the twentieth century saw the outbreak of cultural warfare in Europe. On the one side stood England: traditional, conservative, the image of restrictive morality and good sportsmanship. On the opposite bank stood Germany (and the United States): antihistorical, experimental, technologically oriented, modern. The Great War saw the clash of these cultural identities. Britain and her allies emerged victorious, but at the cost of their own cultural disintegration. Postwar England embraced Germany's modern world. Peter Wimsey's career, we argue, traces the painful process of that modernization.

Many historians, professional and amateur, have addressed the story of England between the world wars. We have taken our tone—and some of our history—from *The Long Week-End,* the work of Robert Graves and Alan Hodge. Both were Oxford scholars, neither a historian in the professional sense. Written on the very eve of World War II, their book provides a contemporary look backward over the previous twenty years, concentrating on the social aspects of Britain's modernization.

Historical information on the period derives from a list of academics far too long to enter here, though we must recognize the critically important work of two scholars. Jay Winter has authored several excellent books on the Great War and its aftermath in Britain; our understanding of the war's impact would prove sadly inadequate without his work. In viewing Sayers's work in this historical context, the concept was pioneered by Terrance L. Lewis in his *Dorothy L. Sayers' Wimsey and Interwar British Society.* Lewis studies Sayers's fiction in the analytical framework of ethnicity, class, and gender so familiar to modern historians.

Turning to the study of Dorothy L. Sayers, we again confront a very long list of most able scholars. Janet Hitchman perhaps paved the way with her most controversial *Such a Strange Lady.* James Brabazon became the first to construct a biography employing essentially all of Sayers's private letters and papers. In our work, we have relied most heavily on the exhaustive research of Barbara Reynolds, whose biography, *Dorothy L. Sayers: Her Life and Soul,* provides the basic life chronicle we follow. Reynolds also edited the two volumes of Sayers's published correspondence, an unparalleled mine of information.

A bewildering array of writers have contributed their thoughts and perspectives on Sayers and her work. Two indispensable collections are *As Her Whimsey Took Her,* edited by Margaret P. Hanay, and *Dorothy L. Sayers: The Centenary Celebration,* edited by Alzina Stone Dale. Dale's research was also the main source of information on Sayers's uncompleted manuscript, "Thrones, Dominations," before its completion and publication by Jill Paton Walsh in 1998.

Our guides through the maze of Sayers material, primary and secondary, published and unpublished, were three in number. Robert B.

Harmon and Margaret A. Burger's *An Annotated Guide to the Works of Dorothy L. Sayers* provides an instructive listing of Sayers's published work organized by type. C. B. Gilbert's *Bibliography of the Works of Dorothy L. Sayers* was especially valuable as a handbook to Sayers's unpublished writings. Ruth Tanis Youngberg's *Dorothy L. Sayers: A Reference Guide* provides an exhaustive listing of secondary perspectives on Sayers, though it is unfortunately becoming rather dated.

Our essential sources for analysis, the Lord Peter stories, are all fortunately still in print. For the sake of consistency, we have employed the large format HarperPerennial series issued in 1993 (with the exception of *The Nine Tailors,* still published by Harcourt Brace Jovanovich). Seeking to expand our analysis beyond this readily available material, we have made extensive use of the unpublished Lord Peter material included in the Marion Wade Collection, Wheaton College, Wheaton, Illinois. Alicia Pearson, assistant archivist at the Marion E. Wade Center, provided invaluable assistance.

Our fervent desire to gratefully acknowledge our more personal debts is tempered by the fear that we may inadvertently leave someone out. We do thank everyone who has offered wisdom and encouragement, to say nothing of patience, to this project. Our editors, Julia J. Morton and Erin L. Holman, have been steadfast in their support from the outset, which has meant a great deal to us. We also owe a great debt to Professor Marty S. Knepper of Morningside College, Sioux City, Iowa, reader appointed by the Press, who said just the right things at just the right times while offering several most-constructive suggestions. Rest assured that our aversion to conjunctions is not her fault.

Closer to home, several people materially assisted in the formative stages of this work. The students in our team-taught Liberal Studies Colloquium, offered in Spring 1997, set us on the track. As the thing took shape on paper, our long-suffering readers, Deborah Kuhn McGregor and Judy Everson, saw us through the early incarnations. We bounced ideas off virtually the entirety of the history and English faculties at the University of Illinois–Springfield (and some others as well), including Cecilia Cornell, Larry Shiner, Bill Siles, Steve Egger, Jackie Jackson, Karen Moranski, Razak Dahmane, and Norman Hinton. John Holtz, Linda Kopecky, and Denise Greene shepherded our odd requests through the library. We burdened the history graduate assistant, Carol Watson Lubrant, with our most abstruse research challenges (When do peaches ripen in England?). The dean of Liberal Arts and Sciences, William Bloe-mer, and his assistant Cherrill Kimbro, saw us through the bureaucratic mazes, while Julie Atwell made certain we met our academic obligations.

Our families exhibited remarkable forbearance with the peculiari-ties of the scholar's existence. Deborah McGregor, Molly Meyersohn, Leaf, Blue, Janna, and Bran McGregor; Corrine Frisch and Nora Frisch; Michael Lewis, Eleanor M. Lewis, Sylvia Lewis, Dora Midman, June McGregor—we bow to one and all.

Two stubborn and opinionated scholars trying to write a single book—this has proved an intriguing experience. Allow us to provide a bit of the flavor of our interaction:

RKM: "I need five or ten pages on the modernist writers, as soon as possible!"

EL: "No problem. Will next Tuesday be soon enough?"

RKM: "Next Tuesday? I need it this afternoon."

EL: "This afternoon? That's not possible. How about tomorrow afternoon?"

RKM: "Well, to be honest, I kind of needed it yesterday."

We are glad that we have brought this to successful conclusion and that we are still friends. We may even teach that class together again sometime.

Introduction:
England, Sayers, and Lord Peter

HE BEGAN EXISTENCE IN THE YEAR 1920, THE INCIDENTAL product of a lively imagination at play. Before bowing from the stage forever some twenty-two years later,[1] he acquired enough flesh and blood to defy the will of his creator. Lord Peter Wimsey—brooding amateur detective, aristocratic man of fashion, talented musician and intellectual, wealthy collector of first editions—had become a recognizable man to legions of readers throughout the western world. His enduring presence is a tribute to the care and genius of Dorothy L. Sayers, the woman who dreamed him up during a long, tumultuous sojourn in Normandy.

Sayers was a striking example of the "new woman" of the early twentieth century, educated at Oxford University and determined to make her own way in the world. Her presence in France in 1920 suggests the nature of her escape from the bonds of Victorian gender roles: she was unescorted, working as assistant to a young scholar whom she wished to love. Sayers, all of twenty-six years old, could only dimly recognize her own participation in the great social upheaval beginning to shape the twentieth century. She was a woman looking toward freedom.

In this second year after the Great War, the traditions of the prewar world were rapidly falling to pieces. Through the twenties and into the thirties, the comfortable, conservative English world of Victoria, and of Sherlock Holmes, would continue to crumble, to be brushed aside in the embrace of the modern. Women stepped up the pace of their long march toward equality with men; aristocratic privilege diminished as democracy grew; the pace of life quickened amidst a perplexing array of communication and transportation potentials; the world grew more exciting and more dangerous. F. Scott Fitzgerald called it the Jazz Age, "the most expensive orgy in history."[2] Robert Graves would remember the era as "the long week-end" between world wars.[3]

Dorothy L. Sayers established herself in these years. She reveled in the limitless possibilities, and sometimes she fell victim to their hidden pitfalls. Her story in some ways encapsulates the social transformation taking place in her time. More important is the story she told of those times, an ongoing saga of crime and detection that so capably captured the energy of postwar Britain. To read the eleven completed novels and twenty short stories that Sayers devoted to the exploits of Lord Peter Wimsey is to return to the "long week-end," when so much was possible and so much was shocking.

The ongoing appeal of this crime literature lies in its characterizations. The mysteries themselves are not terribly difficult to solve—"who done it" is generally obvious, although perceiving how it was done can be something of a chore. Like any true literary artist (and unlike too many mystery writers who rely almost exclusively on plot), Sayers lavished attention on her characters, transforming them from the one-dimensional cutouts inhabiting most popular fiction into representations of real people. Sayers's novels proved far more artistically successful than her short stories for just this reason. She needed the room the novel format offered in order to develop her characters. The short stories, necessarily emphasizing plot, seem one dimensional, suffering in comparison. To comprehend the depth of Sayers's creative ability, attention must focus largely on the novels.

Lord Peter Wimsey was Dorothy L. Sayers's single greatest project. In the two decades she devoted to his adventures, Wimsey grew enormously, reflecting the developing subtleties of his creator's enhanced understanding of her world. In the end, Wimsey was a most reflective man.[4]

He had a great deal to reflect upon. Sayers had placed Wimsey in the aristocracy—from this perspective, he could comprehend the changing British culture. Born in 1890, with one foot in the Victorian era and the other in the postwar world, Peter emerged as a balance of opposites. He became Sayers's literary embodiment of a culture trying hard to accommodate the newly modern.

The salient fact of Peter Wimsey's created life was his service in the Great War. A frontline officer, Wimsey was nearly killed at Vimy Ridge, and he later penetrated behind enemy lines as an intelligence operative. These experiences proved the watershed of his life; like millions of other Britons, he was of the class that saw and would never forget. In the early twenties, this made him a member of a social system containing only one other class: those who had not seen. The miasma of the war permeated the twenties, creating new forces and ideas, smothering the old. The Great War was the benchmark beginning the modern age.

The social transformation so obvious in the twenties was neither as abrupt nor profound as people thought. The war had the effect of darkening memories, making the prewar past seem distant and beyond reach. The movement for women's rights did not suddenly erupt in 1918; its roots extended at least to the 1870s if not as early as the 1790s. The formation of a definable working class interest had been the project of more than a century. The class system still stood for entrenched inequality, though the aristocracy was firmly on the defensive. Men and women continued to enter domestic service, though perhaps more warily.[5]

Yet the landscape, the culture, and the world differed palpably following the armistice. The automobile firmly claimed the roadways, bringing greater independence of occupation and movement to the masses. Faster and more efficient trains, ships, and even aircraft heralded a new era in transportation. Women were everywhere in public—voting, working, wearing saner garments, and attending public entertainments. Just how great a revolution in women's lives occurred is debatable, but the changes were great (and sometimes disturbing) to those living the experience. And laborers, unable to vote before 1870, elected a prime minister in 1924. The world seemed to be turning upside down, even if it was not.[6]

This lively, freer, more democratic world is the backdrop for the Wimsey stories. Dorothy L. Sayers was vitally interested in the changes taking place around her. Absorbing the spirit of her times, she interpreted its meaning and provided a running chronicle of the emergent culture. Indeed, to give her novels a greater sense of immediacy, she often added references to current events to her manuscripts just prior to publication, drawing material from almanacs and newspapers found in the reading room at the British Museum.[7] Using Wimsey as her agent, Sayers could hold a mirror to her culture and offer a critical commentary. Supportive, penetrating, ironic, sardonic, and occasionally bitter, this commentary becomes an engaging window into the maze of that fascinating time. The fiction of Dorothy L. Sayers has become an essential source for the historian and for the literary analyst.[8]

This is a book about Dorothy L. Sayers, her creation—Lord Peter Wimsey—and her portrayal of the coming of the modern age. It is not intended as a biography of Sayers but rather a critical examination of her most popular works in an historic context. Despite an almost overwhelming temptation to the contrary, Peter Wimsey will not be treated as an historic figure but rather as the figment of literary imagination that he is.[9]

Just as Lord Peter is fictional, the stories in which he participates are grounded in "Cloud-Cuckoo Land,"[10] an imaginary world where Peter occupies an elegant flat in Piccadilly Circus, sallying forth to do battle with criminals throughout Britain. Yet Sayers did not create a fantasy world for Wimsey. Peter travels real and familiar English roads and suffers with the rest of Britain through a heady but troubled time. This was a Britain easily recognized by Sayers's contemporaries.

Several themes pervade the Wimsey saga, elements of English life that Sayers considered in novel after novel. The ever-present legacy of the Great War is the most obvious of these. In *Whose Body?*, the first of the novels, the reader learns that Peter is a shell-shocked war veteran and that Bunter, his manservant, served under Wimsey as sergeant in France. In *Gaudy Night*, published a dozen years later, Wimsey takes time from a complicated investigation to yarn with a former serviceman about life in the trenches. The war appears in some guise in every long story; at times, its memory permeates the story.[11]

Another theme, one especially important to Dorothy L. Sayers, concerns women in society. Women play critical roles in virtually all the Wimsey stories. In time, one woman character, Harriet Vane, comes to dominate the action. Sayers was no feminist (as she herself insisted), but she did regard as critical the issue of a woman's right to do as she would with her own life. The women in the novels run the gamut of English society, from traditional housewives to freewheeling Bohemians to fully independent professionals. Sayers took the time to examine their lives, to penetrate their feelings, and to gauge the public's reaction to their activities. If Sayers was herself one of the "new women," she was perceptive enough to recognize that whatever revolution was taking place in English society affected all women and affected women far more than it did men.[12]

Dorothy L. Sayers saw also that the postwar era challenged the very identification of things English. Sayers (and her character, Wimsey) were born late in the Victorian era, products of a complacent society confident of its own superiority. This was the nation of shopkeepers that had brought Napoleon to his knees, launched the industrial revolution, and forced half the world's population to accept British authority. By the turn of the century, this quiet confidence was a bit misplaced, but the average British citizen was ill equipped to see that.

A new cultural premise built of scientific discipline, technological reliance, the dismissal of history, and a determined view to the future flourished in continental Europe and America, challenging the staid traditionalism and sportsmanship projected by the English. "Modernism" had developed initially in Germany, the United States, and in Russia and France among important elements of their populations. This essentially cultural reformation influenced national political behaviors but had little effect on diplomatic and military relationships among nations. The modernist United States could ally with traditionalist Britain to overcome modernist Germany. This military defeat did nothing to arrest the spread of the modernist cultural values embraced by the German people. The war, in fact, accelerated the modernization of Britain. Before the war, the influence of the new was scarcely felt in Britain; after the war, it was everywhere.[13]

This cultural onslaught, characterized by the embrace of technology, the strange new directions taken by the arts, and the compromise (if not outright rejection) of many traditional institutions, threatened the survival of old England. Always a quilt of many classes and communities, England's different groups responded to this newness in different ways. For the Bloomsbury set that Sayers so wickedly satirized in *Strong Poison,* the coming of the modern age meant the freedom to do away with the diatonic scale and scoff at "the prurience of prudery."[14] For the less happy residents of the tiny village of Leahampton, portrayed in *Unnatural Death,* the future meant clinging to the traditional atmosphere of gossip and church doings in the face of fast cars, indiscrete professionals, and a murderous young woman.

At the heart of each Wimsey novel is a vivid and exacting depiction of one or more such communities, from the pathetically pointless aristocrats whom Wimsey joins for lunch in *Whose Body?* to the cloister of women scholars holding forth in *Gaudy Night.* Sayers provides the reader entry into each microcosm, sympathetically displaying the degrees of common cohesiveness and the impact of the modern. How do these communities function? What threatens their survival? To seek the answer to such questions is to approach understanding a Sayers novel.

Technology makes itself felt in every story. Racing cars and motorcycles, airplanes across the Atlantic (in 1923!), constantly ringing telephones, persistently clicking cameras—this is a society increasingly reliant on the wonders of modern technology. More important, and more subtle, is Sayers's treatment of the science permeating the minds of thinking people. Wimsey is quite cognizant of scientific advance, numbering among his friends researchers in several fields. To some extent, he relies on science in his detection work. Yet Wimsey is suspicious of overweening scientific influence, perhaps reflecting the mind of his creator. Although Sayers remained abreast of research theories and incorporated the latest science into several of her stories, she never represented science as an unalloyed good. Too often its practitioners—especially medical practitioners—proved amoral and prone to evil.

Probably this attitude reflected Dorothy L. Sayers's own religious upbringing. Her father was an Anglican cleric who made himself responsible for Sayers's early education. (He began to teach her Latin at age seven.) Religion is not as dominant as some of the themes in the Wimsey novels, but it is a recurring and troubling issue for the main character. Old-fashioned piety is perhaps too simple a sentiment for a man who has suffered the worst of the trenches, yet Peter is enough of a Victorian to feel its pull. The country churches especially—Duke's Denver, Fenchurch St. Paul—are bastions of the old world so endangered by modern culture. Yet they are steeped in the traditions that frame English culture, a culture that Wimsey comes to value more fully in the 1930s as totalitarianism looms. The modern has washed over the English world, but the traditional persists.[15]

The war, the challenge to the Victorian tradition, the changing roles for women, the shifting perceptions of class, the function of communities, the rising influence of technology and science, the steadfastness of traditional culture—these are all themes central to this book. How did Sayers deal with these issues? How did her treatment change over time? How well does her interpretation reflect the realities of her time period? To answer these questions is to gauge the process of modernization as Dorothy L. Sayers understood it.

This is not enough. Certainly Sayers drew from the world she knew and understood. More important, she drew from herself, from her own experiences. Sayers used her popular novels as a vehicle to analyze, to express, and to shake her head at her own life. Her health, her passions, her frustrations, and her triumphs as a woman and a scholar fueled her imagination. So much that happened to Wimsey and other of her central characters had happened first to her. In her suspicion of medical types, the reader sees the consequence of ill-treated sickness that made Sayers's hair fall out. In the story of Philip Boyes, the *Strong Poison* victim, we hear bitter echoes of her love for John Cournos. In the defensive ramblings of Gilda Farren, wife of one of the *Five Red Herrings,* we see an author attempting to establish the necessary foundations for happy marriage. Sayers did not write in a vacuum. In her coordination of the chronology of the Wimsey stories with that of her own life, we see the crosscurrents of experience and inspiration.

Finally, there is the fact of Dorothy L. Sayers's genius as a craftsman with language. Members of the contemporary smart set treasured the Wimsey stories in large part because they were so literate.[16] At Oxford, Sayers received an unparalleled education in language and never betrayed its dictums. She loved to play with language and to experiment with idiom, with point of view, and with the problem of revealing a character's thoughts in contrast to his or her expressed words. Although the conventions of popular crime fiction limited her ability to tinker with modes of writing, she searched continually for ways to better involve the reader in all the levels of her story: the mystery plot, the lives of her characters, their struggles to cope with life's struggle, and the essentially simple humanness underlying all the machinations inherent to crime and its solution.

So this is a book about Sayers as a writer and as a human being, what she saw and felt in the years between the world wars, and how she incorporated the experience into the fictional lives of her creation. It is a history of a make-believe person who lived a real life.

Lord Peter Begins a Career

LIFE WAS NOT EASY IN 1922. AS AUTUMN DREW TO A DREARY close that November, the British nation clung to a kind of wary optimism, a somber hope of the soul. The Great War was truly over, the troops demobilized. Those who would ever return home had done so. Government efforts to ease the transition to peacetime economy met with some success, though a recent slump threatened troubled times ahead. The political situation remained unclear. Lloyd George had resigned as prime minister, and Bonar Law presided for the moment. The next year would bring still another general election. Abroad, a tolerable postwar climate took shape as Germany and Russia stabilized and the Fascists seized control in Italy. It was not an ideal world by any stretch but one in which Britons could only mend their lives and try to go on.

For Dorothy L. Sayers, life experience reflected the national mood. She was young, talented, cautiously confident of the future, yet beset with all kinds of immediate disappointments. She had just ended a tempestuous and unconsummated love affair with writer John Cournos, a memory that would haunt her for years to come. Six months before, she had taken a new job at S. H. Benson's, an advertising firm. Not exactly a soul-satisfying position for a woman with an Oxford University education, but more palatable than the teaching and publishing posts she had tried before. Popular writing had now become an outlet. One detective novel, completed and typed twelve months before, made the rounds of publishing houses while she worked steadily at a second.

There was no pretension to higher literature here, but the writing was great fun and it might someday pay the bills.

The fictional hero whom Dorothy L. Sayers fervently hoped to present to the public was the product of both the mystery writer's convention and her own eccentric imagination: Peter Wimsey, an ingenious amateur detective with an unfortunate penchant for blither. More than two years before, Sayers had invented him, a minor character in a Sexton Blake story she never finished. She began to experiment seriously with the detective genre the following year, and by November 1921 she produced the first Wimsey novel, *Whose Body?* The book finally saw publication in May 1923.

Sayers set the novel in the bleak London of November, presumably in 1922. Although this was to be the first actual public glimpse of Lord Peter, she presented him as a man with a complicated (if largely unwritten) past. The "Battersea Park Mystery" detailed in *Whose Body?* is far from being Wimsey's first case. He has already undertaken enough major investigations to acquire close friends and bitter enemies among the official police. He is also brittle and impenetrably defensive in manner, the consequence of a love affair only barely suggested in the text. One more component is enmeshed in the Wimsey character: his experience as a frontline officer in the Great War. Lord Peter, the reader eventually learns, is a victim of shell shock.

To arrive at this first incarnation of Wimsey, the blithering young ass of November 1922, we must pursue elements of two separate but related natures: the recent history of England and the history of Dorothy L. Sayers herself. Any fictional character is a product of his creator's life and beliefs; this is perhaps more true of Peter Wimsey than most. Wimsey is also a product of the world his creator inhabited, a world haunted by memories and bloodstains.

Sayers was born in Oxford on June 13, 1893. She was an only child, much loved and sheltered by parents who indulged her creative whims from a very young age. Her father was a High Church cleric, headmaster and chaplain at Oxford's Christ Church Choir School. When Dorothy was four, he accepted a parish appointment at Bluntisham-cum-Earith, a remote country town in the fenlands of East Anglia. Educated there by her parents and tutors, Sayers remained at home until the unusually advanced age of fifteen, when she enrolled at the Godolphin Boarding School, Wiltshire. Here she quickly demonstrated her formidable scholastic aptitude, and here also she had her first unhappy encounter with medical practice. Ill with measles, pneumonia, and other ailments through much of 1911, she underwent therapies that caused her hair to fall out.[1]

Despite leaving Godolphin early with illness, she successfully competed for a scholarship to Somerville College, Oxford. Sayers was admitted for the Trinity term in 1912. Somerville, the first Oxford University college for women, was still not allowed to bestow university degrees, but it did offer a thorough grounding in the humanities. Dorothy L. Sayers flourished, becoming one of the leaders of her class and achieving a first in modern languages in 1915. When the university finally relented in 1920, granting women the right to receive the degrees they had earned, Sayers was among the first women's graduating class. The days at Oxford were perhaps the most treasured of her life. The heady intellectual atmosphere steeped her very essence. No matter her subsequent occupation or situation, she firmly remained an Oxford scholar.[2]

The Great War touched the life of Dorothy L. Sayers very lightly. Like many young Britishers in 1914, she did not take the threat of war at all seriously, actually going on holiday in France that malignant August. She escaped to England only after the British Expeditionary Force had assumed positions in northern France; the French army was in full retreat westward. Returning to Oxford for her final year, she found the university in disarray. Most of the male students had enlisted; buildings were given over to Belgian refugees and wounded soldiers. Somerville was moved to new headquarters for the duration of the war, the buildings converted to a hospital. Sayers devoted some time to nursing the sick and wounded but never fully committed herself to this task. She was young, with much of a purely intellectual nature to accomplish. For her at least, the horrors of the Great War were very far away.[3]

Would that such had been true for more of England. While Sayers grew up, attended university, and began the search for a career, the British nation absorbed shock after brutalizing shock as the great conflagration redefined the meaning of warfare. For the vast majority of Britons, the war came to define the routine of existence. Most people were either on the frontline or agonizing for loved ones in danger. The fear was well placed. By November 1918 more than nine hundred thousand English soldiers had died in Europe and Asia Minor. Sayers was one of the very few who did not lose a close friend or relative. It was the tragic end to a century of comparative peace.

As much as anything, the Great War was a consequence of misplaced faith in European cultural superiority. Cultural arrogance led

European nations to carve much of the world into exploited colonies, touching off a competition for resources that left them at each other's throats. Unforgivable smugness and cultural nearsightedness allowed them to believe that they had progressed too far along the path of civilization to descend into general conflagration.

There had been no general European war since the final defeat of Napoleon in 1815. In the ensuing century, Britain leapt ahead of its neighbors, exploiting newfound industrial capacity and establishing a vast overseas empire. The nation's supreme position in world affairs remained essentially unchallenged until the 1890s, when the new German Empire embarked on a military and formidable naval buildup intended to match British strengths. The British felt obliged to respond to this challenge, and the arms race was on.[4]

At this same time Britain went to war against the Boers in South Africa and discovered it had no friends. No continental power supported the effort to extend British imperial authority; several nations openly sympathized with the Boers. Though Britain eventually crushed all resistance, the lesson of the Boer War was not lost. Continued existence of the empire would depend on finding allies among the European powers.

Traditionally, Britain had remained aloof from all alliances, instead practicing "balance of power" diplomacy, ensuring that no one continental nation became powerful enough to dominate all others. Generally this had meant siding with Prussia against the French and probably against the Russians or the Austrians. Now the aggressive rise of Germany had rewritten the diplomatic map. Germany dominated its weaker ally, Austria, and seemed to have attracted Italy to its orbit. France, fearful of this powerful neighbor and recalling past humiliations, had come to an understanding with Russia. Leery of Russia but still more apprehensive of Germany, the British now swallowed hard and came to an understanding with their old enemy of several centuries' standing: the French. Europe had resolved itself into two overarmed camps, waiting for someone to toss a grenade.[5]

The powder keg almost went off any number of times; it finally did so, in June 1914, when a Serbian operative of the "Black Hand" murdered Archduke Ferdinand, heir to the throne of Austria-Hungary, in the streets of Sarajevo. Austria demanded an impossibly grovelling apology from Serbia and attacked when the Serbians did not quite measure up. Russia came to Serbia's defense, which obligated Germany to support Austria. The French had to come to Russia's defense. Europe was at war.[6]

Most thinking people believed that Europe was too civilized to hurl itself into a full-blown conflagration, but they also believed that if war did come, it would be over very quickly. Technology would see to that. The vast network of railroads would allow rapid movement of masses of men, ordnance was louder and far more deadly, and the submarine would destroy overseas supply. Above all, the machine gun would be the irresistible weapon of attack, mowing down resistance as invaders moved across the battlefields. All that mattered was who got the most men, equipment, and supplies to the important points quickest.[7]

Germany had a plan. Rightly assuming that the ponderous Russian military would mobilize slowly, a rapidly moving German army would sucker punch the French, knocking them out of the war before Britain could mount effective aid. With the western front secure, the Germans could then turn to face Russia. Given that Germany faced enemies on two long, separate fronts, this was, on balance, a realistic set of calculations. But the risks were high. This was a gambler's plan, and it required a gambler's nerve to carry it through.

Architect of the German strategy was Count Alfred von Schlieffen, German chief of staff for fifteen years through 1906. Von Schlieffen looked into the souls of his French adversaries and saw character shaped by unthinking aggressiveness and the desire for revenge. The French still smarted from the humiliating defeat in the Franco-Prussian War in 1870. As soon as hostilities broke out, the French would march westward to reclaim the provinces of Alsace and Lorraine, lost to Germany in the war settlement of 1870. This was exactly what von Schlieffen needed to execute his plan. He would place a small residual defense in those provinces, men who would beat an orderly retreat before the French onslaught, drawing the enemy ever eastward. All the while, the main body of German forces would drive through Belgium and wheel southward, falling on the French rear. The vise would close; victory would be achieved.

By the time war finally came, von Schlieffen was long in retirement, his place taken by Helmuthe von Moltke, a good soldier but not one to roll the dice. Von Schlieffen's plan called for an audacity that von Moltke simply could not muster.[8]

The war began early in August 1914. As Dorothy L. Sayers and hundreds of equally foolish tourists struggled to flee from panicked France, the French army acted as anticipated. Wearing glorious red uniforms, they rushed eastward, completely misreading Germany's disposition of forces and its underlying intent. The result was unparalleled slaughter, a German victory so complete as to ruin von Schlieffen's carefully constructed strategy. By August 20, the French were in full retreat westward.

The main German thrust, passing north of the French invasion, crushed "poor little Belgium" in thirteen days. The invasion of neutral Belgium forced Britain to declare war on August 4, but it would be another seventeen days before the British Expeditionary Force could reach the fighting. It was up to the retreating French to rescue the situation.

Retreat was exactly what von Schlieffen had not wanted the French to do. The force on the German frontier was intended to engage the enemy and hold them in place, not bloody them so badly that they moved westward. When the French did that, they encountered the main German invasion coming down from Belgium. The French were in disorder, but they offered enough opposition to bog down the German advance. As the British fell into line, allied resistance stiffened; the German invasion stalled. By September 5 any German hope for quick victory was gone. The two sides spent more than a month trying to outflank each other, a desperate business ending in cold rain with both lines firmly anchored to the North Sea. The troops dug in to escape the constant and brutal hail of enemy ordnance. In mid-October, three hundred miles of trenches stretched from the North Sea to Switzerland. Neither side would move very much over the next four years. The price for that stalemate would be horribly high.[9]

Two months of massive warfare should have been instructive, but many lessons were lost on those in command. They did give up on cavalry charges rather quickly, but the massed infantry assault remained a staple of war for the next three years. "Always attack" was the French mantra; the British accepted this, though no one had an answer for the ugliest fact of the war: the machine gun was the ultimate *defensive* weapon. Time after time, troops were sent over the top in well-organized, open assaults, target practice for a handful of defenders wielding a well-placed machine gun. Death tolls were unforgivable.

The Somme, Vimy Ridge, Caudry, the Marne—lessons in French geography written in blood. Sayers mentions these and other battles of the Great War in her eleven Wimsey novels; contemporary readers recognized the names instantly. These were the places where illusions of advanced civilization dispersed, where men exchanged their faith in progress and glory for the dubious advantages wrought by technological butchery. In the autumn of 1916, while Sayers assumed her first job at the Hull High School for Girls, teaching modern languages and trying to keep her head during zeppelin raids, more than one million men fell in France. By then, dreams of rapid victory had long given way to the harsh realities of a war of attrition. Nobody could win, but everyone had to empty their country of the able-bodied, sending them to the nightmare in the trenches. Too much was already spent; no one dared to lose.[10]

If the French and English lines were hell on earth, the German experience proved worse in the end. A British naval blockade strangled the country, and food became critically scarce. Although the allies did not know it, by 1917 the Germans had to win the war soon or starve. Again Germany decided on a desperate gamble.

The only answer to British naval superiority was unrestricted use of submarines to prevent supplies reaching Britain—an attempt to starve that island first. Whenever the Germans sought to play this card, sabers rattled in the United States. America was the leading "neutral" supplier, England the chief beneficiary. Facing internal collapse, the German high command resumed unrestricted submarine attacks on February 1, 1917, calculating that Britain would surrender before the Americans could mobilize to intervene.

It was a huge mistake. German submarines were unable to make much of a dent in British supply lines, and the United States entered the war on a massive scale. Had the Germans simply held out, they probably would have won. Russia began to collapse early in 1917; by year's end their leadership, elevated by the Bolshevik Revolution, was happy to end the war on the eastern front. The Germans would have faced only France and Britain, both nearing exhaustion.

By spring 1918 the Germans were completely desperate. The tactical leadership of both sides had learned a lot from the three years of debacle. New attack strategies ended the stalemate, and armies began to move. Needing to win quickly, the Germans moved first, shock attacking the British at the Somme late in March. They drove the allies back forty miles toward Paris, but the British lines would not break. The Germans tried again in April and May, gaining vast amounts of ground but failing to rout the enemy. They lost six hundred thousand soldiers in the three offensives.

The Spanish influenza struck as the Germans mounted a fourth attempt. Because of malnutrition, their troops suffered far worse than did the allies from this new horror. The Germans gained only four miles in this attempt. In July they tried one last offensive at the Marne but with no success. German offensive capacity was exhausted, and morale was crumbling. The allied counterattack began on July 18.

In less than two months, British, French, and American forces recaptured all the lands taken by the Germans in the spring. Britain's chief war innovation, the tank, paved the way. Allied ground tactics now bore a curious resemblance to naval deployments, and German resistance slowly melted. Germany's only hope was to maintain a functioning army long enough to achieve a voice at the peace negotiations. The merciless pounding carried on into late autumn, as thousands died fighting Germany's well-ordered retreat. The firing stopped suddenly at eleven o'clock on the morning of November 11 as an armistice was signed. The date was etched in the minds of millions. The killing stopped; the pain would linger forever.[11]

The next year brought "peace"—a hopeless, vengeful, witless peace guaranteed to plunge Europe into war again before long. Allied leaders simply refused to accept that this war had killed the past, that nineteenth-century passions and politics could not recreate nineteenth-century stability. They fell back on nineteenth-century values: nationalist competition and revenge. Germany was humiliated, forced to accept guilt for the war and to pay the entire debt. Stripped of army, navy, and industrial capacity, Germany was left economically moribund. Still, the allies expected this crippled economy to turn over vast sums to support their own national economies. It was a formula for financial disaster, and it worked all too well. By 1931 all of Europe was in massive recession.[12]

November 12, 1918 began a long, anguished process of building a new world. For the war's survivors, there could be no return to the comparative innocence of older days; they had witnessed too much death. Those at home helped as they could, but they too had burdens. Virtually every family in England had lost a brother, a son, a husband, a close cousin, or a dear friend. With the struggle over, long-swallowed grief could be loosed at last.[13]

As Robert Graves observed, only two classes existed in England after the war: those who had served at the front, and everybody else. The gulf between was painfully wide. Neither had the least ability to look into the heart of the other, to feel empathy. For the soldier, the return to civilian life was a shock. The war had further mechanized industry and accelerated the use of motor vehicles. Life was faster. Women were everywhere in public, smoking openly, voicing opinions on political questions (including their own right to vote), wearing clothes that flattened breasts and de-emphasized sexuality, and holding jobs they did not want to leave. Everyone wanted to be nice to the soldiers, but no one knew quite what to say. Everything seemed so different, so hollow.[14]

Society wanted very much to welcome the men back but, at the same time, people did not want to give up what they had gained in the soldiers' absence. Most women returned to the home reluctantly, and a significant few held on to a new life in the public sphere. War veterans found the adjustment to changing women's roles especially difficult. Long stretches of abstinence in the trenches inclined the troops to objectify women as just so many desirable bodies. The idea that British women might desire something more—a job, security without marriage, common respect— seemed utterly foreign.

Return to civilian footing, even in the most elemental fashion, proved difficult. Many soldiers found their old jobs gone, either mechanized out of existence or taken over by others. Pensions and other forms of public aid were inadequate to meet the desperate need. Especially poignant was the exigency of those mutilated by the war. Many walked the streets with missing limbs, wrecked faces, or gassed-out insides. Resentments simmered on both sides of the great gulf.[15]

Most critically, perhaps, the soldiers did not wish to talk about the war or about the loss of life; whereas the rest of society needed to. Nine hundred thousand deaths required public grieving, public remembrance. Bodies of half the men killed in the war were never identified, much less recovered. Following the armistice, Parliament established the Imperial War Graves Commission to oversee the creation of proper cemeteries in France to honor the deceased. Few British casualties returned to British soil. For the nation to bring closure to so stupefying a loss, the British people had to commemorate, to grieve publicly as one. Over the silent protests of thousands of survivors who would just as soon forget, communities throughout England held ceremonies to honor the veterans and to dedicate monuments to those who were gone. Homage to the dead was critical to getting on with life.[16]

The first war memorials were separately sponsored by the religious and lay communities. The business of honoring the dead was traditionally the domain of the religious, but here the Church of England found itself in an awkward position. The Church's chaplains were bitterly resented during the war—they had mouthed all the patriotic guff the soldiers came to hate and they had failed to accompany the men to the front, to the gates of hell. The parsons could do little to compensate for that kind of failure. Any attempt to recall the glory of imperial Britain, the dedicated spirit of Victorian days, met with bemused disaffection. Church memorials were shunned, and overly patriotic monuments fared no better. Lord Peter encounters such a monument in Yorkshire in *Clouds of Witness;* he can only regard "that thing" as incongruous. Like most soldiers, Peter had seen the war through, but not for any reasons of traditional patriotism.[17]

The right chord was struck in London, almost accidentally. The government commissioned Sir Edwin Luytens to construct a temporary monument in Whitehall, centerpiece for a celebratory march by British forces and their leaders during demobilization in 1919. Luytens delivered a spare, geometrical shape, an empty tomb bereft of all religious and patriotic connotations. The cenotaph was simple and sobering, a spare shell over a gnawing emptiness. The work so perfectly reflected public feeling that the government had no choice but to permanently install the monument at Whitehall as a national symbol of all that was lost in the Great War. Dorothy L. Sayers made prominent mention of the cenotaph in two of her novels.[18]

The grief did not end with the dedications and the ceremonies. The war cast a silent pall that lasted more than a decade. But life had to go on. There was much to resolve, much to build, much to face. The transition to peacetime footing led to rampant inflation followed soon by the inevitable contraction of government buying. The resultant recession left many to face criminally high prices with no source of income. Parliament extended unemployment insurance benefits in 1920, demonstrating a sympathetic comprehension that was historically unusual, if inadequate.

There was much unfinished business. The Irish situation demanded immediate attention. The government had quelled a rebellion on Easter Sunday, 1917, but the Irish were clearly fed up with British misrule. The Irish Republican Army organized in 1919. Terrorism mounted. The Government of Ireland Act stabbed at the problem in 1920; one year later came the Irish Free State. In 1921, Parliament also passed an act intended to give the people of India greater control over their own affairs.

At home, a new Parliamentary Reform Act, adopted in 1918, sought to deflect pressures from still other sources of massive dissatisfaction. The Act gave the right to vote to virtually all men over the age of twenty-one and some women over the age of thirty. 1919 brought the Sex Qualification Removal Act, removing bars to public employment on the basis of sex. The government had at last begun to recognize the rights of women, if only in a minimalist fashion. The legal voting age for women was at last lowered to twenty-one in 1928, essentially completing Britain's ratification of democracy.

Working class unrest became endemic in the years immediately following the war, despite the political gains of the Labour party. 1919 saw a national railway strike, the following year a coal strike. Parliament created the Sankey Commission to study the problems of persistent poverty and dangerous conditions in the mines, but little was accomplished. In 1921, the owners locked out the coal miners, resulting in a humiliating reduction in wages.[19]

Troubled times. Dorothy L. Sayers struggled along with everyone else, a young, well-educated (most men would have said overeducated) woman trying to make her way in a tight economy, competing against thousands of returning soldiers who wanted her to go home. Sex Qualification Removal Act or no, England in the immediate postwar era had little room for women in the public economy. Sayers's choices for employment were severely circumscribed by her advanced education and her sex.

She struggled to maintain an optimistic outlook. An intellectual above all else, in the three years after leaving Oxford Sayers published two volumes of poetry, both printed in very small numbers. This, sad to say, was her happiest achievement during the war years. Life after Oxford was difficult to accept. She took the teaching position at Hull but found the work trying and unfulfilling. Next she tried her hand as a publisher's assistant at Blackwell's, the small firm in Oxford that had brought out her own books, only to discover that there was no money in it. Infusions of funds from her father kept body and soul together through the end of the war.[20]

The armistice brought new opportunities. Leaving Blackwell's in May 1919, she took a job as headmaster's assistant at the L'Ecole Des Roches in Verneuil, Normandy. Sayers ventured into French education mainly to pursue Eric Whelpton, an invalided soldier she had met at Oxford. Her love for Whelpton was not encouraged or returned. In 1920 he left France and her life, after offering to sell her his interest in the school. Sayers returned to England soon after. Two more teaching jobs followed, both of them brief, before she took an advertising position at Benson's in May 1922. The job was less than ideal for a woman of Oxford education, but it was far better than staying home. Unfulfilled in her job prospects, unhappy in affairs of the heart, Sayers found some solace by turning to popular fiction.[21]

It was in Normandy that she first demonstrated her interest in detective stories. A friend at Oxford sent her a steady diet of Sexton Blake, that much-bloodied denizen of the mass market pulps. When Eric Whelpton teased her about lowbrow tastes, she announced her intention to enter into a syndicate with college friends to produce new detective fiction and make lots of money. Whelpton seemingly was unimpressed.[22]

Whether the syndicate existed outside Sayers's defensive imagination is difficult to say. One thing is certain: Sayers first attempted detective fiction in Normandy in 1920, trying her hand at a Sexton Blake novel. Like characters in much mass market fiction, Blake was the product of no single author. His publishers purchased Blake yarns from any number of sources, printing them with no author credit at all. Sexton Blake was not so much authored as produced assembly-line style.[23]

The story that Sayers outlined in France was very much a product of postwar conditions—a story built on themes of international intrigue and war-weary mistrust between agents of Britain and France. It was to be firmly in the Sexton Blake tradition: murder and mayhem among the rich and famous, many high speed chases through land, sea, and air, daring escapes by masters of disguise, and the recovery of a valuable jewel after a violent climax. The intrepid Blake must have possessed a hard head to withstand all the blows dealt him in the series.

The unfinished manuscript of Dorothy L. Sayers's effort to produce a Sexton Blake mystery survives intact, providing a glimpse into the genesis of a fictional hero. This fellow named Wimsey was to appear as a secondary character in the adventure. The murder touching off the entire chain of events was to take place in the Wimsey flat in Piccadilly and put Sexton Blake on the trail of the international archfiend, Renault. In his first incarnation, Lord Peter is introduced as the son of the Duke of Peterborough, but much of his later character is instantly recognizable. He is described as a "harmless sort of fellow, I think. Distinguished himself in the war. Rides his own horse in the Grand National. Authority on first editions. At present visiting the Duchess in Herts. I've seen his photo somewhere. Fair-haired, big nose, aristocratic sort of man whose socks match his tie. No politics." Harriet Vane's description of Peter in *Gaudy Night* was not much different.[24]

Sexton Blake is supposed to investigate the murder in Piccadilly, of course, and to follow up the incredible string of criminal events that would ensue. Lord Peter refuses to stand quietly aside. Entering the chase, he flies to Rome to discover that Renault has disguised himself as a woman and intends doubling back to England. Peter cleverly diverts the scoundrel's luggage to Paris, where it is opened, revealing Renault a jewel thief. Sexton Blake then lays a trap to capture the fiend and recover the jewel he has stolen.

Sayers never concluded this story and later chose to forget it completely. It is not difficult to hazard why, though it is the plainest guesswork. For one thing, she left France without Eric Whelpton; the work she did there may have held unpleasant associations. More probably, she gave it up because Sexton Blake was not her own creation but that of a syndicate. More fun was to be had inventing from scratch. Finally, there was the fact that she had invented this fellow Wimsey, an intriguing character. He had shown every capacity for taking over the Blake story. Why not put him to work on his own?[25]

Her first thought was to feature Wimsey in a play. Back in England and teaching at Clapham High School, Sayers roughed out a few pages of *The Mousehole: A Detective Fantasia in Three Flats*. The action was to begin with the discovery of a financier and a woman not his wife dead of carbon monoxide poisoning in the flat above Lord Peter's in Piccadilly. On the scene immediately, Peter was described as "sleek, fair, monocle, dressed in a grey suit, with the exception of his coat, whose place is taken by a luxurious dressing-gown." Peter soon meets Police Inspector Sugg, a familiar antagonist in the published Wimsey tales.

Though Peter has already acquired his eyeglass, his character is not entirely crystallized. At thirty-two he is a bit too old; more importantly, his speech has not yet acquired the clipped pronunciations of East Anglia's upper class: "Excuse me butting in like this Mr. ?—er—I'm so sorry, I really don't know your name, but—is anything the matter? I thought I heard somebody knocking—Oh, dear! (Observing the bodies.) How distressing. Did—er—did they have a fit or something?" Not quite right. Still, Peter readily admits to Sugg that his hobby is "other people's business."[26]

The Mousehole got no further. Sayers dropped the play to take up a more promising premise in January 1921. Years afterward she confided to a reporter that the basic story line for *Whose Body?* evolved at a party, with several friends adding elements to the puzzle.[27] In a letter to her mother, Sayers described the initial idea: "My detective story begins brightly with a fat lady found dead in her bath with nothing on but her pince-nez. Now, why did she wear pince-nez in her bath? If you can guess, you will be in a position to lay hands upon the murderer, but he's a very cool and cunning fellow."[28] She set Peter Wimsey to work to find the "cunning fellow."

The Wimsey character that took shape under Sayers's pen between January and November 1921 became the essential basis for all the elaborations of the following fifteen years. He was the product of a portentous time, a literary transition embracing the best aspects of the lost prewar world while facing the uncertain future with determined cheerfulness. If his amiability is a bit mannered, his air self-consciously light, there is good reason for it. Like English society as a whole, Wimsey has been scarred, perhaps irreparably, by the war.

Just as any writer of detective novels in the twenties, Dorothy L. Sayers had first to acknowledge the formidable influence of Sherlock Holmes, the stereotype for all would-be amateur detectives. Sayers is quite forthright in acknowledging her debt to Arthur Conan Doyle. Five pages into *Whose Body?* Wimsey prepares himself mentally to take on the mystery by announcing, "Exit the amateur of first editions; new motive introduced by solo bassoon; enter Sherlock Holmes, disguised as a walking gentleman." Later, facing up to a small but important error in the observation of minutiae, he calls himself Watson.[29] The name of Sherlock Holmes is invoked in every one of the ten novels that follow.

Wimsey, of course, had to be discernibly different from Holmes, had to be something new in a detective. Where Holmes is tall, rather dark, and ugly, Wimsey is short, fair, and unremarkable to look at, with at least a strong chin. Holmes is of uncertain class but the embodiment of middle-class mentality; Lord Peter is emphatically of the aristocracy. Holmes cares little for wealth or appearance; Peter is a fashion plate with money and a connoisseur of what it will buy. Both are musical virtuosos, though they prefer different instruments (Holmes the violin, Wimsey the piano).

The differences run far deeper than these simple comparisons of characteristics. Sherlock was the evocation of an age, a paragon of all that the Victorian male might aspire to be. He was virtuous and displayed great chivalry toward women, but he was careful to maintain a complete and masterful separation from the opposite sex. He was a man of science, skilled in experimentation, determined to place the work of detection on an empirical footing. Relentlessly logical, he regarded all emotion as weakness. To Holmes, things were just what they were. This made him the court of final appeal, the ultimate source of justice.

Sherlock Holmes was still going strong in the 1920s (Doyle published his last Holmes story in 1931), but he had become an anachronism. These last stories either were placed in retirement settings or were tales of adventure from the good old prewar days. Holmes was no longer the ideal; he had become an impossibility. Peter Wimsey was more the man of the twenties, brilliant but scarred and unsure. Wimsey triumphed through reliance on an uncertain combination of scientific observation, deductive intuition, psychological insight, real assistance from close associates, and occasional good luck. His was a brilliant mind but a mind that acknowledged the existence of factors beyond his control. Wimsey would never be the complete master of a situation.

The difference between the creation of Sir Arthur Conan Doyle and that of Dorothy L. Sayers is manifest in the very tenor of the stories. Holmes was best suited to the short story format: a quick visit to 221B, the proposal of the problem, the logical weighing of the factors to point up probabilities, the testing of the hypothesis, and the exposure of the felon. Apart from Holmes himself, there is little character portrayal; it is extraneous to the plot.[30]

The successful Wimsey stories are the long narratives. (The short stories are enjoyable only if you have read the novels and therefore know something of Wimsey and other participants.) Character development is crucial to the novels. From the very first, solution turns not so much on the analysis of clues as the understanding of character. For a Sayers story to be fulfilling, the readers must have a fairly complex understanding of the people involved. Only the novels provide that opportunity.

At the heart of the first nine novels is Wimsey himself. He emerges from the first chapters of *Whose Body?* as a clever if somewhat unconscientious chatterbox, a blithering talker of the first order. He is capable of celebrating in song when presented a body in a bath, calling a close friend a "fathead," and mercilessly lampooning a dull-witted police inspector. It is difficult to believe he can be completely serious about anything. As the medical student, Mr. Piggott, noted of Peter, "He talked the most fatuous nonsense, certainly, but in a disconcerting way. He didn't dig into a joke and get all the fun out of it; he made it in passing, so to speak, and skipped away to something else before your retort was ready"(188–89).

Wimsey is, however, a man of taste, as even Mr. Piggott (of suspect mercantile antecedents) could attest. We glimpse little more of Peter's belongings than his library in this first novel, but we are immediately made to understand that this "was one of the most delightful bachelor rooms in London." The decor is darkness set off by primrose, the furniture elegant but dutifully comfortable, the wall shelves taken up by priceless first editions bound in leather. A baby grand piano, often used, graces one corner. Oh yes—this is the domain of a wealthy man (26, 189).

And a wealthy, aristocratic man was Wimsey. Sayers determined finally that Lord Peter was the second son of the Duke of Denver, a noble family with roots extending back at least to the Norman invasion. His mother, the Dowager Duchess, is very much in evidence in the story; his father has passed on, leaving the title to Peter's older brother, Gerald. The current duke is a model of convention; like his father, he will not entertain self-made men at Duke's Denver.

Though Sayers does not allude to the fact, Denver and his family are examples of a rapidly vanishing country tradition. The twenties saw a visible contraction of aristocratic landholding as the nobility sought to rid itself of an unprofitable commitment to highly taxed agricultural properties. As the elite divested, both their influence and their privilege among the rural population declined. Sayers envisioned Denver as an exception to this trend, subsequently explaining that Gerald, the wealthiest of England's dukes, could afford to maintain the agricultural traditions at an economic loss. By the end of the series, both he and Lord Peter are convinced that the heir to the title will inevitably sell the properties to Hollywood.[31]

In *Whose Body?* it is Peter who seems prepared to cast away the traditions and entitlements of his station. Gerald is much irritated by Peter's lack of proper aristocratic mien, wants him to "marry and settle down and live quietly, doin' something useful." For reasons left obscure in this first novel, Peter's attempt to conform to the model has been a washout. Now Gerald has to worry that Peter might off and marry a chorus beauty. It is bad enough having him appearing as witness in police court.[32]

Even if he is a "beastly blot on the 'scutcheon," Peter is a beneficiary of aristocratic privilege. In *Whose Body?* we learn little more than that he possesses an Oxford education, and we can infer that he attended the best of the public schools, Eton. "The playing fields of Eton" is a watchword for a standard of upper-class English assumption, a very expression of the culture. It is on the playing fields that young men learned the necessary value of fair play, of being a good sport. The game itself is tantamount, sacred—more important than any individual player. Every participant is expected to adhere to the letter and spirit of the rules while giving all they have to win. At the same time, no player could ever suggest, by word or action, that he was trying to win or even cared about the outcome. Wimsey belonged to a family of sportsmen, skilled hunters who nonetheless had never killed a fox. (Much later in the series, Sayers, speaking of sport through Harriet Vane, observes that the "tom-fool word has got more people in trouble than all the rest of the dictionary put together.")[33]

The sense of fair play stands Wimsey well in his proper social circle but is a definite impediment to his chosen career as an amateur detective. Peter has no impelling reason to chase down criminals; the work is neither dictated by his class standing nor necessary due to straitened circumstances—quite the opposite. The essential justification he offers in *Whose Body?* is simply that investigation is a kind of hobby, a distraction. Not unlike crossword puzzles or other exercises for the mind, criminology provides mental stimulation, exhilaration, adventure (73, 186, 216).

At least that is how matters begin. As long as the body in the bath is an abstract puzzle, the perpetrators faceless, detective work can be an unusually enjoyable kind of game. As soon as suspects acquire identities, become people with traits of character, admirable or otherwise, Wimsey suffers an attack of conscience. Suspecting real people of heinous activity, in some cases (of necessity) unjustly, and snooping into their lives is not playing the game. Peter's closest friend and associate, Police Inspector Charles Parker, makes this plain: "You want to look dignified and consistent—what's that got to do with it? You want to hunt down a murderer for the sport of the thing and then shake hands with him and say 'Well played—hard luck—you shall have your revenge tomorrow!' Well, you can't do that. Life's not a football match. You want to be a sportsman. You can't be a sportsman. You're a responsible person" (159).

This conflict of emotions lies at the core of Peter Wimsey's character throughout his career. At first blush he seems superficial, a man playing a game with life. But he is responsible. He cares about what happens to the people he encounters, even the most evil of murderers. Yet he is also sanguine enough to understand that he possesses unique powers that he must use. His most important duty is to society.

In allowing Peter Wimsey to agonize over such a fundamental issue, Dorothy L. Sayers fashioned a singular kind of popular fiction hero: a man who carefully considers his own motivations and explores the consequences of his actions. Sherlock Holmes, along with most of the great fictional detectives of the postwar era, bows out with the solution of the puzzle, the author paying little more than lip service to the fact that exposure of the criminal will fundamentally alter the lives of many people. Sayers explores this fact. Peter Wimsey's triumphs are muted by the certainty of human suffering to follow.

The reader catches the merest glimpses of Peter's ingrained sense of responsibility in *Whose Body?* Mostly he portrays himself as a regular cheerful idiot, blithely irresponsible about money, appointments, or just about anything. Charles Parker is obliged to warn him that he will never make a true detective "till you learn to do a little work." The one person able to comprehend the necessity of this blither is the great nerve specialist, Sir Julian Freke. Examining Wimsey with the latest scientific instruments, he determines that Peter "must learn to be irresponsible." Wounds exist in Wimsey's brain, producing a "sensitive nervous temperament." The only hope of avoiding further trauma is to avoid opening the old wounds. Peter Wimsey must be frivolous (218–19).

The wounds are a consequence of Peter's service in the Great War. Sayers reveals this to the reader suddenly and unexpectedly. Peter, grasping the solution to the puzzle of the man in the bath, recoils in horror. Abruptly, he is in the manservant Bunter's bedroom, ordering him to keep the lights out, babbling of sappers and artillery. Major Wimsey has returned to the war, to the trenches. His teeth chatter; the terror he feels is palpable. With difficulty, Sergeant Bunter gets his man to bed. Subsequently, we learn that this is the latest of several such attacks, that Peter was "dreadfully ill" in 1918 (171, 173, 214).

From that moment on, the frivolous, babbling Wimsey of the early portions of *Whose Body?* staggers to the finish as a damaged, fragile individual. We learn few specific details of Peter's war record save that he must have done some intelligence work at one point. He "remembered having once gone, disguised, into the staff-room of a German officer." For the rest, he must have served as a frontline officer, as fears of the enemy penetrating his entrenchments lay most heavily on his mind (214).

Just what was the nature of this war that it could lie so deeply ingrained in the aristocratic mind of a Peter Wimsey? Why was Peter's condition so recognizable to Sayers's readers in 1923, a full five years after the war had ended? Why did the fact of shell shock make an otherwise frivolous character so universally sympathetic to the postwar world? The answers lie in the very nature of the trench warfare that comprised too much of the Great War.

The trenches were the war. Strategically, historically, the war was fought elsewhere as well. It can be said quite honestly that the war was lost and won on the seas. But the trenches were the grinding fact of life, a perpetual horror punctuated by occasional moments of terror. When all was calm, as many as a thousand men a day fell victim to sniper fire. Artillery barrage shattered earth and sanity all too often; poison gas wafted across the fields when the wind was right. Technology remained omnipresent, but it had turned its face against humankind. The trenches meant shelter and survival at a dehumanizing cost.

Between 1914 and 1918 Europe's governments issued more than ten million shovels to their infantrymen. The men used them to dig a series of three parallel ditches ten feet deep and three hundred miles long, generally two hundred fifty yards from the enemy. One or more support trenches lay behind the frontline diggings. Some distance behind the support trenches lay the main encampments, with barracks, headquarters, hospitals, ordnance and supply, and so forth. Members of the British Expeditionary Force in France rotated between front lines, support lines, and the encampments, hoping to experience three days of relative quiet for every four days of exposure and danger. The true rotation varied greatly from place to place. There were only a few places where geography realistically gave the enemy any opportunity to attack. Those places were often in an uproar for weeks on end, forcing thousands to endure what seemed eternal frontline duty.[34]

There was literally no language to express what soldiers saw and heard. Enemy artillery laid down sustained barrages with concussive impact to rob men of sleep and sanity, if not life and limb. No-man's-land became a lifeless, barbed-wire hell pockmarked by muddy craters in which wounded drowned. Corpses, often disintegrated, littered the landscape. Rats, sleek and fat, fed lustily.

Three full years of savagery wrought only more of the same. Cold rain, perpetual mud, rats, lice, dysentery, sniper's bullets—those were the lot for a calm and average day. Strategists seemed to have no more answer than to send more men over the top to near-certain death. French forces finally mutinied, refusing to attack anymore. British morale did not sink quite so low, but the war did shatter precious cultural institutions. Well-educated, aristocratic leaders of the military became the blimps—uninformed, uncaring, hopelessly outdated and dull witted. It became impossible for the private soldier to even mouth the platitudes of deference to their "betters" when obedience only got them killed. The last illusions of corporate hierarchy died in the trenches.[35]

Faith in progress and civilization, so central to Victorian thinking, withered in France. The sense of community grew smaller and smaller, defined at last as the mates who shared a dugout while enemy shells shook the earth. Men struggled to sustain some semblance of middle-class values, knowing that it was all an illusion. It was hard to maintain a sporting desire for fair play against an enemy issuing poison gas—better to poison them first. Many dreamed of leave, of returning to England long enough to bed a "nice girl" feeling sorry for a poor infantryman.[36]

Traditional values were displaced by a harsh and cynical humor. Broadsides advocated lice (in a variety of sizes and colors) as pets. Unit newspapers asked the common soldier if he suffered symptoms of optimism. One unit put on a play, written by the soldiers themselves, behind the frontlines. The scene was the trenches, the year 1966. They were all still there, staring across no-man's-land at the Germans. So were their grandchildren.[37]

Dorothy L. Sayers steered a careful but inspired path in concocting Peter Wimsey's war record. To be acceptable to a public acutely cognizant of who had served and who had not, a young aesthete such as Wimsey had to possess a service record. But Wimsey was an aristocrat—dangerous ground. How easy to imagine him a young blimp. By placing him in the frontlines as a major who actually suffered shell shock, Sayers preserved the credibility of his lordly upbringing and education while giving him a real experience of horror shared by millions. And, in refusing to talk about it or dwell on it until forced to do so, Wimsey walked in step with just about every frontline veteran. They had seen far too much that was unspeakable.

The barest hint of service as an intelligence officer provides a bridge between Wimsey the trench officer and Wimsey the detective. Although it is never stated in *Whose Body?* Sayers has successfully planted the possibility that Peter's interest in police work stems from his intelligence work. We are provided little information on the transformation, but it is plain that in 1922, when a man is found in the bathtub, Wimsey has been at this sort of thing before. He is familiar with civilian police methods and with civilian police inspectors. Charles Parker is already a close friend at the beginning of *Whose Body?* and Inspector Sugg his inveterate enemy. Sayers mentions Wimsey's role in the sensational recovery of the Attenbury emeralds but provides no details. (Perhaps this "previous experience" is a partial remnant of the Sexton Blake plot reaching into the new story [14, 216].)

In an essay published in 1937, Dorothy L. Sayers reviews *Whose Body?* finding the book "conventional to the last degree," not at all the clever invention she thought it in 1923. Later, she argues, she had to go to the long labor of making Peter Wimsey "a complete human being, with a past and a future, with a consistent family and social history, with a complicated psychology and even the rudiments of a religious outlook." In casting this revision, Sayers is not entirely fair to herself. Although at times Wimsey's true personality could be discerned only in the barest hints and allusions, all of those elements that she would later require of her main character were established at the outset in *Whose Body?*[38]

If Wimsey was a character ready made to step into the adventure of the man in the bath, much remained to be done before he could occupy a sensible world that his readers would recognize and understand. This was no easy task, given that the familiar world of England seemed to be changing, shifting, and metamorphosing even as Sayers observed it. To provide a proper setting for Wimsey was to capture the bustle and uncertainty of the postwar world.

The year is 1921 or 1922—there is no precise way to date the novel absolutely—but the month is most definitely November, a typical London November filled with leaden skies, frequent and bone-chilling rains, and drizzling fogs. The weather is relentlessly heavy, a severe contrast to the forced lightness of Peter's banter. This is the aura of the immediate postwar world, a world where sympathy and trust are at a premium. A coroner orders the windows opened, bathing his attending audience in cold fog. An attorney of the gentlemanly old school cannot recognize a bona fide visit from the English nobility, accusing Peter of attempting blackmail. Even the postwar beer is lousy. Peter's study is an oasis of civility in the midst of a drear reality, but its master is uncertain. He can only go forward, keeping things light, burying the old wounds, hoping for the best (109–10, 188).

The reader encounters the bustle of modern London at the very outset. The novel begins in the swirling traffic of Piccadilly Circus, as Peter's taxi driver desperately threads past "a 19 'bus, a 38-B, and a bicycle" to gain Lower Regent Street. Wimsey's request to return for a forgotten catalog is more than an inconvenience; it is a request to buck the tide of a transportation network in total disorder. Returning home, he is instantly faced with a telephone call; Peter "sat down to the telephone with an air of leisurely courtesy, as though it were an acquaintance dropped in for a chat." Technology has acquired a life of its own (9–10).

This hectic pace of daily life remains a factor throughout the novel: there is not enough time to do everything. Following up legitimate leads, Peter nearly misses Lady Swaffam's luncheon (his absence might have proved disastrous), and he does miss the Battersea inquest. His confrontation with Julian Freke near the finish occurs as events pass them by—the final procedures leading to Freke's arrest are already in motion.

Wimsey's investigation allows the reader the briefest impression of the dizzying world of international finance. American millionaire John P. Milligan thinks nothing of sailing across the Atlantic to sew up a railroad deal, returning home to have some fun cornering the wheat market in Chicago with his brothers, and then returning to England to give a little talk at Duke's Denver. This is a world where failure of a deal in the Argentines can upset the entire British market, where bankrupt Peruvian oilfields can inspire a flutter of excitement in London. This is all very different from the back-country images of Peter's birthplace where "the local people can't understand much beyond shootin' and huntin'" (75–76, 78–84).

This is also a world where anti-Semitism was all too current and all too familiar. Some critics have levelled the charge of conscious anti-Semitism at Sayers, but this seems a case of reading backwards from present knowledge into the contemporary evidence. Certainly Jewish stereotypes are common in *Whose Body?* Sir Reuben Levy, the ultimate victim of the novel, is a classic stock character. He is treated by essentially all concerned as a man apart: cheap, financially shrewd, ruthless in business dealings yet devoted to family. Everyone in the novel accepts this stereotyping without thought or comment. Peter refers to Sir Reuben as a "wandering Jew," Bunter allows that "a good Jew can be a good man," Peter's mother recalls the difficulties of Christine Ford, a good Christian girl (as her very name implies), marrying a Jew. Later, medical students identify one of the dissection subjects at St. Luke's Hospital as a "Sheeny" by glancing at the physical features. In Wimsey's world, the Jews, resident in England for centuries, were not quite English (47, 56, 65, 195–96).

Incorporating these stereotypes, Sayers mirrored her world, a world that in some ways had learned painfully little. Even after the cataclysm of the Great War, the world could not stand as one. In fact, the war seems to have encouraged ethnic and cultural discrimination. The Germans were still Huns, the Americans uncouth moneygrubbers (such as John P. Milligan), the French altogether too French, and the Jews still Hebrews, a race apart. How easy it was to let those ethnic slurs roll off the tongue in 1922, never thinking twice, never envisioning the evil this heedless behavior could inspire. Too many still blamed the Jews for the death of the Christian savior; too many also blamed Jewish finance for the outbreak of the war. Better to lay fault with the outsider than face up to the responsibility that rested in every European heart. Casual anti-Semitism seemed harmless enough in 1922. Even a woman as educated and sensitive to the human condition as Dorothy L. Sayers could include it in a novel as natural and innocuous behavior. Thirteen years later, she was still surprised to discover that a French translator of *Whose Body?* wanted "to soften the thrusts against the Jews." She felt that the only persons in the story "treated in a favourable light were the Jews!"[39] Unconscious anti-Semitism was a part of life, a condition of mind, an expression of the culture. It put the world on the road to genocide.[40]

If Sayers was unconscious of the danger in her hackneyed portrayal of Jewish people, she was fully cognizant of her approach to questions of science, physical and social. These were an integral part of the coming world, and she did not altogether approve. Science, medical science especially, enters the novel in the person of Sir Julian Freke.

Freke is a classic example of the heroic scientist, attacking the frontiers of ignorance through hypothetically impartial inductive research and application. He is an expert on the human nervous system, a selfless genius whose achievements allow him to successfully treat Russian refugees, careworn financiers, and shell-shocked war veterans. He is also a monster, a man who has placed himself beyond the moral reach of society. At first the Battersea mystery is intractable because it consists of two seemingly separate and unrelated sets of circumstances, both comparatively trivial. It is only when Peter Wimsey, in a moment of deductive intuition, splices the two stories together that he can see the enormity of what has happened. Sir Julian Freke has committed a crime beyond the scope of any moral scruple that Wimsey can imagine (168, 170).

To Freke, human feelings and emotions are products of the body chemistry. There is no altruistic reason to experience guilt or regret; these are aberrations caused by secretions of the body in reaction to outside stimuli. To Freke, the concept of conscience is outmoded and scientifically insupportable. There is no soul, no God to answer to. The man who can understand, who can learn to control his body's chemical reaction, can do anything. He becomes superman, beyond the reach of law or religion (165–67).

Sir Julian was deluding himself. Interestingly, Peter Wimsey employs an essentially (if superficially) Freudian approach to demonstrate the flaw in Freke's reasoning. For all his cold detachment and devotion to pure reason, the great scientist was acting under the influence of one of the most powerful and blinding of all human emotions: jealousy—sexual jealousy. As a young man, Julian Freke thought to marry Christine Ford. He was beaten out by "a little Jewish nobody." For almost a quarter of a century, Freke bided his time, built up his plans with methodological precision. Then came the blow—revenge, at last. What part of Freke's body chemistry had betrayed him and allowed him to cling to this paralyzing emotion? "Sex is every man's loco spot," Wimsey observes. "You needn't fidget, you know it's true—he'll take a disappointment, but not a humiliation" (203).

Sayers would find occasion to return to this theme, both in later novels and in some of her short stories. The message remains basically the same. Science deserves great respect because it has accomplished much for humankind. But, watch out for scientists. By its nature, science embraces no values, provides no sense of morality. In the hands of an amoral scientist, science can become a tool for unparalleled evil.

Having established her essential characters, her settings, and the principal themes, Sayers still had to address the matter of style—no small consideration for an Oxford-educated woman with a degree in modern languages. In her own mind, as well as in the estimation of her own social group, Sayers was "slumming" to attempt popular detective fiction at all. Surely she was more at home with poetic forms if not with the "high" literature of Europe's last thousand years. To write popular literature was to enter a different kind of world altogether, one her training would identify as a much lower form. Yet she was making her daily bread working for an advertising agency by 1922. She needed the ability to communicate with the masses just to survive.

A voracious reader, Sayers familiarized herself with the essential conventions of the detective story by devouring numerous examples, ranging from Sherlock Holmes and Sexton Blake through the novels of E. C. Bentley. To Sayers, the essential ingredient was that the writer "play fair" with the reader. Whatever evidence the fictional detective possesses must be made available to the reader. (Sherlock Holmes did not always do this!) To Sayers, the mystery story was a form of intellectual puzzle that the reader must be given a fair opportunity to solve. The plot must be coherent, the behavior of the characters logical and believable, and the crime accomplished without resort to such legerdemain as unknown poisons, evil twins, or divine miracles.[41]

The story also had to be plainly written. While many of Sayers's readers would derive from the "smart set," a detective story had to appeal to the "middlebrow" taste at least to be successful. This fact severely circumscribed the occasions for literary experimentation. Still, the story Sayers produced for the popular reading public of 1923 demonstrated a cognizance of the rise of the modern in literature.

Modernist sensibilities antedated the Great War, but the war experience provided credibility for their critique of European civilization. The confident assurances of the Victorian age had given way to profound uncertainty: was humanity the agent of cultural change, or its helpless victim? Could Europeans break free from the traps, from the limitations imposed by their own history? That history had dragged them all to the edge of the abyss, a nightmare dug in the ground and called a trench. How was the artist to voice the desperate anxieties wrought by the modern world?[42]

Confronting the cultural crises of the twentieth century, the moderns reflected their uncertainties in the "form and idiom" of their art. In the work of authors such as James Joyce, Marcel Proust, and T. S. Eliot, the principal narrator of the action is not so much an agent as a victim of events: "I" is "acted upon." In composing *Whose Body?* Sayers seems to have struck for a middle ground between the moderns and their non-modernist contemporaries. Her criticisms of society and the world are articulated in the accepted forms of traditional discourse, yet the narrator of *Whose Body?* refuses to remain consistent. Assuming a variety of voices and points of view, Sayers imposes a wealth of narrative perspectives on the action.

The novel begins with what might be described as an imagist poem, perhaps Sayers's only study in that style. For the modern writer, the image is a kind of epigram, capturing, with the speed and the shocking picture of the moment, "an intellectual and emotional complex in an instant of time."[43] The image that Sayers draws to convey the essence of Wimsey is simple enough, but oddly hideous: "His long, amiable face looked as if it had generated spontaneously from his top hat, as white maggots breed from Gorgonzola" (9).

In this case, the image recalls vermin overrunning the trenches, thereby foreshadowing Peter's shell-shocked flashback at the moment when he solves the crime. The Battersea mystery comes too soon after the war; the gruesome horror of the truth is too vivid. The horror of the image ramifies through the text as a whole—the bizarre circumstances of the murder, dissection, and exhumation scenes to come are insinuated in this seemingly innocuous miniature grotesque.

As the image became the staple of modernist poetry in the postwar era, the diffuse point of view came to dominate narrative literature. In the work of James Joyce, Virginia Woolf, or William Faulkner, the standard Victorian narrator seems the victim of an explosion. There is no neutral, steady, reliable perspective, only a multiplicity of ill-defined, partial views supplied by unreliable participants including (and not always especially) the author.[44] This fragmentation occurs in *Whose Body?* as well, though with careful limitation.

Generally on her best British behavior, distanced and omniscient, Sayers nonetheless refused to remain on the outer fringes of her story. She intrudes on the narration first in the form of a few footnotes, then dares more, darting into official discourses during the inquest and then into the voices of the witnesses. When Gladys Horrocks "wished she were dead," she has, for a bare moment, become the narrator of the action. Later, at Lady Swaffham's tea, Sayers injects language such as "soulfully," "anxiously," and "little scream" into the text to accompany the exhalations of Mrs. Tommy Frayle, a woman too inanely worshipful of Lord Peter. Sayers and Mrs. Frayle achieve an odd communion in consequence. The cumulative result of these intrusions is to create a fragmented, almost disembodied narrator; there is no single identifiable narrative voice. This is a far cry from Doctor Watson (125, 150–54).

Although she experiments with modernist perspective, Sayers drew the line at stream of consciousness. Unlike Woolf or Joyce, she seldom speaks the minds of those whose discourse she adopts. This is popular fiction, after all; there are conventions to be observed. Her reluctance to go to this extreme is clearly demonstrated in the stark impact of the few passages where she does enter the minds of her characters, exploring the effect of their thoughts on their emotions. Sayers first applies the technique in exploring the character of Mr. Piggott: "You wondered what the carpet had cost on which Parker was carelessly spilling cigar ash; your father was an upholsterer—Mr. Piggott, of Piggott & Piggott, Liverpool—and you knew enough about carpets to know that you couldn't even guess at the price of this one" (189).

Sayers tried this experiment just one time more in this first novel, allowing the voice of the narrator to speak the thoughts of Peter Wimsey: "The feel of Parker's old trench-coat beneath your fingers was comforting. You had felt it in worse places. You clung now for fear you should get separated. The dim people moving in front of you were like Brocken specters." (223)

The profoundly physical sensations she records separate the narrator from the character even as the words unite their experience. The narrator is not Piggott, not Wimsey, however close the narrator (and the reader) come to sharing the experience. The message is Freudian: there exist unfathomable depths within one's own mind. Viewpoints may shift, but in the last analysis all is relative. Even the world of the fictional detective is ultimately unknowable.[45]

If Dorothy L. Sayers was willing to toy with the relativistic stratagems of the moderns, her detective fiction was rooted in her finely honed sense of the classics, one more characteristic she shared with Eliot and Joyce. Subsequent Lord Peter novels drew heavily from Shakespeare, Wordsworth, Milton, John Donne, and always from Wilkie Collins. In *Whose Body?* the action is framed by references to Dante. As the novel begins, Peter Wimsey is the wealthy and garrulous man about town, off to bid for a Folio Dante to add to his collection. The Folio arrives as the investigation deepens; it is available for inspection by Mr. Piggott as the circle closes around Sir Julian Freke. With resolution of the matter out of his hands, Wimsey attempts to draw solace from Dante. Instead, he determines to confront Sir Julian. By the climax, Sayers has imported images from Dante directly into her story to lend a sense of decency to the grim proceedings at the workhouse burial ground. Wandering amidst the maze of graves, Wimsey clings to Parker's coat sleeve to keep from blundering into "the mass of freshly turned clay" about an open grave.

> Two Dantesque shapes with pitchforks loomed up.
> "Have you finished?" asked somebody.
> "Nearly done, sir." The demons fell to work again with the pitchforks—no, spades.
>
> . . . .
>
> The sound of the spades for many minutes. An iron noise of tools thrown down. Demons stooping and straining.
> A black-bearded spectre at your elbow. Introduced. The Master of the Workhouse.
>
> . . . .
>
> A mutter of voices. The lurching departure of the Dante demons—good, decent demons in corduroy. (223–25)

Then comes confirmation of all the horror Peter Wimsey has surmised. The body exhumed by the Dante "demons"—the gravediggers at a pauper's cemetery—is none other than Sir Reuben Levy, murdered and dissected by Sir Julian Freke. The good doctor is a denizen of the deepest parts of hell.

The extent to which *Whose Body?* anchors the entire body of Peter Wimsey material is striking. Sayers employed many of the characters appearing in the stories time and again, providing Peter a stock community of family, friends, and acquaintances who support his activities. On those later occasions when Wimsey stepped outside the normal bonds of this community, it generally signified that Sayers was allowing Peter room to grow.

Probably the most important of the supporting cast introduced in *Whose Body?* is Police Inspector Charles Parker, Wimsey's only real friend. Parker is Wimsey's complement—a pleasant, generally unexcitable, professional investigator. He lives a rather spartan life. Single, occupying a drab flat in Great Ormond Street, served by an openly judgmental woman who comes in on days, Charles is dependent on the meager salary he earns at Scotland Yard. Wimsey finds him unimaginative and maddeningly cautious, a welcome check to his own flamboyant air. Charles Parker is not Conan Doyle's Doctor Watson nor his Inspector LeStrade. He and

Wimsey are genuinely a team. Parker—steady, plodding, but very intelligent—is capable of performing the grinding police work that Wimsey cannot. His sole source of recreation is reading theological works, commentaries on the Epistles and such. This, he states amiably, is how he learned caution. As Wimsey grows and changes in subsequent novels, Parker grows as well yet remains a touchstone of reality for Peter (26, 67, 156).

Sayers intended Inspector Sugg to be a foil for her team of clever and determined detectives. He is the exact opposite of everything Wimsey and Parker represent, a paragon of bullying stupidity. Presumably Sayers intended Sugg to provide a form of low comedy for the story, a fool engaged to reflect the brilliance of the master. With the presence of Parker at Wimsey's side, however, the ploy does not come off well. It is not that the official police are stupid (Charles disproves that); it is only that Sugg is stupid. Sayers allows him a modicum of dignity in the end and uses him only incidentally thereafter (18, 24).

Two characters appearing briefly in *Whose Body?* recur in several additional works. Early in the novel, Peter and Charles discuss a recent court performance by the brilliant barrister, Impey Biggs. We learn little more here than that Biggs used the inherent uncertainty of medical evidence to secure the acquittal of an almost certainly guilty man, but Biggs is a character Sayers will employ several more times (35).

The reader catches a somewhat fuller glimpse of a character personally closer to Wimsey: his financial friend, the Honourable Freddy Arbuthnot. Freddy's antecedents are by no means clear, but he has money and the peculiar ability to make more at will. His specialty, apparently his sole interest, is the stock exchange, which he knows intimately. He shares with Peter an appreciation of wealth, a fine taste in men's fashion, and a discriminating palate. But Wimsey never spends much time with him, in this story or any other. Freddy does not possess the wide-ranging intellectual curiosity that drives Wimsey (74–78).

Family ties are important in *Whose Body?* Sayers will later broaden and flesh out Peter's relations, but we learn fairly quickly that his father is dead, that his brother is every inch the narrow-minded country squire his father was, and that (unlike Sherlock Holmes) Peter has a mother, one who takes an active interest in his adventures. The Dowager Duchess of Denver is one of Dorothy L. Sayers's most memorable characters. After a few pages with her, it is not difficult to discern the source of

Peter's ability to prattle on. Small, plump, and good-humored, she is not nearly as circumvolved in speech in this first novel as she will later become, but she is very elliptical, jumping from one subject to the next as thoughts strike her, not quite at random (52, 277):

> By the way, such an odd thing's happened about the Church Restoration Fund—the Vicar—oh, dear, here are these people coming back again; well, I'll tell you afterwards—do look at that woman looking shocked, and the girl in tweeds trying to look as if she sat on undraped gentlemen every day of her life—I don't mean that—corpses of course—but one finds oneself being so Elizabethan nowadays—what an awful little man the coroner is, isn't he? (115)

For all that, she is shrewd and quick to think on her feet as well as a fountain of strength in a crisis. Charles Parker calls her "wonderful," and Peter agrees. She is the first of several strong older women that Sayers will introduce, eventually establishing a discernible pattern of interpretation. Dorothy L. Sayers admired Victorian women with spirit; they pointed the way to the "new woman" of the twenties (223).

One last critically important stock character takes shape in *Whose Body?* We do not yet learn that Bunter has a mother in Kent and that he was one of eleven children, but we do come to understand very quickly that the presence of this most capable manservant is crucial to Peter Wimsey's survival. It is not simply that Bunter buttles, that he supervises Wimsey's wardrobe, that he cooks and cleans for him, that he serves as technical assistant in Wimsey's investigation. Mervyn Bunter takes care of Lord Peter with carefully cloaked affection. This is no small thing, once the reader comes to understand Wimsey's precarious emotional health. Severely correct, "a truly terrible manservant," Bunter understands his place and has no desire to transgress his role. When Peter threatens to sack him, merely to provide him the opportunity of venting an honest opinion of his master, Bunter allows that even then the wall of servitude would not crumble. He is a servant and must never express an ill opinion of his noble employer.

The relationship of manservant to master was one of the few remaining anachronisms from days of rigid social hierarchy then rapidly disappearing. There was real inequality here. Even "in these democratic days" of the early twenties, Lord Peter and Bunter would never meet eye to eye as equals. Yet they would be intimate associates in a long string of adventures.

Although Bunter is a servant, this is not to say he is servile. Sayers drew him as a capable and complex individual, dropping hints from the start that Bunter is a man of many talents. Most obvious is his skill and devotion to the craft and art of photography. Bunter's work with the lens provides a material basis for the connection of the two ends of the Battersea mystery. This is something he is quite passionate about; one of the few cracks in his otherwise correct facade occurs when he respectfully proposes the purchase of a "Double Antistigmat with a set of supplementary lenses." The care he takes in photographing evidence appalls others of his caste. To destroy a possible clue is to do "as much as my place is worth," but one gets the impression that the sentiment is even more Bunter's than his master's.

For all his formidable correctness, Bunter is capable of exercising great charm within the context of his own class. A few soft and encouraging words make Mabel (Sir Reuben Levy's kitchen maid) his steady assistant. Bunter will exhibit his way with women in several more stories. But he is able to gain the confidence of male servants as well. With a little show of friendly drink and comaraderie, Bunter induces Cummings (Sir Julian Freke's man) to relate a detailed picture of events in the household. Sayers employs this episode so as to elicit not only clues to the mystery, but to demonstrate by comparison how truly superior Bunter is as a manservant. Bunter's letter also certifies his unswerving, unquestionable loyalty to his master, the "bloody little fool," Wimsey: "May I take this opportunity of expressing my grateful appreciation of your lordship's excellent taste in food, drink, and dress? It is, if I may say so, more than a pleasure—it is an education, to valet and buttle your lordship." (178) Note the perfect correctness of Bunter's grammar—in every sense (25, 64, 179–85).

Taken together, this company of stock characters lends dimension to Peter Wimsey's imagined life. Moving among a community of familiar figures, Wimsey's activities present the reader with a sense of returning to familiar ground with each future story. Peter is more than a detective; he is a human being with a close, if trying, family. His investigative work brings him into close contact with the official police, but he has other friends as well. The supreme loyalty of so superior a servant as Bunter also implies an important fact about Wimsey: he is a superior individual.

Dorothy L. Sayers worked on *Whose Body?* throughout much of 1921, finishing the manuscript in November and paying seven pounds she could ill afford in order to have it typed. She was not terribly sanguine about its prospects, writing her mother on November 8 to say, "I don't suppose anything will come of it. I haven't the least confidence in the stuff, which is a pity, because I really enjoy turning it out." She had already begun work on a second novel.[46]

Her skepticism seemed justified for a painfully long while. Lord Peter made the rounds of publishing houses, was taken up by an agent who promptly died, and got nowhere through the first half of 1922. Finally an American publisher nibbled. After some protracted agonies, the book was brought out by Boni and Liveright, New York, in May 1923, and T. Fisher Unwin, London, in October. Response was modest but enough to continue. Peter Wimsey was on his way.[47]

Lord Peter Discovers the Possibilities

MUCH OF THE ORDER AND GOOD SENSE TO BE MADE OF A life comes in retrospect. The triumphs grow in magnitude, the small agonies of existence assume a proper proportion, and the sense of grind and ennui dominating the day-to-day reality are forgotten. By 1928 Dorothy L. Sayers had achieved national recognition as a popular author. It would be easy to fasten onto the stepping stones to this success, overlooking the agonies of her life history. For Sayers, altogether too much of the previous seven years was spent in her own carefully fashioned purgatory. Portions of that bleak reality found their way into the works she produced during the period.

If the years 1922 to 1928 were too often a kind of private hell for Sayers, they were a time of restless transition for England as a nation. The modernizing trends apparent in British society at the close of the Great War accelerated in the middle twenties. The old political order underwent severe modification as the parties embraced democracy; the economy adjusted unevenly to the rise of new expectations, and the disappearance of others. All in all, the world seemed to go faster.

Though evolving over several decades, democracy was altogether a recent innovation in English life. The political privilege of hierarchy was banished; the people supposedly governed their own fate through their elected representatives. When Parliament lowered the voting age for women to twenty-one in 1928, adult suffrage became nearly universal. The newly created political context was bound to be unstable; Britain changed prime ministers six times during the 1920s.

Somehow, greater political power did not translate into happier lives or even increased economic security for the mass of people. Recovery from the slump of 1922 was slow and sporadic. Growth enterprises such as entertainment and the motor industry did all right, but the industrial backbone of the nation, the mines and the transportation systems, staggered from one crisis to the next. In many ways, regulating the economy was out of British hands entirely. As long as Europe forced Germany to make reparations, the economic health of that nation severely affected the economic vitality of the rest. When recession left Germany too poor to make the required payments in 1923, the French army occupied the Ruhr Valley, extracting the cash through main force. This made matters that much harder for the Germans and, in the end, for everyone.[1]

Responding to the demands of a democratized electorate, Parliament did what it could to ease the persistent unemployment at home. In 1923 it passed a Housing Act intended to grant public subsidies for construction and alleviate the chronic housing shortage; in 1925 it passed a Widows Pension Act. The Electricity Act of 1926 extended public funds to provide the entire nation the convenience of modern electrification. By 1928 the government had to face up to the fact that poverty had become endemic and was not likely to go away. A "De-rating" Act altered the national tax collection system, bringing much-needed relief to distressed areas in the form of lower taxes.

All of this was well intended, but what the government dispensed with one hand, it withdrew with the other. This was still Britain, a nation that saw itself as the world's bank, the very birthplace of fiscal responsibility. True to the rock-hard nineteenth century credo that the only real money in the world possessed intrinsic value, Britain was returned to the gold standard in 1925. Gold had been abandoned temporarily as a wartime measure, allowing circulation of a freer money supply to promote industrial growth. Restoring the gold standard naturally had just the opposite effect: a bad economic situation got worse. In July of the same year, Parliament compounded the problem, legislating an end to the subsidization of the coal industry.[2]

Britain's laborers were hit hard by these measures, the miners especially so. Already reeling from the lockout of 1921, a new round of wage reductions, coupled with increased production demands, drove them to the wall. On April 26, 1926, the miners went out on strike. The rest of organized labor in Britain followed them.

Throughout the early twenties, there had been considerable discussion of the newfound political power of labor. With all laboring men (and some women) enfranchised, the Labour party had assumed genuine national importance. Their man, Ramsey MacDonald, had briefly occupied the position of prime minister in 1924, only to be ousted by a slender margin later that same year. With the conservatives firmly in charge of the traditional political machinery, it seemed time to flex laboring muscle, to see who really was, or should be, in control. The miners' plaint became a shared burden of every union member. The Trades Union Council called a general strike of all unions for May 3, 1926.

The general strike lasted nine tumultuous days. Amid dire press warnings of Bolshevism run rampant, the union rank and file obeyed the summons almost universally. They not only shut down most heavy industry but also the public transportation system and the regular newspapers. Initially London was in mass confusion. Commuters could not get to the office in the usual way, traffic snarls became immense, and some had to walk as far as twenty miles to work from the suburbs. Rumors of socialist revolution mushroomed, as there were few newspapers to provide accurate information. The conservative middle-class paper, the *Daily Mail* (Sayers consistently referred to a paper called the *Daily Yell* in her novels), was printed in France and flown to England bearing such headlines as "The Pistol at the Nation's Head." Indeed, one of the chief logistical mistakes of the strikers was their inability to properly publicize their side of the story. All the sympathetic newspapers were victims of the strike.[3]

If this was revolution, it was of a curiously amiable kind. For all the high feelings and massive inconvenience, there was little violence. Strikers destroyed some property but not much; scabs damaged more by trying to run machines they did not understand. The strikers made no attempt to shut down vital services or government functions; the government used no military force to bring matters to a close (despite advice to this effect from Winston Churchill). The general strike was a nine-day wrangle. No one would ever forget it, but it did not leave much of a visible mark.

Divisions within the ranks of labor brought the thing to a rapid end. Political labor leaders including Ramsey MacDonald thought the general strike was disastrously bad tactics, while others had doubts about its legality. The Trades Union Council began negotiating with government representatives almost immediately and soon decided to abandon the Miners Union to its fate. They called off the general strike as of May 13. A few trades, more embittered than the rest, held out for an additional five days. Breathing a national sigh of relief, Britain slowly returned to business as usual.

The miners, more radical and more desperate, surrendered after six months. The wage reductions left them scratching a living from inadequate gardens and stolen livestock. By the early 1930s, more than a quarter million miners had emigrated. For those who remained, poverty in the mining districts dug itself in for a long stay. Parliament responded by adopting the Trade Union Act, making national strikes in sympathy with local union actions illegal. No more general strikes would be allowed. Organized labor raised no objection. The general strike was a rousing confirmation of British tradition: the people would not surrender to the demands of labor. They would just muddle through peaceably, putting up with whatever was necessary so life could go on pretty much as always. The times might be changing, but forcing change along was not the English way.[4]

Given Dorothy L. Sayers's keen eye for contemporary detail and her determination to give her books a sense of immediacy, it seems peculiar that none of her novels so much as mentions the general strike of 1926. She does make curious reference to news of rioting in far-off China, in *Unnatural Death*. "Everybody seems to take it very casually," her character states. "If all this rioting and Bolshevism was happening in Hyde Park, there'd be a lot more fuss made about it."[5] This observation is ostensibly uttered in the spring of 1927, one year after the general strike. The comment is curiously reminiscent of the strike, yet somehow it seems unrelated to the great events of the previous year.

In later stories Sayers makes consistent note of the economic hardships plaguing the nation, but she seems more attentive and sympathetic to the problems of agriculture. Lord Peter essentially makes no contact with the organized working man or woman, though he does at times meet working people.

There may be very good reasons for this omission from the novels. Sayers herself was college educated and politically conservative, albeit something of a social radical. She might conceivably have had some sympathy for the miners' problems, but their world was so foreign to hers that empathy was impossible. Then, too, she had created Peter Wimsey as an aristocrat; his opportunities to hobnob with the working classes were severely limited. To maintain consistent character, it would be difficult for Peter to deal with working people without some condescension, however inadvertent or unintended. It was better just to avoid the whole thing.

The more compelling reasons for the omission of the general strike lay closer to Dorothy L. Sayers's heart. The years 1923 to 1926 were especially difficult ones for her. Her second novel, *Clouds of Witness,* gave her considerably more difficulty than the first. Events that Sayers had sketched out to occur in 1923 did not reach print until 1926. A big hole had opened in the envisioned Wimsey career. More critically, Sayers was emotionally wounded by personal woes during this long period. One love affair had closed in 1922, but she continued to pick at the scabs in 1924 and 1925. A second affair ended disastrously with the birth of an out-of-wedlock child in January 1924. She finally found some happiness late in 1925 and married on April 13, 1926, about three weeks before the general strike. She never made mention of the strike in her correspondence. Chances are, she took in stride the inconvenience during the strike of staying home more often.

Dorothy L. Sayers probably met John Cournos, the first of her wretched lovers, through mutual friends among London's Bohemian crowd in 1921. Older, mysteriously foreign, a gifted intellectual and writer, Cournos was almost everything Sayers could dream of in a man. He was a Russian Jew, born in Kiev in 1881. When he was ten his family emigrated to the United States, where he became a rags-to-riches story. He rose to an assistant-editor position in Philadelphia before moving to England as a freelance writer in 1912. There he joined a literary community that included William Butler Yeats and Ezra Pound; he produced a highly regarded novel, *The Mask,* in 1919. By this time he had become a man of "advanced views."[6]

As a minister's daughter and an Oxford student, Sayers had led a fairly sheltered life. Her first hope of love, Eric Whelpton, spurned her. Cournos then crossed her path with the impact of an explosion. She fell passionately in love, determined to marry Cournos and have children with him. Cournos was not interested—at least not that interested. He believed in free love, he said, and would never marry. Bed would be all right, after a visit to the "rubber shop" (Sayers's disdainful euphemism for birth control). In the meantime, he used his modicum of highbrow success to impugn much of Sayers's own literary activity, especially her creation and development of Lord Peter. Cournos was in fact the devil's own snob. On one night the couple traipsed through half of London, looking for a movie he would condescend to watch. He did not like the one they chose—too lowbrow. Sayers, nursing blisters, was less than awed by his unrelentingly fastidious attitude.[7]

Frustration piled on frustration, and the unhappy affair dwindled out in 1922, when Cournos left for the United States. Bitter and still virginal at age twenty-nine, Sayers quickly fell in with an unemployed motorcycle mechanic named Bill White. Not caring "tuppence" for the man, Sayers gladly visited the rubber shop, but the birth control failed. When *Whose Body?* reached print in May 1923, she was two months pregnant. White could make no commitment and soon passed out of her life. Desperately anxious to keep the pregnancy a secret from her parents and her employers, grinding out a living in advertising, Sayers had hit bottom. She took two months' leave from Benson's in November 1923, ostensibly to write, actually to have her baby in secret. She gave birth in a nursing home on January 3, 1924, named the boy John Anthony, and turned him over to a cousin to raise. Fortunately, proceeds from the sale of *Whose Body?* paid all the expenses. She returned to work, determined to make enough to give her child the best circumstances and education possible. There was little else to look forward to. Then she found out that John Cournos had married in America.[8]

The man had abandoned all his principles. Not only had he married, but his wife was an author of detective stories. Hearing of his temporary return to England in the summer of 1924, Sayers determined to write him a letter. What followed was a most extraordinary correspondence, as Sayers poured out the love and wrath consuming her soul. "I love thee still," she admitted, "and as you've no use for me I must be in a very stupid and false and painful position." The pain burnt into the pages of her letters. She confessed that "If I saw you, I should probably only cry— and I have been crying for 3 years now and am heartily weary of the exercise."[9]

Sayers destroyed Cournos's half of the correspondence, but it is easy to infer his remarkable insensitivity from her replies. He degraded her popular fiction efforts, showed no sympathy or understanding over her pregnancy, and even mocked the choice of names for her young son. The man really was despicable. Sayers wrote him at least thirteen letters before the exchange ended in October 1925. By that time, she had met her future husband.[10]

No one knows exactly how Sayers met Atherton "Mac" Fleming. He was a journalist by trade but worked sporadically because of chronic illness—he was a veteran, still suffering the effects of shell shock. The war had changed him profoundly, so much that his first wife had recently divorced him. When able to work, Fleming was a more than capable writer. In 1919 he had published a sensitive and helpful little volume titled *How to See the Battlefields,* an aid to families coping with losses from the war. He also painted, produced excellent photographs, and was very skilled at cooking. Moreover, he was a good-looking fellow. He apparently triumphed over Sayers's anguished passion for Cournos; Mac and Dorothy married in 1926, no more than ten months after their initial meeting.[11]

The writing of *Clouds of Witness* is framed by Sayers's two destructive love affairs, the birth of her son, and her marriage. The book was the longest in production of any Wimsey novel—more than four years passed between its inception and publication. The turmoil of her personal life in part explains the delay, but still more was at work. The novel itself gave her trouble.

The story line that eventually took shape as *Clouds of Witness* was a far more ambitious project than the Battersea mystery. Set principally in two disparate locations, London and Riddlesdale (in Yorkshire), the action revolved around a member of the upper nobility accused of murder. Sayers was nothing if not attentive to accuracy of detail, and a plot such as this required considerable research. She knew little of the Yorkshire country, recognizing only that it was so different from town as to be almost a foreign country. This dictated much research into northern customs and beliefs. Eventually she vacationed in the district, hoping to absorb the local color more fully and correctly.[12]

Murder among the aristocracy was a tough nut to crack as well. Sayers sought to appeal to the international taste for scandal in high places by placing Gerald Wimsey, Peter's older brother, the Duke of Denver, at risk. But a peer cannot be tried in the common courts; the only possible jury of his peers was the House of Lords. This was an intriguing spectacle to portray during the democratic bloom of the 1920s, offering readers a window into the hierarchical past. Sayers worried that a mystery built on the arcane traditions of the British aristocracy might be too much for American readers, but she plunged ahead.[13] She detailed some of her research into the subject in a letter to Cournos, written in January 1925:

> I spent a beautiful sunny afternoon in the B. M. [British Museum] today, reading up the trials of Lord Cardigan and Lord Pembroke. Lord P. was a splendid picture of London night life in 1678. He had a row with a man in a pub in Haymarket and knocked him down and kicked him. The man died and Lord P. was had up for murder. . . . Anyway, the Lords brought it in manslaughter, and the culprit "pleaded his clergy" and so got off scot free!!! The whole tale is characteristic![14]

Such careful research into the antecedents of her stories became characteristic of Sayers.

Carrying on the research and writing amid the travails of heartache and the demands of work, Sayers completed the novel early in 1925. As she had feared, her American agent did not care for it. She explained the situation to Cournos: "[The agent] doesn't like the new book and . . . I shall either have to chuck it up or re-write great chunks of it—and you can imagine how much I shall enjoy going over that old ground again.— I hope Anthony and I don't come to the workhouse! but it's so hard to work. It frightens me to be so unhappy."[15] Somehow, she persevered. In some ways, she flowered. After purchasing a motorcycle in 1925, she rode out the long miles of the great northern highway alone to visit her parents at Christchurch (where her parents had moved in 1916), scandalizing the neighbors by standing out behind the rectory to smoke cigarettes. A working woman with a motorcycle and a secret sexual past, Dorothy L. Sayers had become an advanced woman—and a successful author. T. Fisher Unwin of London published *Clouds of Witness* in February 1926, two months before she married Mac Fleming.[16]

Clouds of Witness shared much in common with its predecessor, *Whose Body?*, but it still represented something of a departure. The community of actors assembled to carry the action of the first novel largely continues in the second, with a few intriguing additions. Several of the stock characters are fleshed out, and Wimsey himself acquires some new qualities. Most important, however, is a shift of emphasis. In *Whose Body?* all of the principal actors are men. *Clouds of Witness* is the first story in which the activities of women become critical.

First and foremost is a new stock character, Peter's sister, Lady Mary Wimsey. Mary, five years younger than Peter, is drawn as a thoroughly modern woman. Her rich golden hair is bobbed, her actions are the product of headstrong decisiveness, and her opinions, if a trifle confused, are decidedly her own. If her considerable financial inheritance is controlled by her brother, she is willing to forego it to escape the lifeless obligations accompanying her title. She would rather work as a secretary for a socialist.

Other witnesses describe her relationship with Dennis Cathcart, her fiancé and the victim of foul play at Riddlesdale, as "offhand" and undemonstrative. This was due in part to the fact that the two did not really love each other, but "that sort of thing was the fashion nowadays."[17] Mrs. Pettigrew-Robinson, another of the guests at Riddlesdale Lodge, "had never liked Lady Mary; she considered her a very objectionable specimen of the modern independent young woman; besides, there had been that very undignified incident connected with a Bolshevist while Lady Mary was nursing in London during the war" (37). Lady Mary's mother, the Dowager Duchess of Denver, had not thought much of Mary's nursing efforts during the war either. Mary could have performed far more valuable work elsewhere, but she was simply dying to get up to London, on whatever pretext (124).

Much of the confusion that created the Riddlesdale mystery is the fault of Lady Mary Wimsey. She had agreed to marry Cathcart as a convenience to escape the dreary conventional life of the aristocratic lady, "opening bazaars and watching polo and meeting the Prince of Wales" (160). Naturally reluctant to actually enter into a loveless marriage, she jumped at the chance to elope with a former lover, the Bolshevik George Goyles. As luck would have it, the night of their proposed elopement is also the night that Dennis Cathcart chooses to commit suicide. First Goyles discovers the body and runs off, then Gerald Wimsey finds the body, and finally Lady Mary discovers her brother bending over the body. Contriving to give evidence at the inquest in such a way as to shield Goyles, Mary manages to incriminate her brother, the Duke. Thus begins the march to all the rigmarole of a capital trial in the House of Lords, the first in more than two centuries.

Peter readily admits that he does not know his sister well. First he went to Eton, followed by Oxford, the war, and the studied separation from the rest of the family in Piccadilly; the two had shared little contact before the death of Cathcart. But Peter is well aware of the family's exasperation with Mary, a difficult and independent woman of twenty-eight who refuses to settle down in an acceptable fashion. When Charles Parker allows his infatuation with Lady Mary to show a little too plainly, Peter details the situation: "—to put it on the lowest grounds, do think what it might have been! A Socialist Conchy of neither bowels nor breeding, or a card-sharping dark horse with a mysterious past! Mother and Jerry must have got to the point when they'd welcome a decent, God-fearing plumber, let alone a policeman. Only thing I'm afraid of is that Mary havin' such beastly bad taste in blokes, won't know how to appreciate a really decent fellow like you, old son" (221–22). A determined, independent woman in her late twenties with a "beastly bad taste in blokes"—Sayers must have modelled Lady Mary on herself.

As matters resolve, Mary proves herself a decent sort. She goes to incredible lengths to protect Goyles, obscuring investigations by one brother intended to save the other, eventually claiming to be the murderer herself. But when Goyles exposes himself as a hypocritical, unworthy ass, Mary at last tells the truth. From that point on, she is a stout ally in the investigation, joining forces with her mother to protect the other mysterious woman in this case, the stunning Mrs. Grimethorpe. Sir Impey Biggs is bemused. "Time and trouble will tame an advanced young woman," he intones, "but an advanced old woman is uncontrollable by any earthly force" (258).

Mrs. Grimethorpe is not an advanced woman. The wife of a brutal Yorkshire farmer, trapped in the remote rural confines of Grider's Hole, she is a prisoner of conventions not merely belonging to Victorian days but extending back to the evil days of feudalism. A more stark contrast to Lady Mary would be difficult to imagine. Mary is petulant and more than a little difficult, but she is capable of running her own life. She is the image of light, golden-haired, and pleasantly mannered. Mrs. Grimethorpe, as her name suggests, is reflected darkness.

We do not even discover Mrs. Grimethorpe's given name. She is surpassingly beautiful, a true Helen; this is both her sole identity and her cross. Men seem to share a universal reaction to her, seeing only "a broad white forehead under massed, dusky hair, black eyes glowing under straight brows, a wide passionate mouth—a shape so wonderful that even in that strenuous moment sixteen generations of feudal privilege stirred in Lord

Peter's blood" (97). Gerald's reaction seemingly was much the same; at risk to life and reputation, he slept with her at least twice. She had consented to the Duke's overtures because he was kind to her, a welcome change from her husband's ferocity.

A traditional woman in the bondage of a traditional marriage, Mrs. Grimethorpe is a true victim. Every emotion save fear has been savagely extinguished; she exists only as an object, a beautiful object to light up the eyes of men. She confesses to her liaison with Gerald only after Peter confronts her with incontrovertible evidence. When at last she does volunteer to testify in the Duke's behalf, to risk the murderous wrath of her husband in order to save her lover, it is a gesture of despair. "I am a lost woman," she says (216).

Here, in the characters of two very different women, Sayers sketches the range of the socially possible in the postwar era. If Lady Mary is the "new woman," forthright and decisive, Mrs. Grimethorpe is her antithesis, a creature at the mercy of the wills of men. Lady Mary's path is filled with complications and obstructions; she can make her way only with difficulty. But at least she is in control. Mrs. Grimethorpe can only react to whatever is set before her. More often than not, such choices as she has are equally poisonous.

Sayers does allow Mrs. Grimethorpe an escape in the end. The accidental death of her husband—killed in the act of trying to do her in—at least frees her from the tormented marriage. Mrs. Grimethorpe now has autonomy, justly inherited with her husband's property. She grasps the meaning of this freedom in a spontaneous decision to buy a scarf:

> "I have money," she said. "I took it from his desk. It's mine now, I suppose. Not that I'd wish to be beholden to him. But I don't look at it that way."
>
> "I shouldn't think twice about it, if I were you," said Lord Peter.
>
> She walked before him into the shop—her own woman at last. (285–86)

The reader never discovers whether Mrs. Grimethorpe can sustain this tentative beginning. She announces her intention to return to her own people in Cornwall. One suspects that it will take more than that to make her an advanced woman. Can she really strike out on her own, run her life without the imprisoning walls of subjugating vow and obligation? Perhaps the best we can hope for is a more prudent second marriage.

If Mary Wimsey and Mrs. Grimethorpe represent the extremes of possibility for women in the twenties, the two settings of the story may be said to represent the extremes of country and town. While London and Paris are at the center of the modern age, Riddlesdale, Grider's Hole, and the market village of Stapley remain enmeshed in a world increasingly alien to people like Mary Wimsey.

The mystery begins at Riddlesdale, but the reader is privy to the action only at second hand. Peter Wimsey is in Paris, preparing to enjoy the advances of modern civilization after three months in Corsica. Among the conveniences is the availability of the *Times,* delivered expeditiously each morning from London by air. Basking in the latest luxuries offered by the Hotel Meurice, Lord Peter studies the paper, entranced by transcripts of the inquest into the death of Dennis Cathcart.

The tragedy grew out of one of the hoariest and most privileged of aristocratic customs, a hunting party. The Duke of Denver, his sister and her fiancé, and several wealthy friends descended on the Yorkshire countryside to shoot birds in obscene numbers. Surrounded by surly folk who need to get on with making a living, they are accepted for the money they bring and the structures of social power they represent. They are not of the Yorkshire country and do not wish to be. They desire only those advantages appealing to privileged taste. In Gerald's case, this includes exercising the right of seigneur with the wife of a local farmer.

The images of the Yorkshire countryside are reminiscent of the nineteenth century if not far earlier. The people of Stapley have been touched by the Great War, have dedicated a monument to the fallen, but it is a tasteless oddity to the eye of Peter Wimsey. The rhythms of the village are intensely agricultural; at any time but market day the streets are mostly deserted. The people are clamlike. When they do speak, it is in a terse local dialect approaching rudeness to a southern ear. The only person with whom Lord Peter can truly communicate is Timothy Watchett, an innkeeper born and raised in London.

Moving from Stapley into the countryside is to step further back in time. The moors are drawn as forsaken wasteland, fit habitat only for birds and rabbits. Trails (much less roads) are almost nonexistent; unpredictable fogs make the going treacherous in the extreme. At the far end of the moor (for Peter and Bunter, at least) lies Grider's Hole and its deadly bog, "Peter's Pot." The bog comes straight out of *The Hound of the Baskervilles* and suggests how little Sayers knew of such places. Real bogs do not behave at all in the manner she describes.

Grider's Hole—the very name suggests sinking backwardness—is something out of the unlamented agricultural past. The operation is a large one, embracing a variety of meat and dairy productions, driven with an iron fist by the black-hearted Mr. Grimethorpe. His wife and child live in mortal terror of his wrath; the hired help tread softly in his presence. It is a smoky, dark, and tyrannical domain, rejecting such signs of modernism as electricity or the consideration of women's roles. In practical reality, Mrs. Grimethorpe has as much recourse as a slave.

The tragedy that takes place at Riddlesdale is of course the responsibility of the local officials, but it is not a community event. The hunting party are outsiders in trouble—one dead, another accused of his murder. The locals will draw considerable entertainment from their predicament ("Why, it'll be better'n a funeral to 'em," (39) as Freddy Arbuthnot observes), but it will not in any way affect their lives. It is horribly easy to envision families like the Grimethorpes living on in that quasi-feudal fashion for decades after the Riddlesdale mystery fades from memory.

The initial police investigation exemplifies the local perspective. Before the Scotland Yard man arrives to take charge of the investigation, the coroner and the local constable "were already as thick as thieves, had fixed the inquest for that morning—which was ridiculous—and arranged to produce their blessed evidence as dramatically as possible" (43–44). Here was an opportunity to get one back at an aristocracy frivoling in the midst of people working hard to make ends meet.

It is not merely that the local officials are spiteful. Toiling out in the backwaters of modern Britain, they are also just a little bit backwards. Despite Peter Wimsey's fame as an investigator, he is received "frigidly" by the police superintendent at Ripley. Peter is hoping to obtain his cooperation in following up a Riddlesdale clue. He ends up telling the man how to do his job:

> Lord bless us and save us, man . . . you're not goin' to waste your time lookin' for the number-plates. . . . Now, forgive me, Superintendent, for shovin' along with my opinion, but I simply can't bear to think of you takin' all that trouble for nothin'—draggin' ponds an' turnin' over rubbish-heaps to look for numberplates that aren't there. You just scour the railway-stations for a young

man six foot one or two with a No. 10 shoe, and dressed in a Burberry that lost its belt, and with a deep scratch on one of his hands. (76)

One can almost hear Wimsey pining for the efficiency of the London police force. When Scotland Yard does get its chance, they turn up the man among the teeming millions of London in less than twenty-four hours.

The mystery that begins in the traditional climes of Yorkshire ends in the bustling international world of the twenties. Charles Parker crosses to Paris where he unravels the sad tale of Dennis Cathcart's financial miseries in the wake of the Great War. Another clue turns up at an elegant jewelry shop on the Rue de la Paix. Still, Charles is relieved to return to London. Paris is perhaps a little too advanced—the hotel rooms are all centrally heated.

For better and worse, London forms the center of Dorothy L. Sayers's modern world. Here is Wimsey's home and his study, the very essence of civility with its black and primrose walls, vases of chrysanthemums, and latest editions of all the papers. Here too is the Soviet Club, with its abominable food, its Bohemian atmosphere, and its free-thinking clientele, amiably freeing literature "from the superstition of syntax" while plotting to convert "the Army and Navy to Communism" (141, 139). The distance from London to Yorkshire is more than geographical.

In this novel at least, Peter Wimsey is far more at home in up-to-date London than in the Yorkshire countryside. Although brought up in rural surroundings at Denver, he is astonishingly maladroit in his investigations up north. His usual blither makes no impact at all at Ripley or Grider's Hole, and he is fully responsible for losing himself and Bunter in the fog on the moor. He really should have known better.

In London, Peter is on a first-name basis with the chief of Scotland Yard, Sir Andrew Mackenzie. All of the facilities of the law are at his disposal. Moreover, he moves easily and efficiently across the range of London scenes, demonstrating a cultured taste at the Inns of Court, amicably adjusting to the unusual service and fare of the Soviet Club, and dealing ingenuously with the demands of the modern press. He is most decidedly a town man, willing to brave the deprivations of Yorkshire to prove his brother's innocence but preferring the comfort and variety of city life.

The story's conclusion finds Wimsey a most modern man indeed. The final bit of evidence necessary to clear Gerald turns out to be in America.

After rushing about to secure the necessary travel papers in less than a day's time ("and they say the English can't hustle" [229]), he boards a passenger liner bound for New York. The return journey edges even closer to the limits of the possible; he flies the Atlantic in a two-seater plane piloted by a pioneer airman. This is January 1924, more than three years before Lindbergh's solo flight to Paris. Teams of pilots had achieved the feat a couple of times at that point, but it was surpassingly dangerous, especially in winter.

Examined in the context of all eleven novels, the Wimsey character of *Clouds of Witness* stands apart in interesting ways. He is somewhat consistent with the Wimsey of *Whose Body?* The essential biographical details remain the same, and he is still given to the same maddeningly breezy chatter, even at the most serious moments. He has learned not to look on detection as a game, at least where his brother's innocence is concerned, and he does take somewhat greater care in examining material evidence. Still, he relies on intuition, on chance connection of unrelated details, to see his way to a solution. And, true to his name, he remains a study in lightness:

> To Lord Peter the world presented itself as an entertaining labyrinth of side-issues. He was a respectable scholar in five or six languages, a musician of some skill and more understanding, something of an expert in toxicology, a collector of rare editions, an entertaining man-about-town, and a common sensationalist. He had been seen in Hyde Park in a top hat and frock coat, reading the *News of the World*. His passion for the unexplored led him to hunt up obscure pamphlets in the British Museum, to unravel the emotional history of income-tax collectors, and to find out where his own drains led to. (93)

In the one moment of serious reflection Sayers allows him, Peter contemplates "(1) The vanity of human wishes; (2) Mutability; (3) First Love; (4) The decay of idealism; (5) The aftermath of the Great War; (6) Birth-control; and (7) The fallacy of free-will" (90). Certainly there was a great deal for a pensive man to consider as the challenge of the modern world unfolded. In *Clouds of Witness* Sayers simply did not allow her hero to think about such conundrums very much.

In fact, Lord Peter differs most in this novel in that he has become intrepid. One gets the feeling that Dorothy L. Sayers must have read one

Sexton Blake too many. The story begins quietly enough, with Peter merely exhausted after a twenty-four hour journey by air, railroad, and automobile just to reach Riddlesdale. Before the novel is half over, he has been shot, breaking his collarbone and taking a severe knock to the head in his fall. He is infernally cheerful the following morning, despite a roaring headache. The collarbone apparently requires no sling or bandage, as Peter is investigating in Stapley three days later without visible hindrance. The upshot of that inquiry is to fall into the bog at Grider's Hole, coming oh so close to dying. He is saved by main strength, hauled out by his arms. The pain to that broken collarbone must have been excruciating, but no mention is made of it. And then, of course, the story ends with Peter flying the Atlantic in foul weather, risking his neck one more time to bring back the evidence that will absolutely clear his brother. Sexton Blake must have wept with pride when he read about it.

Peter is a markedly more sexual animal in *Clouds of Witness* as well. We catch the merest glimpse of the personal catastrophe that had left him so fragile the previous year; he had "got the chuck from Barbara"(49), apparently in 1918. But he had spent three months in 1923 admiring "the wild beauty of Corsican peasant-women" from afar, returning then to Paris to heed "the call of the blood"(9)—poor Peter. Called to Riddlesdale before he could get fairly unpacked in Paris, he came up first against the spectacular Mrs. Grimethorpe and then the even more spectacular Simone Vonderaa. "I seem to be gettin' so susceptible," he muses.

> "When Barbara turned me down—"
> "You're cured," said his friend brutally. "As a matter of fact, I've noticed it for some time."
> Lord Peter sighed deeply. "I value your candour, Charles," he said, "but I wish you hadn't such an unkind way of putting things." (282)

Lord Peter's blood must have been absolutely screaming by the time Gerald was cleared.

Charles Parker proves himself susceptible in this novel as well. Perhaps hoping that at least in fiction two decent people might find happiness in each other, Sayers created the bare beginnings of a romance between Parker and Mary Wimsey. Charles is smitten with Mary from the very first, to the point that it actually affects his detective judgment—an exceedingly rare thing. Blind to the worst of Mary's lies and subterfuge, he defends her actions in the face of the brutal facts that Peter sets forward. A horrible moment comes when Mary actually confesses to Cathcart's murder. Charles knows she is doing it to shield another man; he knows she is lying, and he knows that it is highly irregular for him even to listen without cautioning her. A difficult situation for a man in love. A worse moment comes when Peter catches on; Charles is naturally defensive, and an ugly scene ensues before Peter assures his friend that all is well, at least as far as he is concerned.

An intrepid Wimsey, a romantic Parker—the Lord Peter series would have been vastly different had these trends continued. The climax of the story proves another aberration, a four-alarm ending with a verdict from the House of Lords, an attempted murder, a car crash, and finally Wimsey and Parker getting stone cold drunk with Freddy Arbuthnot. The fragile, sensitive Wimsey, mindful of the consequence of his discoveries, is virtually nonexistent in this novel.

This anomaly among the Wimsey novels took four years in the making; for the most part they were the most miserably unhappy years of Dorothy L. Sayers's life. That might well explain the story's curious turns. Bereft of romance and adventure in her own life, she turned to fiction to supply what she ached for most.

Two additional stock characters make important impressions in *Clouds of Witness*. Sir Impey Biggs, casually mentioned in the first novel, becomes a major player in the second. The barrister primarily responsible for Gerald Wimsey's defense before the House of Lords, Biggs proves a formidable figure. Shrewd, sagacious, and bullying, he will stop at nothing to obtain an acquittal—he does not want the truth, he wants to win the case. Lord Peter is confirmed in his belief "that the professional advocate was the most immoral fellow on the face of the earth" (178). After he gets Denver off with what turns out to be the truth, Sayers employed Sir Impey Biggs in significant roles in at least two more of Wimsey's cases.

The Wimsey family solicitor, Mr. Murbles, is a lawyer of a decidedly different stripe, "a real gentleman of the old school."[18] As a retained attorney, his job is to provide the family good counsel in the legal aspects of day-to-day living. Murbles is perfectly attuned to the task, a cautious and wise man with a keener devotion to abstract justice than has Sir Impey. The solicitor is a throwback, an older man firmly ensconced in the conservative traditions of the Victorian age. Lady Mary is the first woman to dine in Murbles's chambers in twenty years—women traditionally had little need or comprehension of a lawyer's services, and Murbles was not one for feminine companionship.

Sayers made ample use of this newly drawn figure, as did Peter Wimsey. For all the differences in their age and outlook, the two men share opinion on the most fundamental things of life: excellent food and discriminating drink. In the two novels to follow, this "wise old bird"[19] becomes an integral part of the investigating team headed by Lord Peter Wimsey and Charles Parker. Peter must rely on Murbles's impeccable knowledge of wills to find a reason for the "unnatural death" Sayers invented for her third novel.

In her last letter to John Cournos, dated October 18, 1925, Dorothy L. Sayers admitted to being "rather nervous" over a new mystery story she was preparing to write. The letter was in fact devoted exclusively to the craft of mystery writing, a cold departure from the bitter anguish of her past correspondence. Sayers had by this time gotten to know Mac Fleming, achieving a happiness that would cure the bittersweet passion she had poured into the Cournos letters. More assured of her own worth, she seized the opportunity to discuss the challenge of the mystery novel with the "jaded intellect" of her former lover.

Sayers argued that the best detective stories to date had been two dimensional, citing the work of Conan Doyle, Freeman Wills Crofts, and Austin Freeman as examples. Even an ostensible novel such as *The Moonstone* by Wilkie Collins "was not intricate and not altogether in the round." Detective stories were "on the whole most effective when done in the flat and on rather broad lines." Yet, it was in this letter that she confessed her daring intention to break with this most productive tradition, to write a story "combining the appeal to the emotions with the appeal to the intellect." The new story showed signs of "becoming 'round."[20]

This new story was to become *The Dawson Pedigree,* more generally known as *Unnatural Death.* Although Sayers initiated work on this third novel just as her personal life began to show signs of improvement, the effects of the preceding years of unhappiness are readily apparent. The "roundness" of *Unnatural Death* is manifest in its darkness. For all that the novel is set in springtime, the world Sayers creates is largely cheerless, beset by tragedy, greed, and steady, creeping evil.

Mary Whittaker is the most cunning and determined villain that Dorothy L. Sayers ever created, a woman who stops at nothing. Sayers enhances the sense of Whittaker's evil presence by providing only the merest glimpses of her person. The reader sees her once through the eyes of Miss Climpson (Peter's operative), and twice again—although we are not made aware of it—in her disguise as the soon-to-be-divorced Mrs. Forrest. For the rest, she operates at a distance, committing abhorrent crimes with cold-blooded determination. She murders her great aunt for her money and two young women to keep that fact hidden. She tries also to polish off the lawyer who provided innocuous advice, then Wimsey, disguised as the over-nervous Mr. Templeton. Her greed extends to cutting off a poor relation—a clergyman, yet!—without a farthing, and then attempting to pin all her crimes on him. Mary Whittaker is the ultimate rapacious female, the "new woman" run amok.

That Whittaker is a thoroughly modern woman is emphasized from the very beginning. The first description Peter Wimsey hears makes no bones about it: "Oh, a very nice, well-educated, capable girl, with a great deal more brain than her aunt. Self-reliant, cool, all that sort of thing. Quite the modern type. The sort of woman one can trust to keep her head and not forget things."[21]

Mary Whittaker is in fact a professional woman, a nurse trained in London at the "Royal Free." Her status as the "new woman" is subsequently confirmed by the discerning eye of Peter's confederate, Miss Alexandra Climpson: "She was totally out of place among the tea-tables of S. Onesimus. With her handsome, strongly marked features and quiet air of authority, she was of the type that "does well" in City offices. She had a pleasant and self-possessed manner, and was beautifully tailored—not mannishly, and yet with a severe fineness of outline that negatived the appeal of a beautiful figure" (59). By story's end this nice, handsome woman will be revealed as evil incarnate, in part because of her sex.

> "When a woman is wicked and unscrupulous," said Parker, sententiously, "she is the most ruthless criminal in the world—fifty times worse than a man, because she is so much more single-minded about it."

"They're not troubled with sentimentality, that's why," said Wimsey, "and we poor mutts of men stuff ourselves up with the idea that they're romantic and emotional. All punk, my son." (245)

Two men make these observations in the context of the story, but a woman wrote it all. Here, in a sense, is the ultimate argument for equality of the sexes—a woman is just as capable as a man of appalling malevolence.[22]

Sayers had several themes in mind as she painted the repellant career of Mary Whittaker. As a budding writer of detective fiction, Sayers hoped to create a new kind of criminal mastermind whose deeds were so subtle in motive and means as to be almost undetectable. For more than half of *Unnatural Death*, it is questionable whether any crime has been committed. When a motive for murder at last introduces itself, it is still unclear how in the world Whittaker actually killed her aunt. Had she not plunged into criminal lunacy, attempting to murder every person with information about her motives, Mary would never have seen the inside of a jail.

In the face of the remote but unremitting danger emanating from Mary Whittaker, Peter Wimsey and Charles Parker return to the more sober and sensitive characterizations Sayers originally created for them in *Whose Body?* There is no mention of Mary Wimsey; the romantic interest is for the moment buried. Charles is twice described as "nondescript." His role for the first half of the novel is that of rational skeptic—he doubts that Mary Whittaker has committed any crime at all. Once Wimsey garners enough evidence to suggest otherwise, Parker then assumes his role of grinding professional, interviewing (if he must) every lawyer in London. He is the ultimate professional, unimaginative but industrious.

Peter Wimsey's usual capacity for blither reaches truly arresting proportions during the investigation. Random images occur in the midst of critical conversation: "Far from it, as the private said when he aimed at the bull's eye and hit the gunnery instructor" (25). The puzzle of Whittaker's method for murder inspires Peter's best (or worst):

"I am baffled, Watson (said he, his hawk-like eyes gleaming angrily from under the half-closed lids). Even I am baffled. But not for

long! (he cried, with a magnificent burst of self-confidence). My
Honour (capital H) is concerned to track this Human Fiend (cap-
itals) to its hidden source, and nail the whited sepulchre to the
mast even though it crush me in the attempt! Loud applause. His
chin sank broodingly upon his dressing-gown, and he breathed a
few gutteral notes into the bass saxaphone which was the cherished companion of his solitary hours in the bathroom."[23]

Again, as in *Whose Body?*, the babbling masks a troubled soul. This
entire case existed because Wimsey stuck his curious nose into matters
that did not concern him. Two innocent young women die in consequence. The puzzle Wimsey must face is more than the resolution of a
crime. It is a moral dilemma. Mary Whittaker's first crime was to kill a
terminally ill old woman to secure money the woman wanted her to have
anyway. Was that so bad? Legally it was murder, but morally? When
Wimsey investigates, believing this to be the ultimate case, he sets off a
chain of new killings. Is he responsible for the deaths of Bertha Gotobed
and Vera Findlater?

In some desperation, Peter on the spur of the moment turns to a vicar
for advice. The priest reassures him, contending that the murderer's own
guilty conscience eventually would have led to more violence, whether
Peter had interfered or not. Mollified, feeling less "rotten," Peter takes
his leave. But the priest has seen through him with remarkable clarity:
"Mr. Tredgold watched him as he trotted away among the graves. 'Dear,
dear,' he said, 'how nice they are. So kindly and scrupulous and so vague
outside their public-school code. And much more nervous and sensitive
than people think. A very difficult class to reach.'"[24]

Wimsey bears the burden of responsibility for the remainder of the
novel. He must put a stop to Mary Whittaker, both to arrest the evil she
perpetrates and to halt the chain of events he has set in motion. Faced
with the possibility that Whittaker may claim one more victim before
the police can take her, he breaks into sobs. There is no drunken celebration to end this story. Wimsey is cold and sick, fully prepared to
believe that the world is ending.

Beyond the dogged determination of Parker and Wimsey, beyond the
shadowy wickedness of Mary Whittaker, a still more remote yet crucial
personality lingers: Whittaker's first victim, Agatha Dawson. Already

deceased when the novel begins, this stubborn, independent, crafty old woman occupies the very center of the text. In celebrating Agatha Dawson's fierce determination to live, Dorothy L. Sayers expanded on a theme becoming increasingly critical to the body of her popular fiction: the role of individualistic Victorian women in preparing the ground for modern women.

The first of these women is Peter's mother, the Dowager Duchess of Denver. After playing a central role in the first novel, she is reprised in *Clouds of Witness,* where her relentless command of the complexities of spoken English dismays all opposition. The Duchess is discerning and practical, perfectly able to see through her daughter's subterfuges, her son's blither, and George Goyles's empty rhetoric. She does not need to do anything so complicated as investigation; she merely sees—and knows.

The Duchess makes occasional appearances in subsequent novels, but she gives way to a series of truly ancient standard bearers: Agatha Dawson of *Unnatural Death,* Felicity Dormer of *The Unpleasantness at the Bellona Club,* and Cremorna Garden of *Strong Poison.* Each of these women is drawn as an anachronism: a fiercely independent, industrious, and successful survivor of the Victorian age. Here are women who refuse to buckle under to the conventions of the nineteenth century. They defy the marriage plans laid out by their families, they refuse to depend on men for their existence, and they die possessed of considerable wealth earned by their own wits. The crux of each novel is defined by their legacies, pecuniary and otherwise.

Dorothy L. Sayers well understood that the system of gender roles emerging in the postwar world was very much a relic of Victorianism, however far women may have gone in stretching social taboos. Caricatures of the backlash against the "new woman" are sprinkled here and there throughout *Unnatural Death.* A coroner lectures on "the prevalence of jazz and the immoral behaviour of modern girls," the highly moral Mrs. Cropper speaks of all the goings-on "with lots of girls as they are," and Vera Findlater—no intellectual heavyweight—complains of men denigrating "modern young ladies who want the flappers' vote." The struggle for equality was still all uphill (127, 113, 185).

The roots of the struggle that took shape in the twenties were anchored well back in the Victorian era and before, at the beginnings of the Industrial Revolution. To be sure, sexual divisions of labor and role predate industrialization. The horrors of Mrs. Grimethorpe's existence suggest the kind of sexual exploitation that can emerge in remote agricultural settings. But industrialization severely aggravated the sexual division by physically separating men and women for much of the day. In the pre-industrial era, home and work were located in the same space, generally under the same roof. The baker, the carpenter, and the store-keeper worked out of his (or, sometimes, her) home. The entire family contributed to the success of the enterprise: the husband as head of the family and director of the business, the wife as deputy director, fully prepared to assume responsibility and direction when necessary, the children, servants, and laborers contributing as required.[25]

By centralizing commercial production, industrialization changed the locus of work. People left home to earn a daily wage, now walking steps, blocks, or even miles to work in a bakery, a carpenter shop, a store. Home became wholly domestic, and "productive work" was something done in a completely different place.

Coping with this revolution in basic lifestyles, people in the nineteenth century cast about for new models of proper behavior, a morality fitted to the industrial world. Developing middle-class images of propriety would become the essential ingredients defining "normal" behavior by Victoria's time. "Normal" meant that men went out to win the bread, while women stayed home to manage the household. Never mind that thousands of working women had produced within the home for centuries and would go into the shops and factories as the nineteenth century unfolded. The dominant culture determined these women to be culturally marginal, unrefined, and morally treacherous. If they possessed a grain of breeding, they would desire only to get out of the factory and into the home, where they belonged. To the middle-class Victorian, the ideal woman was a dependent woman. Articles in popular journals, stories in mass circulation magazines, and fashionable novels sought to reinforce this stereotype and its attendant assumptions.[26]

The culture seriously conflated sexual characteristics (matters dictated by biology) and gender functions (roles allotted the sexes by the culture without real biological justification). Women were regarded as little more than baby producers. They therefore had no need of education, no place in business or the professions. To educate a woman was to endanger her reproductive capability; it was held that overexcitement of the brain would cause the ovaries to atrophy. Women were to emphasize their femininity, entrapping their bodies in elaborate dresses, innumerable petticoats, and unyielding corsets, all to accentuate (or create) the shapely bosom and the hourglass figure. Here sex was emphasized, even as the culture demanded that the passions be sublimated.[27]

If the culture demanded (and sex supposedly dictated) that women belonged in the home, the defined characteristics of maleness would naturally lead to opposite behavior. Only the man was fit to sally forth into the workaday world, where competitive aggressiveness was natural and necessary. Men were assumed to be predatory and indiscriminate, outdoing their competitors in business. Left to themselves, they would also pursue sexual relations whenever and wherever possible. It was up to the good woman at home to put a stop to that.[28]

The woman's—the wife's—role was to be the fountain of virtuous purity. She would maintain the home as a shelter from the cruel world outside; she would exercise her virtue to keep her man on the straight and narrow. In a sense, her husband became her oldest child, subject to the same lessons in virtue exercised on their children. She was expected to be submissive at the same time, to tolerate the necessary sexual union within the home. It was the duty of every couple to increase the population of the empire. Still, for a good woman, sex was something to endure, not to enjoy. Ladies did not move.[29]

With the division between the sexes so firmly engraved, strange things were bound to develop. Men and women became truly estranged. Some women suffered from a malady (considered medical in the nineteenth century) that caused them to become hysterical whenever their husbands tried to bring them to the bed. Knocking them out with chloroform was one solution. Other women were kept so completely unaware of the basic functions of sex that they did not know what their husbands expected on their wedding night. (Consider passages from *The Devil is an English Gentleman* by John Cournos, describing a series of love scenes in which a man and woman lie together, she absolutely clueless of what he wants. The scenes were inspired by memories of his unhappy and celibate affair with Dorothy L. Sayers, which took place in 1922.)[30]

This, of course, was the kind of extreme reaction that could be expected to occasionally occur, given the narrow confines of the culture. What really went on behind closed bedroom doors in more than ninety-nine percent of Victorian married households is anybody's guess; there is virtually no evidence documenting actual behavior. One suspects that matters moved along pretty much as they had for the past hundred thousand years—some men and women happy, others less so. Culturally, what mattered was the public face that Victorians attached to such primal human behavior. The Victorians claimed that sex was dirty, and the ideal was to avoid it as much as possible.[31]

Therefore the middle-class English Victorians often chose to accentuate the divisions between men and women. In addition to the natural distinctions of biological function and the new economically imposed divisions of role, middle-class people chose simply to avoid their opposites. Women gathered in exclusive social circles for purposes ranging from giving birth to reforming public behavior. Men viciously ridiculed women's associations, claiming intellectual and organizational superiority, but women organized and endured all the same. What time men did not spend in business pursuits they often spent at their clubs (no women allowed), sometimes not coming home for weeks at a time. More fortunate men (and a very few women) separated themselves for far longer duration, adventuring in the wilds of Africa, Asia, and the Americas.[32]

Separation became the ideal. If sex was dirty, the best men were those who avoided it, using the energy to build railroads or explore the Himalayas instead. Small wonder that Sherlock Holmes was the middle-class hero of late Victorian times. He was the ultimate in energy and self-control, and he was utterly sexless. Like all good men, he was the perfect gentleman, chivalrous to a fault when he had to deal with women. He simply did not trust them, having no use for persons who supposedly based all decision making on emotion and intuition. Like any ideal Victorian man, Holmes was a logical reasoner.[33]

The ultimate male adventure was to go to war. Serving the nation, fighting for a glorious cause, separated from women yet fighting to protect their lives and virtue—what greater glory could a man ask? If a man were truly fortunate, he might go to the war and get killed. This was the sublime heroic sacrifice, and it saved him the doom of returning home, getting married, and falling into dirty ways. Only the good die young, you know. In August 1914, the young men of Britain were eager to march off to fight the Huns; the women cheered them, urged them onward. Oxford was nearly emptied of students. The supreme moment for a sexually divided culture had come. Five long years later, a great many Victorian assumptions had fallen by the wayside.[34]

In Agatha Dawson, Dorothy L. Sayers created a woman embodying some characteristics of Victorian culture while completely flaunting others. Certainly Agatha avoided men, but to a remarkable extreme. Born in 1852, she decided early "to be an old maid . . . and be ever so happy, without any stupid, tiresome gentlemen."[35] She took a house with her cousin, Clara Whittaker, a true Victorian anomaly. Clara Whittaker ran a thoroughbred horse business, doing exceedingly well despite the jealous opposition of various men in the district. A sharp and shrewd business woman, Clara Whittaker also rode to the hounds, easily keeping pace with male participants even well into her sixties. Agatha Dawson did not possess the same adventurous spirit or business acumen, but she was fiercely loyal to Clara. Maintaining the forms of convention in a decidedly non-Victorian arrangement, Agatha managed the household, serving as an able domestic partner to her cousin.

When Clara Whittaker died in 1922, Agatha Dawson inherited the vast fortune that Clara had accumulated. There was some jealousy over this; again, Clara had shocked convention by passing over Whittaker family members to leave the money to her partner. Agatha Dawson continued in the tradition of their partnership, defying the advice of interfering males such as lawyers, toughing out a hideous bout with cancer, and doing things her own way. When her very distant great niece, Mary Whittaker, attempted to trick her into signing a will, she very neatly checkmated the entire scheme. She was not terribly bright, but she was determined and very independent. She was also a decent human being, defying the prejudice of her housekeeper and neighbors to entertain cousin Hallelujah Dawson, "a man of colour."[36] In the 1920s, such determination and independence were the qualities the "new woman" sought to emulate. It was the Clara Whittakers and Agatha Dawsons of the nineteenth century who carved out the path.

In her next novel, *The Unpleasantness at the Bellona Club,* Sayers highlights the story of Lady Felicity Dormer, another survivor of the bizarre dictates of Victorian convention. Felicity Dormer was the vivacious daughter of a poor upper-class family. Such money as there was went to purchase a commission for the family's only son; the parents shamelessly matched the daughter with an old and decrepit (but rich!) member of their class. Felicity would have none of it, stooping to the middle class to elope with (God forbid!) a button manufacturer. The family never forgave her, cutting off all ties and denying her existence. She lived quite happily, however, becoming a wealthy and titled woman with a true zest for life. She succumbed to pneumonia, contracted after watching a fireworks display, at the age of seventy-eight. Here is another woman cut from the mold of Agatha Dawson, a woman who finds happiness by defying the culture and pursuing her own path. A truly independent spirit, she was genuinely successful.[37]

Sayers returned to this theme again in her fifth novel, *Strong Poison*, this time celebrating the career of the notorious Cremorna Garden, profligate singer and actress who climbed the social ladder to wealth using her sex appeal. Modelled on the career of adventuresses such as Lillie Langtry, she was the kind of woman who took everything offered and gave away nothing, ending up as the respectable Mrs. Wrayburn, with untold wealth and a mousy husband firmly under her thumb.[38]

Dorothy L. Sayers probably derived her enormous respect for spirited and unconstrained women from the women of her own family. Her mother, Helen Leigh Sayers, though a parson's wife for much of her adult life, held strong convictions and took real responsibility for running family affairs in the face of her unworldly husband. Sayers could also look to two aunts, Mabel Leigh and Gertrude Sayers, for prototypes of defiant older women.[39] One more from this mold emerges in *Unnatural Death*: the redoubtable Miss Alexandra K. Climpson.

Sayers is coy in introducing Miss Climpson, allowing Parker (and the reader) to believe that Lord Peter has taken a mistress. The woman living at the top of six flights of stairs at St. George's Square is a complete surprise, "a thin, middle-aged woman, with a sharp, sallow face and a very vivacious manner."[40] She is not Peter's mistress but his operative, a woman of diligence, quick wit, and keen perception. Because she is middle aged—a "spinster made and not born" (184)—she is privy to sources of information that no man could ever harvest: the boarding houses and tearooms where older single women congregate. Gossip is the pastime of choice, an incomparable source of genuine news. Through no fault of her own, Miss Climpson has long been an involuntary denizen of this world. She is one of the "surplus women" the newspapers loved to pity and deride in the years following the Great War. Sayers was all too aware of the horrid meanness in such an existence; her own Aunt Gertrude Sayers was a victim of its clutches. Gertrude "lived peripatetically as a 'companion' to various old cats, . . . aimlessly doing what when done was of little value to God or man." Dorothy L. Sayers could only thank God she had been spared such "frustrate unhappiness."[41]

Miss Climpson is a definite victim of the prevalent Victorian attitudes toward women. Possessing a genuinely fine native intelligence, she could have been a professional woman of surpassing ability. Her "poor father" did not believe in education for women, not even the rudiments of law or business practice. His daughter was therefore condemned to a pointless existence as chaperone, travelling companion, and common boarder. Her one reliable companion has been her own good conscience, honed through years of steadfast religious devotion. She and Lord Peter share equally in the good fortune that they have found each other.

At the time of *Unnatural Death,* Miss Climpson has been working for Wimsey some six months. Generally she investigates newspaper advertisements, searching for attempted frauds or worse. But Peter recognizes the depth of her talents and plants her in the middle of complex investigations, such as the Agatha Dawson murder, when the situation warrants. In her own convoluted, enthusiastic way (a product of her "roaming Catholic" devotion [226]), she sees directly into the heart of Mary Whittaker and goes about gathering the evidence to prove murder. It is Miss Climpson, acting from instinctive revulsion, who first confronts Whittaker. Lord Peter could not have solved the case without Miss Climpson, though it is conceivable that she could have worked it out without Lord Peter.

Perhaps in the spirit of these rebellious women, Dorothy L. Sayers became noticeably less disposed to tolerate the easy prejudices of her age as her career in popular writing developed. Echoing the nascent anti-Semitism of the society portrayed in her first novel, she had impeccably captured the Francophobia gripping Britain in her second, incorporating commonplace anti-French platitudes into several conversations in *Clouds of Witness.* In doing so, she summed up the feelings of the British public quite well; mistrust of the French extended back at least nine hundred years and was not about to be overcome by any recent alliance, however successful. In fact, postwar Britons tended to blame the French as much or more than the Germans for the appalling death tolls of the war. Robert Graves summed up the popular outlook when he stated that no one wished the Germans any harm in the twenties, but all were prepared to fight the French. Still, in the same book, Sayers did soften her unthinking stereotype of the Jews, mentioning only that Mrs. Grimethorpe's unusual beauty was not of English origin; it must be a "touch of Jew."[42]

Easy stereotypes give way more completely in *Unnatural Death.* In portraying Agatha Dawson as a brave and gracious old woman, Sayers openly attacks the unthinking prejudice that lumped all dark-skinned people—Africans, Argentines, Esquimaux, Hindus—into one mass of un-British, inferior humanity. The Dawson family housekeeper is scandalized and quits when Agatha invites a man of "pleasant, slightly aquiline features and brown-olive skin of the Polynesian"(155) into the home. Miss Dawson's position is that the man, whatever his color, is a blood relation and a Christian minister and deserves to be treated as such—a sentiment with which Sayers plainly agrees. The Reverend Hallelujah Dawson, a man of "humble and inoffensive" appearance, turns out to be the most decent and pious soul in the novel.

Sayers also chose in this novel to address—however obliquely—the issue of homosexuality. Although none of the characters in *Unnatural Death* mention the word or any of its euphemisms, two lesbian relationships form the core of the story. On the one hand, it is Vera Findlater's "pash" for Mary Whittaker that alarms Miss Climpson, suggesting that Mary's homosexuality is integral to her "unnatural" makeup. Yet Sayers treats the long-lived same-sex relationship between Clara Whittaker and Agatha Dawson with compassion and respect, implying that theirs was a thoroughly understandable and honorable love. There seems some ambivalence in Sayers's underlying message, as if she cannot make up her own mind on the subject. Certainly Sayers encountered homosexual relationships in her own life. Among the Bohemian set, same-sex affairs more generally came into the open during the 1920s. By 1930, Sayers had apparently accepted them as a positive; Harriet Vane's closest friends and supporters in *Strong Poison* are a lesbian couple.

Apparently by conscious choice, Sayers has softened her opinions— and those of her characters—in considering issues of race and sexual relations. While such displays of tolerance are not an entirely consistent feature of the stories to follow, the common prejudice that Sayers so fully incorporated into the first two books does largely disappear.

A new London publisher, Ernest Benn, brought out *Unnatural Death* in September 1927, less than two years after Sayers began plotting the story. This was a vast improvement over the four years of agony poured into *Clouds of Witness*. Satisfied in marriage, she was now able to devote more energy to creative work. The writing itself also became more rewarding. Recognition and sales grew, enabling her to negotiate a relatively lucrative contract with another British publisher, Victor Gollancz. Before proceeding to the work for Gollancz, however, she was obligated to produce one last volume for Ernest Benn. She pushed "the

'Bellona Club' story ahead for him"; *The Unpleasantness at the Bellona Club* appeared just ten months after *Unnatural Death*.[43]

This fourth Peter Wimsey novel is a very brave piece of work and a direct product of Dorothy L. Sayers's marriage to Mac Fleming. Eight years before, she had chosen to portray Lord Peter as a shell-shocked war veteran. Now she was married to such a man and privy to his moods, his memories, and his pain. She chose to face this ticklish subject head on, to write a novel about the impact of the Great War on human life.

The war is an omnipresent fact of life in her two previous novels, a presence mentioned but never dwelled upon. In *Clouds of Witness,* the maidservant Ellen, doing the laundry at Riddlesdale, vividly recalls her sorrow over poor Bert, her "young man what was killed in the war." In London, a ragged news vendor remembers Peter Wimsey as the major he helped to pull out of a shell hole at Vimy Ridge. Most of all, it is the war that creates the desperate set of circumstances leading to Dennis Cathcart's suicide. Heavily invested in properties and securities throughout Europe, he saw his Russian and German credits disappear in 1914, while his proceeds from the French vineyards were suspended for years together. Unable to shore up the situation while serving at the front, he turns to cardsharping, a "rotter's game." His mistress deserts him anyway, and in despair he pulls the trigger—one more victim of the Great War (73, 247, 265).

In *Unnatural Death,* the action takes place in 1927, nine years after the war's end. Here the characters look determinedly forward, expressing much concern over flappers and the ways of the modern world. Yet the war has cast its shadow over this story as well, exacting its grim toll on the Dawson family of the Hampshires. John Dawson, Agatha's first cousin and her only close relation, died at the front in 1916. "A cruel business that was . . . and nobody the better for it" (147).

Despite the repeated presence of the war's aftereffects, Sayers did not confront the conflagration directly in either story. Wimsey seems cured of the remnants of his shell shock—perhaps the three months in Corsica did him good. His personality is still balanced on the knife edge, especially in *Unnatural Death,* but the reader is not allowed past the blithering mask to view the scars of those years in the trenches. Like all true veterans, Peter prefers not to speak of the war.

This reticence still marks his character in *The Unpleasantness at the Bellona Club*. The story begins, significantly, on November 11, 1927, the ninth anniversary of the armistice. Peter is at the Bellona Club to attend a private dinner to honor the memory of a close friend killed in the war. He has weathered the public ceremonies honoring the veterans and mourning the dead, and he is heartily sick of the whole business. Commiserating with another veteran, he expresses the wish of virtually every man sharing their grisly experience: "All this remembrance-day business gets on your nerves, don't it? It's my belief most of us would be only too pleased to chuck these community hysterics if the beastly newspapers didn't run it for all it's worth. However, it don't do to say so" (2).

Peter has done with the war, and he sincerely wishes the war was finished with him. But he can only express these sentiments at places such as the Bellona Club, within the hearing of the war-experienced and no one else. Nine years after the fighting has ended, these men form a special and exclusive kind of community, prone to emotions only they can fully understand.

The Bellona is a refuge for war casualties. There is "Tin-Tummy" Challoner, with his "spare part" from the second battle of the Somme; the secretary, Cuyler, with his one good arm; and the cloakroom attendant with "a Sam Weller face and an artificial leg." Worst of all are those without visible scars, the men who look and act "normal," men desperately wounded deep in their emotions. The Fentiman brothers, George and Robert, are prime examples (34).

To all appearances, Robert Fentiman has escaped the war without a scratch, physical or psychological. He is of a military family and was quite the hardened soldier at the front, a "regular army type." His brother remembered him "at that ghastly hole at Carency, where the whole ground was rotten with corpses—ugh!—potting those swollen great rats for a penny a time, and laughing at them. Rats. Alive and putrid with what they'd been feeding on. Oh yes. Robert was thought a damn good soldier" (128).

For all his physical and mental hardihood, Robert came away from the war a damaged soul. His sense of gentlemanly honor was gone. When his ninety-year-old grandfather dies suddenly, killing his chance to inherit thousands from Lady Dormer, Robert immediately bends to fraud, concealing the death and dishonoring the old man's body by hiding it in a telephone booth—on Armistice Day! He compounds this unholy fraud by systematically lying to Peter Wimsey about his grandfather's last night on earth. When Wimsey at last exposes him, Robert explodes with laughter. He has no finer feelings left.

Brother George is in worse shape. Most of the time he is feeling visibly awful. His insides are "gassed out," his nerves shot. Perpetually paranoid and complaining, he cannot hold a steady job but must depend on his wife's income. This only aggravates matters, robbing him of his sense of honor and worth. Too often he is bitterly critical of his wife, a good woman with untold patience and a determination to work hard for both of them. At heart, George knows this, but he is incapable of returning honest respect and love. The war has gassed it out of him.

. To have any hope of at least maintaining a normal appearance, George must avoid stress. He sits quietly nodding as his ancient grandfather (a veteran of the Crimea) lectures him on proper behavior. The grandson controls himself with difficulty; the old man has no idea what George has suffered, what he must now avoid. Tension mounts with old Fentiman's death and becomes unbearable when it is proved murder. The old shell shock returns; George Fentiman's nerves run amok. He ends up at the police station confessing to a killing he did not commit, convinced he is possessed by the devil.

Though he finds their actions deplorable at times, Peter Wimsey fully comprehends what has shaped Robert and George Fentiman. He is of the same community and is perhaps capable of similar behavior. Millions of men honed by the war would understand in just the same way. When the body of old Fentiman is discovered sitting by the fire in the Bellona Club's sitting room, George dissolves into hysterical laughter. The older members are horrified by this undignified display. "Only the younger men felt no sense of outrage; they knew too much" (7).

The sense of what is lost is best provided by a close friend of the Wimsey family, the elderly Colonel Marchbanks. Having lost a son in the war, Marchbanks is a sensitive and sympathetic soul, but still his perspective is different:

Sometimes, Lord Peter, I think that the War has had a bad effect on some of our young men. But then, of course, all are not soldiers by training, and that makes a great difference. I certainly notice a less fine sense of honour in these days than we had when

I was a boy. There were not so many excuses made then for people; there were things that were done and things that were not done. Nowadays men—and, I am sorry to say, women too—let themselves go in a way that is to me quite incomprehensible. (335–36)

Peter has no response to this. An honorable man himself, he shares the Colonel's sense of dignity. But the war, the Great War, has left its mark on him.

Although a tale of murder, with all the usual trappings of the modern detective story, *The Unpleasantness at the Bellona Club* was something more. By weaving the most painful of sentiments into the text, by drawing fully rounded portraits of human beings still suffering from their wounds, Sayers gave her readers an opportunity to genuinely contemplate a long-forbidden subject. There were essentially no books about the interior view of the war written between 1918 and 1928. Soon after would come Remarque's *All Quiet on the Western Front,* followed by Graves's *Good-bye to All That* and countless others. Dorothy L. Sayers had ventured down a courageous path.[44]

Sayers was not interested merely in the war and its effects on those who participated; she wished to consider its impact on the whole of society. To this end, she returned to two familiar themes: the influence of scientific dogma and the emerging roles of women in the modern world. Her depiction of each is in some way shaped by the presence of the war-wounded characters populating the novel.

Scientific theory was news in the latter half of the 1920s. The idea that medical intervention could in some way not only improve health but actually cure society's ills arrested attention. In the Fentiman mystery, this idea takes the form of research into glandular imbalances. Peter Wimsey is conversant with the subject, possessing "a number of scientific friends who found him a good listener" (220), but the true expert is Doctor Penberthy, Harley Street physician and medical man at the Bellona Club. A war veteran himself, Penberthy is sensitive to the special needs of the combat veterans who make up much of his patient list. He understands not simply their physical ails but their emotional difficulties as well. Still, he is fed up. He would much rather do something more glamorous, more rewarding. Penberthy is an earnest and determined practitioner who closely follows the latest research; his own analysis is "original" and "suggestive." His dream is to abandon the poor-paying demands of regular practice and establish his own research clinic devoted to the study of glands. His vision of treating both disease and criminal tendency through glandular injections is very attractive—the wealthy high society Rushworth family is "all over glands" (220, 181).

Penberthy is prepared to do anything, including murder, to get his clinic. Sayers has to some extent repeated here the essential theme of *Whose Body?* the scientific visionary utterly without a sense of social responsibility. Not only does he kill a ninety-year-old man to prevent him inheriting money which would otherwise go to his fiancée, he then turns brutally on the woman, accusing her of sexual mania to get rid of her and conceal his own crime. This is a man after Julian Freke's heart.

Of the first four Peter Wimsey novels, one is resolved by suicide; in the other three, the killers are all medical practitioners. Dorothy L. Sayers's concern with the dangers of unregulated science was a recurring focus in her work. If nerves and glands were news, the public needed to be wary. (The book apparently had some impact in this respect; Sayers received a letter from a medical man asking for information about gland research after the book was published.) It is possible, too, that Sayers was gently avenging herself on the medical profession for memories past. Their treatments, after all, had made her later adolescence a traumatic experience. What young woman would want to lose her hair?[45]

If the solution to *The Unpleasantness at the Bellona Club* mirrors that of *Whose Body?* the comparison must end there. In this fourth novel, Sayers has evolved a far more complex story line, a "rounded" story in which Peter Wimsey must carefully consider the psychological profiles of several persons, including himself, to arrive at the proper solution. This represents an extension of Peter's character, as evidenced in his interactions with three young women integral to the plot.

The long grasp of the war has shaped the lives of Sheila Fentiman, Marjorie Phelps, and Ann Dorland in powerful ways. Each is struggling to make her way in the world, only to run up against impediments of a kind not so common in the world before 1914. Yet each is unique, and Peter Wimsey must deal with each in a different fashion, talking to them "like ordinary human beings."[46]

Sheila Fentiman is as much a victim of the war as is her husband, George. He had been a caring and supportive husband when first they married, but he had returned from the trenches a mental and physical wreck. This placed the economic, as well as the emotional, burdens of the family squarely on her shoulders. George could not hold a job. Sheila tried running a tea shop, but the slump took care of that. Heavily indebted, she must now work long hours on the outside, only to return to a demanding and guilt-ridden husband. He wants them to be a traditional family: he out earning a paycheck, she keeping the house. She perhaps seems to want the same thing. This is impossible, and he takes it out on her, accusing her of being one of those "advanced women," prone to "all this jazzing and short skirts and pretending to have careers." Poor Sheila—her hair is going prematurely gray, she has to take medicine for her heart, and her husband envisions her "flying off to offices and clubs and parties." Small wonder she wept for the injustice of it all. One quality of the war's effect is plain: even in the dawn of the age of the "new woman," not every woman wanted to work outside the home. Some simply had to (81–95).

Wimsey, alas, can see both sides of this unresolvable conflict. In his own defense, George does admit that it is his "filthy temper," spurred on by his damaged nerves, that makes him so rude to Sheila. Peter can only understand and forgive, agreeing that "She's damned fine, old man" (81–95). But his sympathies really lie with Sheila. "It always gives me the pip," said Wimsey, "to see how rude people are when they're married. I suppose it's inevitable. . . . I've asked people, you know—my usual inquisitiveness—and they generally just grunt and say that their wives are sensible and take their affection for granted. But I don't believe women ever get sensible, not even through prolonged association with their husbands" (105). When George Fentiman has an attack and disappears, Wimsey rushes immediately to Sheila's aid, ignoring the pointed suspicion of neighbors to provide real sympathy and comfort. Sheila loves her war-damaged husband and will stand by him, no matter what. Peter can only give his hand to support such real affection.

What provoked George Fentiman's remarks about "advanced women" was a discussion of Ann Dorland, the rival claimant to Felicity Dormer's thousands. Dorland is only a distant relation of Lady Dormer, but the old lady, desiring some youthful fresh air about the house, had plucked her from a life of comparative poverty, inviting Ann to share her substantial house at Portman Square. In return for her companionship, Lady

Dormer provided Ann Dorland a considerable allowance and perfect freedom to do as she liked, even giving over the glass-roofed billiard room on the first floor for use as a studio/laboratory.

On the surface, Dorland seems the epitome of the new woman, moving among the Bohemian artists of Bloomsbury, pursuing love affairs, and expressing herself first through painting and later through a self-taught interest in scientific research. But, for much of the novel, the reader never views Ann Dorland directly. Images and stories about her are filtered through a variety of witnesses, none of whom seem to really know her very well. She is not very popular among the Bloomsbury set, possessing little real artistic talent and taking her brief romantic flings all too seriously. The servants in Lady Dormer's household find her artistic and scientific interests something of a nuisance. Apparently Ann does too, as she has all but given up on them by the time the murder investigation begins. When the reader at last does encounter Ann Dorland, reluctantly and gracelessly answering the pointed questions of Charles Parker, she appears thoroughly unlikable: bitter, sulky, and rude.

The truth is that she is a young woman without the faintest idea of what to do with herself. She has money but has not been educated to appreciate what it can do. She is interested in art but is herself artless. She has achieved freedom and found it empty. For Ann Dorland, the choices offered women in the twenties are still too narrow. She is shockingly conventional to the Bloomsbury Bohemians, far too rebellious and independent to settle into the old Victorian mold (even if she could find a way to do it). The war may have opened doors for women, but this particular woman cannot figure out what to do once she has walked through.

Peter Wimsey is the one person in the novel capable of seeing Ann as she really is. Examining her sad attempts at painting, he sees through the flawed brushwork to catch a glimpse of frustrated devotion. He intuits the entire ugly story: the love affair with Penberthy, the callous rejection, the bitter shame. Catching up to her, he displays the simple charm and honesty required to coax the whole story from her. In the process he discovers that, for all her pathetic lack of finish and poise, she most definitely has brains. And, as matters turn out, she also has a natural sense of good taste. She wins Peter's deepest respect by refusing a dinner of lobster and champagne, also by recognizing that the Romanée Conti 1915, while exhibiting considerable potential, is not yet a good wine. Like the wine, Ann Dorland is an unfinished product, possessing the proper spirit, but not yet finding her place. She will come into her own one day (300–27). Peter foretells her future:

> Not an artist, not a bohemian, and not a professional man;—a man of the world. . . . That is the kind of man who is going to like you very much. Look! that wine I've sent away—it's no good for a champagne-and-lobster sort of person, nor for very young people. It's too big and rough. But it's got the essential guts. So have you. It takes a fairly experienced palate to appreciate it. But you and it will come into your own one day. . . . But your man won't be at all the sort of person you're expecting. You have always thought of being dominated by somebody. . . . But you'll find that yours will be the leading brain of the two. He will take great pride in the fact. And you will find the man reliable and kind and it will turn out quite well. (322)

Difficult though it may be to believe, Sayers brings the novel to a symmetrical conclusion by allowing Ann Dorland the opportunity to dominate Robert Fentiman. (Given the shape of his moral values, he needs dominating.) Ann will follow the spirited footsteps of her elderly companion and patron, the Victorian rebel Felicity Dormer. Eschewing society's expectations, she will marry a man of the world who will allow her to come into her own as a human being.

A happier contrast to the struggles of Sheila Fentiman and the awkward uncertainties of Ann Dorland is provided by Marjorie Phelps, successful sculptor and Lord Peter's guide to London's Bohemia. Marjorie, a "pleasant-looking young woman with curly hair" (135), is wiser than most in her set. Without compromising her essential art, she has established herself in a line of original yet saleable figurines that enable her to pay the bills and live in reasonable comfort. Her approach to Bohemia is practical and a little cynical. She tracks the love affairs and scandals of the Bloomsbury crowd with amusement, indulging herself when she considers the danger minimal. She is perfectly at home at Chelsea parties where the chianti is too thin and the men too obvious, but she is also prepared to appreciate the exquisite gentility of a man such as Peter Wimsey. She is perhaps Sayers's ideal for the new woman: intelligent, independent in spirit and judgment, and a productive member of society. With no pecuniary need for a man's support, she is able, at least to a point, to make her own choices in love. She is perfectly willing to take on Peter as a husband, not because of his wealth or title, but because he is a truly loveable man. Unfortunately, Peter cannot return the compliment. If "a great liking and friendship were enough, I would—like a shot" (341). He knows that she would be unsatisfied. Her life in most ways complete, Marjorie Phelps must marry for love and nothing less.

Dorothy L. Sayers steers Peter Wimsey himself further down the path toward love in this fourth novel. Demonstrating little interest in women in *Whose Body?* Peter shows himself to be dangerously susceptible in *Clouds of Witness*. By the time of his strange encounter with Mary Whittaker in *Unnatural Death,* he has become the very picture of experienced eligibility, "rich enough, well-bred enough, attractive enough, and man of the world enough"(180) to attract the attentions of an array of women. Although Peter indulges no passions during the Bellona Club episode, the reader is made aware of his manifest attractions through his effect on Marjorie Phelps. By this time, Sayers's chief character was thirty-seven years old. How long could he hold out against the Marjories of the world?

Sayers does begin the process of making subtle changes to Peter in this fourth novel. He is still proficient in classic blither ("Like the lady in Maeterlinck who's running round the table while her husband tries to polish her off with a hatchet, I am not gay."[252]), and he is still painfully aware of the consequences posed by his investigations. Sensing real unpleasantness, he tries to warn Murbles off a close inquiry into old Fentiman's death right from the beginning. When it proves murder, he is the sole agent to perceive the essential psychology of the event: Penberthy is undeniably guilty, but his one-time fiancée, Ann Dorland, is not. And of course, he remains burdened by memories of the war, recalling dealing himself countless hands of "Patience" in a nursing home in 1918 just to avoid the repercussions of thinking.

He is still Wimsey, and the mystery is still a Sayers mystery, but the formula has begun to change. Most notably, Lord Peter goes it alone for much of this story; the highly effective team of Parker and Wimsey begins to dissolve. Peter uncovers the murder essentially on his own, requesting only minimal help of a technical nature from Parker. When the murder is out and Charles enters the case, he and Peter proceed to not one but two ugly rows over interpretation of character and evidence.

Parker becomes an impediment to Peter's honest handling of the case; to save Ann Dorland, Wimsey must checkmate his friend's headlong determination to stick to facts as facts.

The two will never work together as an integral team again. Charles Parker remains Wimsey's most intimate friend (and eventually becomes his brother-in-law), and he continues to participate heavily in some of Wimsey's investigations. But Peter has grown autonomous as a sleuth. Charles Parker slips into the role of supporting character as Wimsey takes over the stories more completely.

The reason for this mutual adjustment seems to lie with the better understanding of basic human psychology that Sayers has created for Lord Peter. The nuances of human motivation and human reaction become increasingly important in the later novels, and only Peter is prepared to meet them. This is a pivotal theme in the conclusion to *The Unpleasantness at the Bellona Club*. The true resolution to the mystery rests with the reader's ability to share Peter Wimsey's basic comprehension of human foible. "Who done it" is pretty obvious once the facts of General Fentiman's death are known. The old man died unexpectedly of a heart attack; Penberthy is the only man with both means and opportunity to do the murder. The problem lies in his motivation: how would he profit from the old man's death? The obvious answer is that he was in collusion with Ann Dorland. If Fentiman died, she would inherit Lady Dormer's money, and she and Penberthy would marry, start a clinic, and live happily ever after. Only Peter can see that this obvious solution is not right. A mechanical explanation of the facts, however accurate, is just not enough.

More important, he sees that merely proving the obvious solution wrong is not going to save Ann Dorland. Before meeting Ann, Peter is prepared to swear that she is innocent. Any conclusion assuming her guilt simply will not fit the emotional facts of the case as he understands them. Unfortunately, the material evidence Wimsey uncovers may acquit Dorland in a court of law, but it will not protect her in the court of public opinion. Even were she declared innocent by a jury, the tag of "murderess" would follow her for the rest of her life. For Ann to be truly spared, Penberthy must be forced to take full responsibility unequivocally onto his own shoulders where it belongs. In this case, Sayers allows matters to arrive at a neat and satisfactory conclusion, with Penberthy signing a full confession and taking a gun to his head (318–39).

Probably influenced once again by her marriage to a journalist, Sayers has become more aware of the impact of publicity on public opinion and the danger this might hold for the unlucky individual held up to its scrutiny. Newspaper headlines influence earlier stories, but in the Bellona Club case, reporters actually discuss the evidence with Wimsey and Parker, digging up dirt and speculating on the outcome. Their fierce determination to uncover a story that will sell—no matter the cost to those involved—becomes a more pronounced element in the drama. In recognizing the ravages of journalists, Sayers again demonstrates that she is not satisfied to present merely a mystery puzzle to the reader. She wishes to explore the range of experiences inherent in any association, however innocent, with a capital crime. In this spirit, she examines Ann Dorland's (and Lord Peter's) dilemma.

The devastating effect of assumed guilt, especially unjustified guilt, becomes a critical theme for Dorothy L. Sayers as the Wimsey saga continues. In many ways, *The Unpleasantness at the Bellona Club* is a transitional novel. The story embodies the familiar Lord Peter, the sagacious and sensitive war veteran with the marvelous investigative talent. Yet this mystery also begins the exploration of much in his character that would become familiar in the stories that follow. With the accent on his loveable eligibility and his fine-honed appreciation of the psychological, Peter Wimsey's character had taken on new dimensions— with good reason. Sayers was about to launch him into one of the strangest romances in the history of popular detective fiction. At its heart will lie that burden of perceived guilt, a cruelty that tests Wimsey not only as a detective but more essentially as a human being.

Lord Peter Acquires a Soul

FOUR PUBLISHED NOVELS, A NEW CONTRACT, REPLETE WITH commission for both a personal collection of short stories and an edited anthology—Dorothy L. Sayers arrived as a popular author in 1928. The success may have brought some sense of inner security and peace, but it afforded no guarantee against the noise and turmoil integral to getting on with life. The years 1928 and 1929 overflowed with tumult, bringing personal tragedy, household upset, domestic anguish, and critical career choices. Sayers weathered the challenges, but the storms affected her outlook and left her clinging to resignation as a comfort. The storms would change Lord Peter Wimsey as well.

Certainly it was a tumultuous time. News from America on October 29, 1929, terminated whatever hopes Europe might have entertained of returning to real prosperity. The great Wall Street crash plunged the western world into economic depression to be cured only by money spent on rearmament. The long weekend and the good times, such as they were, had begun to move inexorably toward a dangerous close.[1]

As Sayers prospered from the proceeds of four volumes published between September 1927 and November 1928, Britain as a whole showed signs of severe economic strain. A financial scandal in 1927 became a harbinger; James White, controlling owner of the Beecham Trust, manufacturer of patent medicines, without warning killed himself with chloroform. This highly visible public figure—the master of the opulent life style with his most modern office, his yacht, his fancy meals, and his theatricals—had run up debts of more than six hundred thousand pounds that he could not pay. Several trusting financiers drowned in red ink when the bills fell due.[2]

Business ethics of the period were revealed in the 1929 trial of Clarence Hatry, kingpin of the Hatry group. A dealer in bonds and securities, Hatry and four associates juggled the finances of several companies and individuals, supposedly working "to harmonize opposing personalities" and thereby smooth the path of finance. Unfortunately, the group was caught midjuggle, having issued valueless securities as a stopgap to harmonize the debts within their own company. The whole thing came crashing to the ground; Hatry and friends received long prison terms. Comparatively few were monetarily hurt in this particular crash, but the investigation did reveal the shaky ethical nature of the British financial system as a whole. Though the Hatry group had legally recorded worthless pieces of paper as if these possessed honest value, most business observers felt they had really done nothing wrong.[3]

The American stock market crash of 1929 impacted the British market almost immediately, though the effects were not as readily apparent. Unlike their American counterparts, average English citizens had not speculated much in stocks and bonds; the damage was limited to the fortunes of a small coterie of London financiers. The ensuing depression did nothing to help Britain's already limping economy, but there was no panic, no utter ruin. The next decade in Britain was to be merely the "troubled thirties"; the government did what little it could to ease endemic local pain in the face of international economic woe. A general election in 1929 brought Ramsey MacDonald and the Labour party back to power. They responded to the chronic monetary illness by passing a Local Government Act and a Coal Mines Act and by opening diplomatic relations with the Soviet Union. Lord Beaverbrook crusaded for a return to free trade as a cure for Britain's troubles, but he got nowhere.[4]

As always, Dorothy L. Sayers was extremely cognizant of the national situation, drawing on the headlines of her times to provide her novels a sense of immediacy. In *Strong Poison,* the root of the difficulties leading to the murder of Philip Boyes is a financial scandal of the kind that rocked Britain in 1927 and again in 1929. The Megatherium Trust, an echo of the Beecham Trust and the Hatry Group, went belly up sometime in the late 1920s, making attorney Norman Urquhart a monetarily desperate man. Lord Peter's friend, the financial wizard Freddy Arbuthnot, had warned his friends off the Megatherium "before the band began to play."[5] Peter's operative, the ever-resourceful Miss Murchison, knew the history of the great disaster even more intimately. Her employer had been described:

> The brilliant financier who juggled with so many spectacular undertakings was juggling for his life under circumstances of increasing difficulty. As the pace grew faster, he added egg after egg to those which were already spinning in the air. There is a limit to the number of eggs which can be spun by human hands. One day an egg slipped and smashed—then a whole omelette of eggs. The juggler fled from the stage and escaped abroad, his chief assistant blew out his brain, the audience booed, the curtain came down, and Miss Murchison, at 37, was out of a job.[6]

Sayers had invented the story of the Megatherium Trust by blending the essential facts of the Beecham Trust scandal and the Hatry case with a little judicious fiction. Readers of this novel in 1930 knew exactly what she was about.

Victor Gollancz had made Sayers financially secure by that time. He had written out of the blue in 1927 to offer her a contract for a set of new mystery novels and also to edit a series of anthologies featuring the best in detection, mystery, and horror short stories.[7] Her response was what might well be expected from a struggling young author: "Yes, rather, of course, like a shot! It's most frightfully good of you to suggest it and I should love to do it. . . . It ought to be hugely successful— I'm awfully thrilled!"[8]

Gollancz and Sayers quickly agreed that she should edit and write the introduction for *Great Short Stories of Detection, Mystery, and Horror,* which reached print in September 1928. After completing *The Unpleasantness at the Bellona Club* for Benn, she plunged to work on a collection of short stories featuring Lord Peter, the first of nine volumes of Wimsey material published by Gollancz. She had achieved security at last.[9]

Lord Peter Views the Body was published in November 1928. Twelve stories of uneven quality composed the collection; Sayers had struggled mightily to arrive at these. Writing to Victor Gollancz in late November

1927, she listed nine stories existing and estimated that she would need to write five more to bring the volume to the requisite eighty thousand words. One of these five, "The Inspiration of Mr Budd," was eventually omitted.[10] Over the next few months, several ideas for additional stories came and went; one still exists in fragmentary form. In August she wrote to her parents to announce that she had purchased "a wonderful trick chair, with a back which reclines at all angles on pressure of a button. . . . The idea is that when I come home tired in the legs after a day at the office, I should be able to sit in it with my feet comfortably up and write stories about Lord Peter."[11] To that point, Sayers found the chair more sleep inducing than inspirational.

Of the dozen stories finally chosen for inclusion, none is in any way remarkable. A handful create mild interest because they provide detail on some of Lord Peter's early cases, but they in no way advance the reader's understanding of the character or of his community. The lead story, "The Abominable History of the Man with Copper Fingers," is set in New York City in April 1920, making it the earliest of Wimsey's cases to find print—a creepy pulp thriller. The second, "The Entertaining Episode of the Article in Question," apparently takes place almost exactly two years later. Sayers seems to have borrowed somewhat from her unfinished Sexton Blake story; the villain, a female impersonator, speaks masculine French, tipping Peter off that she/he is an international jewel thief. The introduction to this insipid story mentions several additional cases that Sayers never intended to record. She was merely borrowing a page from Conan Doyle.[12]

In "The Vindictive Story of the Footsteps that Ran," Sayers again seized an opportunity to explore the failings of science. The story takes place on a hot summer day in 1921, when Wimsey and Bunter assist a Doctor Hartman with his medical experiments. The doctor's reaction to a murder committed in the flat above only points up his inadequacy:

> "What is wrong with the doctor's theories, Bunter?"
> "You wish me to reply, my lord, that he only sees the facts which fit in with the theory."
> "Thought-reader!" exclaimed Lord Peter bitterly.[13]

Again, the man of science is blind to his own inadequacies, a danger to his fellow human beings.

There is no evidence to date the year of "The Undignified Melodrama of the Bone of Contention," but it seems right to place it in the late autumn of 1922, just after the events of *Whose Body?* Peter is desperately in need of rest, and his desire to visit country friends and swap war yarns in a harmless way makes sense in the aftermath of a last unexpected episode of shell shock. This story is one of the best of the short works, perhaps because it is by far the longest, running almost seventy pages. It is also notable because it is one of the very few stories in which Bunter and the other stock players make no appearance whatsoever. Of the rest, only "The Learned Affair of the Dragon's Head" creates mild interest because of the introduction of a new stock character: Peter's "ten-year-old nephew, Viscount St. George," the Duke of Denver's son and heir. The story itself is a rather tepid treasure hunt.[14]

The one intriguing story in *Lord Peter Views the Body* is the last, "The Adventurous Exploit of the Cave of Ali Baba," and that for most unusual reasons. The tale is straight out of the pulps, as Peter goes underground for two years to get the goods on a highly organized criminal syndicate specializing in theft. The gang kills when they have to, and Peter very nearly becomes the latest victim when he is unmasked. The Wimsey portrayed here has much in common with the intrepid daredevil of *Clouds of Witness*, decidedly out of sync with the creation developing in the novels.[15]

"The Cave of Ali Baba" could be summarily dismissed as a potboiler, save for one factor: its dating. In a letter written in 1933, Sayers advised Harold W. Bell, an American enthusiast and Sherlock Holmes scholar, that "as regards the dates—I'm afraid I usually mix these up on purpose, to prevent people like you from attributing the events narrated to any particular year!"[16] This was not altogether true. The two earliest novels are difficult to date exactly, and several of the short stories are maddeningly vague, but Sayers grew more explicit and precise in later works.

As a kind of working hobby, Sayers had taken an interest in the dating of Arthur Conan Doyle's Sherlock Holmes adventures, entering into a long correspondence with H. W. Bell.[17] Sayers considered his *Sherlock Holmes and Dr. Watson: The Chronology of their Adventures* the most complete attempt to unravel this really arcane subject. However, anyone familiar with Doyle's cavalier approach to the subject of dating (or consistency in the names of his characters!) has to realize how impossible the task really is. Many have tried, and one set of guesses is really as good as another. To produce a comprehensive chronology of the Holmes adventures, the scholar simply must be arbitrary somewhere. The debates center on where best to be arbitrary. In her own work, Sayers came to be the antithesis of Doyle's approach, despite protests to the contrary. The events ascribed to *Unnatural Death* are definitely set in the spring of 1927, and it is difficult to conceive that *The Unpleasantness at the Bellona Club* took place at any time other than the late autumn of the same year. Several references in these works and others place Peter's birthday in 1890, providing a continuous frame of reference. In sharp contrast to Doyle, Sayers took assiduous care over her dates, consciously constructing a biographical chronology of Wimsey's adventures. That is what makes "The Cave of Ali Baba" so curious.[18]

The story begins with a faked announcement of Peter's death. The newspaper obituary announced that he was killed at age thirty-seven while hunting in Tanganyika in December. The staged death therefore takes place in December 1927, just after the events surrounding the Bellona Club mystery. For the next two years, Wimsey poses as an ex-footman named Rogers to gather evidence against the syndicate, which he finally exposes. Presumably, these events take place throughout 1928 and 1929, a view supported by the fact that Sayers never set any other cases during this period. The difficulty is that this story—highlighting appallingly melodramatic events of 1929—appeared in print in 1928. Sayers was describing events that would take place in Wimsey's imaginary future.[19] This has to be the ultimate form of creative biography.

Sayers perpetrated a similar trick in the novel *Strong Poison*. Peter, weighed down by the most critical investigation of his career, spends Christmas with his family and their friends at Duke's Denver. Almost without exception, the bluebloods gathered together prove overbearingly insensitive to Peter's aspirations and fears. Sayers introduces this ordeal by stating that "Wimsey was accustomed to say, when he was an old man and more talkative even than usual, that the recollection of that Christmas at Duke's Denver had haunted him in nightmares, every night regularly, for the following twenty years."[20] The difficulty is that *Strong Poison* was not published twenty years after the imagined events. In fact, the novel was released just scant months after the Christmas of 1929, when this fictional nightmare occurred. Again, Sayers was looking into Peter's future, giving him twenty years of life that none of his enthusiasts had yet lived.

This peculiar playing with the dates on the part of Dorothy L. Sayers would be nothing more than a strange anomaly, had she done it only once or twice. Yet she consciously tinkered with the concept of time in a variety of subtle and inventive ways during the next few years. She cast Wimsey into the future, she pushed him into events of the more distant past, and she arranged events of later novels to fit within the time frames of those already published. And she did this with a purpose. By placing the Wimsey adventures in the proper time sequence that Sayers created for them, the reader can observe both the proper evolution of his character and the expression of his author's deepest beliefs on the most important of all subjects: the nature of human love.[21]

This complicated fictional chronicle was a further product of the complicated tangle that Sayers's life continued to be. Although contracts with Gollancz and American publishers brought the promise of steady publication, financial security did not bring happiness. After eight years and half a million words, Sayers was growing a bit restless with the demands of Lord Peter. Writing the kind of breezy chatter that had become his trademark was wearying work, and his defined role and station in society did rather narrow his opportunities to uncover really unusual criminal activity. In "Gaudy Night," the essay written in 1936 to explain the origins of the tenth Wimsey novel, Sayers recalled that she entered into the writing of *Strong Poison,* the fifth novel, with every intention of marrying him off and having done with him.[22] Her correspondence for 1928 and 1929 offers no indication of such a series-ending intent. It is difficult to believe that she would turn off her bread winner just as the future was looking so bright.

Sayers did enter into a new writing partnership at this time, branching out to experiment with the mystery genre in novel ways. Her associate was (of all things) a physician, Doctor Robert Eustace Barton. Barton had previously cooperated with a number of mystery writers, providing proper scientific background material for L. T. Meade and Edgar Jepson. Sayers included examples of their works in her first anthology for Gollancz, then wrote to Barton to express her admiration. They met and subsequently corresponded, evolving an intricate plot turning on the distinguishing characteristics of natural and synthetic muscarine, a poison derived from mushrooms. Sayers spent much of 1929 writing *The Documents in the Case,* a mystery story told through a collection of "primary" documents—mostly letters and diary entries written by the participants. Though she included Sir James Lubbock, a stock character from the Wimsey series, in *Documents,* she had from the beginning ruled out the inclusion of her great detective:

> Dear Dr. Barton . . .
>
> I am so glad you like Lord Peter. I certainly don't intend to kill him off yet, but I think it would be better to invent a new detective for any tales we do together. . . . Lord Peter isn't supposed to know a lot about chemistry and that sort of thing, and it would mean inventing a doctor or somebody to help him out. Also, I'm looking forward to getting a rest from him, because his everlasting breeziness does become a bit of a tax at times![23]

Had the book proven an unqualified critical success, the career of Lord Peter might well have been different—and much shorter. Sayers herself felt that she had made a hash of the narrative, and then she discovered that Barton's information regarding muscarine was seemingly incorrect. The novel was a twice-flawed fiction. Sayers would turn to Barton for medical information for later stories, but a potentially creative alliance ended with just the one book. *Strong Poison,* written in tandem with *The Documents in the Case,* would become the latest rather than the last Wimsey story.[24]

Both books were written in an atmosphere of personal trial and tragedy. On September 20, 1928, just a few weeks after Dorothy wrote to tell her parents of the automatic chair, her father, the Reverend Henry Sayers, died of pneumonia at age seventy-four. This was the first time death had touched someone close to her, and the loss came hard. Father and daughter had been especially close through the years; he had supported her, emotionally and financially, in all her career struggles and had lived just long enough to see the beginnings of her great success. True, she had been something of a wayward child, forced to hide some very large sins from the devoted old clergyman, but this as much as anything demonstrated the depth of her love.[25]

The grieving was difficult, and with it came responsibility. Sayers's mother and her Aunt Mabel really had no one else to turn to. After the burdensome fuss of the funeral, Dorothy and her husband began to search for a quiet home out of town that they could share with her mother and aunt. As Dorothy had to return to her responsibilities at

Benson's, much of the actual search activity fell to Mac, who was still unable to work steadily. Thanks largely to Fleming's efforts, they quickly located "a pretty old Georgian house in Witham, Essex,"[26] some forty miles northeast of London. Dorothy purchased the property herself, combining funds left her by an uncle with a loan from her mother. Helen Leigh Sayers and Mabel Leigh would occupy the house as rent-free tenants, while Dorothy and her husband continued to live in town.[27]

Fleming took the lead role in readying the house for occupation, struggling with the unremitting gloom and unrealistic goals of Dorothy's mother to the brink of a nervous breakdown. His own health was not good, and his mother-in-law was prey to persistent depression. Helen Sayers did not cope well with her sudden loss. Dorothy explained the situation in a letter to her cousin: "He bored her to death for forty years, and she always grumbled that he was no companion for her—and now she misses him dreadfully. That's life, I suppose."[28]

With Mac's attentive help, the two sisters took up residence in December 1928, with Dorothy arriving on the 24th to help celebrate Christmas. The arrangement, stressful as it was, lasted just seven months. In July 1929, Helen Sayers fell ill with an intestinal blockage. She died on July 27, just ten months after her husband. With the loss of both parents so unexpectedly, the sudden void in Dorothy's life seemed unbridgeable.[29]

Sayers had written several times to her mother since 1926, sharing her successes and expressing her fears. She wrote at times of more than nettlesome matters—the ongoing difficulties in her relationship with Mac Fleming. Her husband was a most unhappy man, and this made life with him very trying. While Dorothy L. Sayers's career flourished, his own went nowhere. He had given up reporting for *The News of the World,* attempting to freelance but working only sporadically. He was subject to nervous attacks and digestive problems, and each winter brought a nagging cough—a chronic effect of poison gas, Sayers suspected. In several depressing ways, she had come to play Sheila Fentiman to his George. She was the major breadwinner, and he had difficulty accepting that.[30]

Still deeper emotional problems were at work as well, problems Sayers could not share with her mother. For the past five years, Dorothy's son, John Anthony, had been in the care of her cousin. At the time of their marriage, Mac Fleming had agreed that the couple should soon assume responsibility for the boy's care. Fleming had even promised to adopt John Anthony and raise him as his own. When her father died in 1928,

Dorothy made a will reflecting this promise and hope. Yet her son was never adopted and never brought into their home to live.[31]

Fleming's excuses rested on his ill health. He did seem to worsen with each year, showing little stamina or ability to work on any project for very long. He talked of writing a cook book, an idea that Sayers encouraged, as he was most wonderfully adept at cooking despite his own stomach problems. The actual work went at a snail's pace. Mostly he seemed to need prolonged periods of relaxation. Before marrying Sayers, he had made a habit of taking his vacations in the west of Scotland, at Gatehouse of Fleet in Kircudsbrightshire. Now Sayers accompanied him, spending her days peacefully writing while he pursued the activities he enjoyed most: painting, fishing, and betting at the races. Fleming at times remained in Scotland when Sayers was required to return to her work at Benson's.[32]

When her mother died, Sayers and Fleming decided to leave London and take up full-time residence at the house in Witham. Her success as mystery writer and editor gave her enough security to leave Benson's for good in August 1929. Though the move out and away from the press of the city must have been something of a relief to Mac's health, the success and notoriety achieved by his wife most emphatically was not. He became increasingly impossible to live with. By 1933 Sayers was seriously considering leaving him.[33]

Dorothy L. Sayers was definitely a star on the rise by 1929, with a new and successful novel, a collection of short stories, and an edited anthology to her credit over the previous twelve months. She had even found time to return to "higher" forms of scholarship, publishing a translation of *Tristan in Brittany* with Ernest Benn in July 1929.[34] Freed from her advertising work at Benson's, she was now able to devote her full attention to writing, generally developing at least two projects at more or less the same time. But it was a triumph tinged with bitterness, as the course of her life refused to run smoothly. The grievous loss of both parents, the memories of ill-fated love affairs, the presence of an ill and trying spouse— all of this and more occupied her attention. Much of the psychological burden found its way, in one form or another, into her Peter Wimsey stories. Even Wimsey on vacation was drawn from the real-life experiences of Sayers and Mac Fleming. Lord Peter's questions about life and its duties were those Dorothy L. Sayers would ask.

Three Wimsey novels grew out of the personal anguish felt by Sayers in the years following the deaths of her parents. They were written at different times—*Strong Poison* was published in 1930, *The Five Red Herrings* in January 1931, and *The Nine Tailors* in 1934—to meet very different needs, but each in some way addressed the same complex of fundamental human issues. To emphasize this fact, Sayers carefully wove the time element of the three novels together: all of Peter Wimsey's activities in all three books take place over a period of fourteen months, between December 1929 and January 1931. Writing to a devoted enthusiast in January 1934, she warned that "*The Nine Tailors*, by the way, goes back a few years to an almost pre-Harriet period."[35]

The Nine Tailors was indeed pre-Harriet. "Harriet" is Harriet Vane, former lover of Philip Boyes and his accused killer. She is also the flame that sets Peter Wimsey's heart afire. He sees her for the first time, in *Strong Poison*, in the dock, standing trial for her life. The narrative obliquely refers to the fact that Peter had been away a long time ("The Cave of Ali Baba"); Parker had investigated the Philip Boyes murder without him. Rushing to his mother, Peter announces: "Look here! here's the absolutely one and only woman, and she's being put through a simply ghastly awful business and for God's sake come and hold my hand!"[36]

The trial of Harriet Vane for the arsenic murder of Philip Boyes ends in a hung jury in December 1929. Sayers is exceedingly clear about the dates of this mystery, placing several references tracing the exact chronology of events into the mouth of the judge summarizing the case against Harriet Vane. When Harriet wins her reprieve, it will be one month, more or less, before a new trial can commence. Peter has that long to uncover evidence that can clear her. Working desperately and haphazardly, he pushes the investigation as far as he can take matters himself by the week following Christmas. Then he must place the active work in the more than capable hands of Miss Climpson for a week. In the novel, Sayers observes that "to chronicle Lord Peter Wimsey's daily life during the ensuing week would be neither kind nor edifying."[37]

As a matter of fact, Peter in that week drove off to celebrate New Year's Eve with friends at Walbeach in East Anglia, only to involve himself in an automobile accident near the tiny Fens village of Fenchurch St. Paul. The automobile had nothing seriously wrong, just a broken axle. Forced to stay overnight at the church rectory, Peter takes part in the

New Year's bell peal, "no less than fifteen thousand, eight hundred and forty Kent Treble Bob Majors."[38] Unbeknownst to Wimsey or anyone else, he takes part in killing a man in the process. Thus begins the story Sayers lays out, with great affection and sensitivity, in *The Nine Tailors*. Again she is most careful to emphasize the exact dates of the adventure. There can be no doubt that this is New Year's Day, 1930. Sayers makes no reference to the events of *Strong Poison* in *The Nine Tailors*, although Lord Peter and Bunter do enter into an interesting exchange. Peter wishes to know if his manservant has ever rung a church bell:

> "Only once, my lord, and on that occasion an accident was only narrowly averted. Owing to my unfortunate lack of manual dexterity I was very nearly hanged in the rope, my lord."
> "That's enough about hanging," said Wimsey, peevishly. "We're not detecting now, and I don't want to talk shop." (13–14)

Presumably, the doom threatening Harriet Vane was very much on his mind.

By two o'clock on the afternoon of New Year's Day, Wimsey and Bunter are once more on the way to Walbeach. As this first of four sections of the story ends, the two meet an ex-convict walking toward Fenchurch St. Paul, but they think little of the incident.

Lord Peter's participation in *Strong Poison* picks up following the successful mission of Miss Climpson. He now sets in motion the machinery that will reveal the real killer of Philip Boyes, the exact motive, and most importantly, the method. Harriet Vane goes free. As the novel ends, she and Peter most decidedly do not fall into one another's arms; Dorothy L. Sayers is much too good a novelist to allow that to happen. Much bitterness of feeling will have to be resolved before Peter will have any chance with Harriet. Sayers eventually gave some inkling of the early days following Harriet's freedom from prison, in *Gaudy Night*:

> During the first year or so after her trial, she had not wanted to appear anywhere, even had she then been able to afford the frocks to appear in. In those days, he had taken her to the quieter and better restaurants in Soho, or, more often, carried her off, sulky and rebellious, in the car to such roadside inns as kept reliable cooks. She had been too listless to refuse these outings, which

had probably done something to keep her from brooding, even though her host's imperturbable cheerfulness had often been re-paid only with bitter or distressful words. (62)

In the Wimsey chronology, the action returned to occurrences record-ed in the second and third parts of *The Nine Tailors*. Events pick up in Fenchurch St. Paul as Easter nears. One of the most respected members of the community, Sir Henry Thorpe, has died, and the sexton must re-open the grave where Sir Henry's wife had been interred just a few months before. Overturning the earth, he discovers a strange, unidentifiable body hidden in the grave. Church and law enforcement are perplexed; Peter Wimsey is invited to investigate. Over the next two months, he unravels as snarled a string of events as he will ever face; the solution is a sad nightmare for all concerned. He would as soon leave Fenchurch St. Paul behind forever, but he has, in the process of the investigation, become the executor for a large fortune bequeathed to Sir Henry's daughter, Hilary Thorpe. The obligation weighs heavily.

The late summer of 1930 finds Lord Peter vacationing with Bunter at Kircudbright in Scotland. Peter is a familiar character in those parts, turning up annually to take advantage of the fine weather, spending his time alternately fishing or playing very decent golf. Kircudbright is the kind of brilliant, mellow, almost wild country that readily attracts the landscape painter; Peter is accepted by the considerable artistic commu-nity as a harmless if untalented eccentric. When one of the artists, the truly obnoxious Campbell, falls prey to murder, Wimsey gets an oppor-tunity to display the talents he does possess. Seeing through *The Five Red Herrings*, he successfully traces the killer's every movement, some-thing five different local police officials cannot duplicate.

Insofar as Wimsey's life story is concerned, this particular investiga-tion does not amount to terribly much. True, Wimsey does refer to his inductive triumph as "the proudest moment of my life," one in which he can at last "feel like Sherlock Holmes" (260). But the case is barren of the psychological and social conundrums that mark so many of the novels. In fact, *The Five Red Herrings* would scarcely be worth men-tioning in the context of this most emotionally challenging year of Lord Peter's fictional life, save for one incident. Unravelling the disappear-ance of Farren, one of Campbell's many enemies, Peter enters into a long conversation with Mrs. Farren regarding the necessary elements for a successful marriage. In view of the tempestuous time he was having with Harriet Vane, strategies for pursuing wedded bliss must certainly be on his mind.

The year 1930 approaches its close. Out of loyalty and respect for young Hilary Thorpe, Peter returns to Fenchurch St. Paul to celebrate Christmas. *The Nine Tailors* reaches an apocalyptic climax as the murderer is at last revealed. The strange, unhappy chain of events claims another victim, and the Fens are flooded, washing away the sin and exposing once again the fragile stupidity of humankind.

Dorothy L. Sayers employed a short story, three full novels, and a small portion of a fourth to tell the story of those horrendous fourteen months. By the time she had completed the tale, the Peter Wimsey that emerged had become almost her perfect model of a human being. He was a man after her own heart, exceedingly talented, everlastingly cheerful, and, in the depths of his soul, very unhappy. His greatest asset was supreme patience, aided by a calm acceptance of what was.[39]

For a period in 1929 and early 1930, *Strong Poison* became almost a stepchild of Sayers's fertile imagination. While she lavished attention on *The Documents in the Case,* the latest Wimsey novel seems to have bumped along, plaguing her sense of artistic fair play. Perhaps, as she later claimed, she did enter into the story "with the infanticidal intention of doing away with Peter; that is, of marrying him off and getting rid of him."[40] If so, she discovered in the process the stubborn depths of her own conscience as an author. She discovered also what a resilient and well-polished character Peter had become. He simply refused to marry the woman as matters stood.

The novel that she sent (without fanfare) to Victor Gollancz in April 1930 was conceived as an integrated detective fiction and love story. As a mystery, the plot is an intriguing return to old ground. For the third novel in a row, an elderly woman's will provides the motive for murder; this time a lawyer becomes the professional consumed by temptation. Norman Urquhart has lost his cousin's legacy gambling on the Megatherium Trust. His only hope of avoiding discovery, therefore, is to do away with the cousin—Philip Boyes. As in *Unnatural Death,* the perpetrator of the crime becomes obvious to the reader rather quickly. The difficulty is, how was the murder done? Sayers has left clues all through the novel for those with knowledge and imagination. From the very first, Urquhart is described as possessing "smooth dark hair," while his

"skin was pale and curiously clear, except for a number of little freck-
les, like sun-spots" (111). These were the visible symptoms of his habit-
ual intake of arsenic, and in the end they will betray him.

For reasons dictated more by the romantic side of the story, Peter is
unusually helpless in *Strong Poison*. The climax is vintage, as Wimsey
works late into the night to assemble the pieces necessary to comprehend Urquhart's crime. The scene is reminiscent of *Whose Body?* where
Peter, alone in his study, surrounded by literary clues, suddenly and intu-
itively understands the whole of the Battersea mystery. Yet this is practically the only valid comparison between the two cases. In *Strong Poison*,
Peter does not crumple with nervous shock. More importantly, he does
not ferret out the disparate puzzle pieces himself; they are carried to him
by a series of operatives. He relies on Charles Parker to retrace Philip
Boyes's last night in Bloomsbury, Marjorie Phelps to guide him through
London's Bohemia, Miss Murchison to investigate Urquhart's law office,
Blindfold Bill to teach Miss Murchison the use of burglar's tools, and
Bunter to investigate Urquhart's household. Above all, he relies on the
endlessly resourceful Kitty Climpson to get a look at the will in question,
the last testament of the notorious Cremorna Garden. Peter can only
stand and wait, an endless agony of waiting for the others to do what is
necessary. Small wonder he thought of becoming a hermit.

As Peter's operative, Miss Climpson is much the same character as in
Unnatural Death, though her responsibilities have grown immensely. She
began work for Lord Peter as a lone agent late in 1926; three years later
she is in charge of a "cattery" employing dozens of "superfluous women"
(49–50) in a variety of investigations. Still, when the work to be done is
critical, Peter will rely on no one else but Miss Climpson herself. Ordering her to drop all usual assignments, Peter orders her to Windle, in
Westmoreland, where she must again consign herself to boarding house
life, becoming just another elderly spinster looking for friendship.

Kitty Climpson's conscience has come a long way since the Mary
Whittaker investigation. She now assumes the role of invading spy without the least flicker of remorse (save on Sunday!), and she embarks on a
campaign of deliberate falsehood completely at odds with her religious
beliefs. In short, Miss Climpson poses as a spiritualist medium. A paranormal investigator has taught her all the tricks of the spiritualist char-
latan's trade. She has learned her lessons well, completely taking in Miss
Booth, Cremorna Garden's foolish nurse.

The long passages describing the series of seances carefully orchestrated by Miss Climpson seem a bit out of step with the rest of *Strong Poison,* as if Dorothy L. Sayers had an axe to grind and was seizing an opportunity. Sayers's position is manifestly clear: "The apparatus of planes and controls, correspondences and verdical communications, astral bodies, auras and ectoplastic materialisations" (181) were an insult to the intelligence. The descriptions of seance become one long demonstration of how the shrewd can easily dupe the guileless. Miss Climpson, cloaked in spiritualist disguise, gains access to Cremorna Garden's will by the most obvious falsehoods. The nurse, perfectly faithful and anxious to communicate with the spirit world, never suspects a thing.

Perhaps Sayers felt it her duty to set the mystery-reading public to rights regarding the paranormal. It had to be more than a little embarrassing that the most famous detective author of all time, Sir Arthur Conan Doyle, had become an evangelical spokesman for spiritualism. The man was so easily fooled: he pronounced genuine the most obviously doctored photographs of little girls "playing with fairies"; he endorsed and defended patently fraudulent mediums; and he proclaimed his second wife to be a strong medium, though no less a person than Harry Houdini knew she was fooling herself.[41]

In the modern world of the 1920s, belief in spiritualism was something of a throwback. Spiritualism had flourished originally during the Victorian era, a weird kind of rationalist approach to the subject of afterlife. Advocates referred to it as "paranormal science," an attempt to fuse standard Christian belief with Darwinian discoveries. The Church of England condemned the idea, as did the biological and physical scientists. Spiritualism appealed to a small but steadfast subset of the population.

Until the Great War. When more than three-quarters of a million young men died abruptly and horribly, when loved ones had not even the opportunity to view them in death or to say a proper farewell. Arthur Conan Doyle's own case stood for many. His son Kingsley died in combat, as did his brother-in-law and his own brother. When a close acquaintance told him that she had received mediumistic messages from her three brothers, all killed at the front, Doyle was ready to believe. He attended seances in which he believed he spoke with his son. Healed in part by the experience, he began to spread the word. As the creator of the ultimate rationalist, Sherlock Holmes, Doyle inspired many to believe it was all true. Spiritualism gathered strength in the early twenties.[42]

Sayers had lost no one close to her in the war. Death did not touch her much at all until the sudden loss of both parents in 1928 and 1929. Now, during the writing of *Strong Poison,* death was very much on her mind. Plainly, spiritualism was no answer for her. Lord Peter may have been less the rationalist than Sherlock Holmes, but his creator had her head screwed on right. Like Miss Climpson, Sayers knew the tricks, and she "had wondered greatly at the folly and wickedness of mankind" (182).

Yet by ruthlessly playing on the folly of Miss Booth, Kitty Climpson managed to successfully complete her mission for Lord Peter in just eight days. Did the end justify the means? Miss Climpson can only fervently hope so and salve her conscience by warning Miss Booth to look out for charlatans. Peter is not even bothered by the question. By whatever means necessary, by whatever tools available, human or otherwise, he must triumph. Ten years of devotion to the cause of justice demanded no less. And there was also the romantic aspect to consider.

Strong Poison provided the first genuine love angle for Lord Peter Wimsey. Obviously he had panted after women before but, in Harriet Vane, Sayers sought to create the ultimate woman for Wimsey. For reasons not immediately made clear, Peter falls for her at first sight (perhaps the two years spent as the ex-footman Rogers have increased his susceptibility). His thoughts after actually speaking to her for the first time suggest how completely she mirrors his dreams of desirable womanhood:

> Her skin is like honey—she ought to wear deep red—and old garnets—and lots of rings, rather old-fashioned ones—I could take a house, of course—poor kid, I would damn well work to make it up to her—she's got a sense of humour too—brains—one wouldn't be dull—one would wake up, and there'd be a whole day for jolly things to happen in—and then one would come home and go to bed—that would be jolly, too—and while she was writing, I could go out and mess around, so we shouldn't either of us be dull. (47–48)

Peter's thoughts perhaps embody Sayers's own ideas of the necessary ingredients for a successful marriage.

So who is this Harriet Vane? The reader learns a few salient facts during the judge's summing up at her murder trial. Her eyes were "like dark smudges under the heavy square brows" (1). Comments on her physical attractiveness throughout the novel are much influenced by questions of her guilt, but she is definitely not beautiful in any classic sense. She was born in 1901; at the time of the trial, both her parents had been dead for six years. She made her living as a detective novelist. Peter's mother thought her books "rather clever" (30); they sold steadily if unspectacularly. As a popular writer, she moved easily among the Bloomsbury crowd, attracting several close friendships and, eventually, the amorous attentions of Philip Boyes. Boyes had made a career of his advanced ideas on issues including free love — he would not marry Harriet but wished her to live with him. After much anguished hesitation, she consented, only to see Boyes alter his own views after a year, asking her hand in marriage. Showing herself to be the true denizen of modernist society that he had implored her to be, she took his proposal as an insult and left him.

In sum, Harriet Vane is a rather plain woman with brains and a good deal of mental toughness. The loss of her parents had been a difficult blow, but she was making ends meet, dependent on no one. Her principles are Bohemian, but they are principles and she sticks to them. She is an enigma and a paragon of the modern woman. She most decidedly would not be every man's dream of feminine companionship; her brains alone would repel more than half of maledom. But she is the perfect answer to the enigma that is Lord Peter — perfect in every way except, of course, for the fact that she is on trial for murder.

Harriet is in many ways an amalgam of the three young women caught in the light by the Bellona Club affair. Like Ann Dorland, Harriet is not physically striking, though she does seem to carry herself with more grace. She is also bereft of parental advice, making her own way in the world and making mistakes. But, like Marjorie Phelps, she is a successful Bohemian, dependent on nothing but her own skill to support herself. She is capable of deep and passionate love, but it must be on terms acceptable to her. And, like Sheila Fentiman, she knows the pain of a mentally abusive relationship, however much her partner may actually love her. Add to these attributes a large dollop of Dorothy L. Sayers's own personality — Harriet is a mystery writer who has suffered much wounding of the emotions — and the character to emerge sums up much of her creator's views on the problems of women in the postwar era.

Knowing what will eventually come of the Wimsey-Vane macabre waltz of the emotions, it is very tempting to read backward from later books to assess the Harriet Vane of *Strong Poison*. In this novel she is not quite the mirror of Dorothy L. Sayers that she will later become. There is, for example, no mention of her attending Oxford University nor of her being raised in a remote village. The most autobiographical aspect to Harriet in this story is the repellent tale of her relationship with Philip Boyes.

Philip Boyes was the devil of an excrescence, a conceited, self-absorbed prig who demanded not love but worship from all who knew him. He had talent as a writer but used it to offend more than to enlighten, expressing the most "advanced" views in a clever but tasteless fashion. Believing that a talent such as his own should be supported by his lesser friends and relatives, he sponged without shame as a kind of natural right. Peter Wimsey almost wishes the man alive, just so he could have the pleasure of kicking his bottom.

All in all, this was a pretty good summary of Dorothy L. Sayers's opinion of John Cournos. If Cournos lives in the culture today, it is because of this portrait, spread through so much of *Strong Poison,* and for no other reason. His own books are long dead.[43]

If Sayers created Harriet Vane as a match for Peter Wimsey, then she had to alter Wimsey to meet his match on equal terms. At the same time, he had to remain consistent, generally speaking, with the Wimsey of the four previous novels. What emerges is a character pushed to the edge by circumstances of his own choosing. In falling so completely for this nearly doomed woman, he reveals the essential fragility of his own being. For eleven years since the war, Peter has been looking resolutely forward, riding the crest of his own supreme self-confidence in the abilities necessary to his chosen field. Now, for the first time, it all really matters. He absolutely must be the investigative genius he envisions himself to be, or the woman he loves will be lost to the gallows. The thought is terrifying and enervating. Peter flounders at the task, trying one desperate gambit after another, grasping futilely at straws. It is more because of good luck—and the faithful help of those resourceful others—that the real murderer is flushed. At no time is Peter the master of this situation. Confronted with Harriet Vane, even his usual sangfroid falters; he comes very close to saying the wrong thing on more than one occasion. Like anyone facing love in desperate circumstances, Peter is changing:

Whether his present enterprise failed or succeeded, things would never be the same again. It was not that his heart would be broken by a disastrous love—he had outlived the luxurious agonies of youthful blood, and in this very freedom from illusion he recognized the loss of something. From now on, every hour of light-heartedness would be, not a prerogative, but an achievement—one more axe or case-bottle or fowling piece, rescued, Crusoe-fashion, from a sinking ship. (89)

Lightheartedness might become more difficult to achieve, but Peter's ability to jabber on remorselessly and inanely does not desert him. Several times in this novel, Sayers allows Peter to rise to heights of blither that have to be fully read to be believed. An especially notable point arrives when Peter demands to know Charles Parker's intentions regarding his sister Mary, a throwback to Victorian conventions made necessary not by Mary's expectations but rather Parker's. Peter and Charles are on opposite sides in this particular case, a situation that both find a little awkward, but this does not stop Wimsey from urging Parker to join the family:

> "For the last five years or so," said Wimsey, "you have been looking like a demented sheep at my sister, and starting like a rabbit whenever her name is mentioned. What do you mean by it? It is not ornamental. It is not exhilarating. You unnerve the poor girl. You give me a poor idea of your guts, if you will pardon the expression. A man doesn't like to see a man go all wobbly about his sister—at least, not with such a prolonged wobble. It's unsightly. It's irritating. Why not slap the manly thorax and say 'Peter, my dear old mangel-wurzel, I have decided to dig myself into the old family trench and be a brother to you?' What's stopping you? . . . Cough up the difficulty, old thing, and we will have it removed in a plain van. Now then!" (166)

Encouraged by the sincere message beneath this blither, Parker dissolves his Victorian reluctance to intrude himself into the aristocracy; he and Mary both are aggravatingly grateful to Lord Peter. Wimsey finds it difficult to remain lighthearted in the presence of the "imbecile happiness" (169) of the now-devoted couple. His own chosen still faces the executioner.

During this same Christmas season, Peter discovers that he is to stand up with Freddy Arbuthnot, who, after seven years, is finally going to marry the late Sir Reuben Levy's daughter, Rachel, in a synagogue. Sayers thus succeeds in tying up all the significant loose ends of past romance in the series within the space of forty pages. Undoubtedly she wished to remove all potential distraction from the critical romance of future stories, that of Peter and Harriet. Possibly, too, she merely wished to provide some happiness to at least some of her characters, given what was happening to Peter—and to herself.

Blindly searching about for some handle on the death of Philip Boyes, Wimsey is forced once again to call upon the assistance of Marjorie Phelps, his guide to London's Bohemia. Peter rightly feels embarrassed asking Marjorie to help him rescue his one and only, but with only a month to investigate, scruples of any kind have to go to the wall. He and Marjorie sally forth into the Bloomsbury district, keeping the taxi waiting just in case. What follows is one of the most marvelous burlesques in popular literature. Sayers had previously intimated much about Bohemia. This time she provided the reader a genuine taste.

The first stop is at the Kropotkys'—"pro-Boyes, Bolshevik and musical" (81)—where Peter wishes to interview Boyes's best (only?) friend, Ryland Vaughan. The atmosphere is beyond reckoning. The heat stifles, kippers simmer in an open pan, a piano and violin duo perform a clashing tone piece on "the Piccadilly Tube Station," and the uncountable crowd converses through the murk in shouts by necessity. Entering into the spirit of the thing, Peter finds himself condemning the diatonic scale and the octave as sentimental conventions of the bourgeoisie. Marjorie drags him off to meet Vaughan, who is seated morosely on the floor "eating caviare out of a jar with a pickle fork" (84). With little urging, Vaughan plunges into bitter reminiscence about Boyes. He has no doubt that Harriet Vane poisoned his friend. In saying so, he reveals something very significant about Bohemia: "Oh, she did it all right. Sheer, beastly spite and jealousy, that's all there was to it. Just because she couldn't write anything but tripe herself. Harriet Vane's got the bug all these damned women have got—fancy they can do things. They hate a man and they hate his work. You'd think it would have been enough for her to help and look after a genius like Phil, wouldn't you?" (84–85) This monologue has shades of George Fentiman. Yes, even in the Bloomsbury District, men could find it difficult to accept that women had brains, ability, or the wherewithal to do far more than serve some man, genius or not.

The fact was, for all its playing at Bolshevism and its discussion of freedom from traditional structures, the vanguard of art and literature in London during the period was itself mostly molded by convention. The freedom to experiment with both form and content, to push the culture in new and (seemingly) outrageous directions, was there. Surely it was happening elsewhere, even before the war. Igor Stravinsky's *Le Sacre du printemps,* a step into uncharted artistic territory, had been performed in London by the Ballet Russes, to a mixed response, in the spring of 1913. In Spain, Picasso was dissolving the conventions of sketchboard and canvas. James Joyce (an Irishman, of course), had published *Dubliners* in 1914, *A Portrait of the Artist as a Young Man* in 1916, and *Ulysses* in 1922. William Butler Yeats (another Irishman) began his career employing the conventional poetic forms but shifted to a dramatic modernism not long before the Great War. T. S. Eliot (an American, God forbid) published the modernist poetical masterpiece, *The Waste Land,* in 1922. And Virginia Woolf (a Briton, but not one who had served in the trenches) added a feminist perspective to the modernist approach in novels such as *Mrs. Dalloway* (1925) and *To The Lighthouse* (1927). What these artists shared was an intimate sense of limited audience—the mass culture would never understand them; they were doomed to misunderstanding and alienation.[44]

The influence of this modernist outpouring on Britain was surprisingly minimal. As much as anything, this was due to the power of association—the modernist critique was too intimately identified with a Prussian *kultur* that emphasized a love of technology, a breaking free from the limitations defined by the historical past, and an embrace of mythic images. To the conservative Briton, this conjured up visions of sacrilegious Hunnish fantasy and sexual deviance. When D. H. Lawrence's *The Rainbow* was published in 1915, the book was banned under the Defense of the Realm Act for just those reasons. Germany—and Germanness, even more so—was the great enemy. Though the war itself would lead to severe doubts regarding traditional British cultural values, the sheer price of victory made most Britishers—even the avant garde—reluctant to embrace *kultur* too openly. The result was a most tepid embrace of modernism among the cultural adventurers practicing in Britain.[45]

This is best illustrated by the careers of the "war poets": Siegfried Sassoon, Wilfred Owen, Herbert Read, Robert Graves. These men shared much of the modernist vision: the attack on form, the breaking of convention, the rejection of tradition. All had been practiced adepts of the familiar forms of English poetry before the war. The experience of the war itself smashed this out of them, left them groping for forms and expression that could in some way convey the madness they experienced. Take, for example, the third stanza of Wilfred Owen's "Insensibility":

> Happy are those who lose imagination:
> They have enough to carry with ammunition,
> Their Spirit drags no pack.
> Their old wounds, save with cold, can not more ache.
> Having seen all things red,
> Their eyes are rid
> Of the hurt of the colour of blood for ever.
> And terror's first constriction over,
> Their hearts remain small-drawn.
> Their senses in some scorching cautery of battle
> Now long since ironed,
> Can laugh among the dying, unconcerned.[46]

This is a fractured poetry: the uneven metre, approximate rhyme scheme, and clanging imagery, the elusive to nonexistent structure; these are not according to Lord Tennyson's tastes. Yet it was the war that created the need for such a harsh poetic landscape, as men educated in the conventions found them lacking for the situation. Driven by horror and artistry, they invented. The red smeared the vision, tortured the verse.

The war poets wrote for a very exclusive club, however. Peter Wimsey was a member, as were Mervyn Bunter and the Fentiman brothers. These were the men who had served in the trenches and knew firsthand the emotive images the poets tried so hard to capture on paper. Like the modernists, the war poets wrote essentially for one another and others like them; there was no hope or expectation of communicating with the mass audience of nonveterans, especially women. They were, both in their art and their experience of the war, alienated men.[47]

Little of this new war poetry found publication during the war itself, but several of the poets produced (or, in the case of those who died in the war, had produced) collections during the 1920s. Their appeal was minimal. To the educated, the work was too much at variance with accepted convention; to the mass, it attempted to communicate an experience most had not shared or would just as soon forget. At best, they prepared the path for Yeats and Eliot, true modernists intruding from outside the culture. At worst, not one of them was accepted as a true British poet, then or since. These were the sons of Britain with the greatest affinity for the modernist stance. Britain simply tolerated them.[48]

And so even the freewheeling discussions of "free love, D. H. Lawrence, the prurience of prudery and the immoral significance of long skirts"[49] — the Bloomsbury set so familiar to Dorothy L. Sayers, Marjorie Phelps and Harriet Vane—could produce little of lasting value. Within Bloomsbury, Virginia Woolf struggled determinedly for the common cause of women, but there were too many copies of Philip Boyes and Ryland Vaughan and John Cournos in this bunch. Shockingly conventional in their unconventionality, these were men barren of real inspiration or real genius. It was better to write standard detective fiction, write it well, and take pride in this constrained creation.

Every reactionary inspires an action, and the Bloomsbury world of Harriet Vane proved the rule. Anxious to obtain a more or less complete understanding of this particular world, Peter allows Marjorie Phelps to lead him to Joey Trimble's, the stronghold of Harriet's supporters. This is exactly the same show—chaotic heat producing little light—save that Harriet's most fervent friends are not present; Sylvia Marriott has sprained her ankle. They find her at home with Eiluned Price, the antithesis of Ryland Vaughan. "Eiluned's anti-man," Sylvia explains, "but a very reliable person" (91).

Eiluned Price, whose artistic talents are suggested but not revealed, is indeed fed up with male types, especially the ones to be found in Bloomsbury. She is willing to abide Peter only because he is going about the positive good of clearing Harriet. Still, she tests him, demanding to know if he needs "masculine refreshment," refusing to allow him the gentlemanly act of carrying the tea kettle. Peter adjusts, adopting "an attitude of passive decoration," and manages to draw Price's perspective on the Vane-Boyes relationship:

> "There never was much money, except what Harriet made. The ridiculous public didn't appreciate Phil Boyes. He couldn't forgive her that, you know."
>
> "Didn't it come in useful?"
>
> "Of course, but he resented it all the same. She ought to have been ministering to his work, not making money for them both with her own independent trash. But that's men all over. . . .

Women geniuses don't get coddled, . . . so they learn not to expect it." (92–93)

Harriet Vane's bitterness ran deeper than even the crushing disappointment of her failed love affair. A woman of talent, she understood
all too well that her own genius was largely unappreciated among her
peers. This was the quality she shared most with her creator: her determination to follow her own muse in the face of opposition and ridicule.
Unlike Eiluned Price, Harriet had not allowed her bitterness to become
complete. She would not stoop to hate the men of her own set. She did
draw strength from the few women who defied the classic sexual bigot-
ry of Bloomsbury males, just as Sayers drew strength from her female
friends. Even Bohemia still wore Victorian blinders; women of talent
needed to support one another as much as they could.

What kind of match is that of Harriet Vane and Peter Wimsey? In
Strong Poison, it is very difficult to tell. The thing they most visibly
share is the shadow of the hangman's noose, an arresting reminder both
of Harriet's ill luck and Peter's peculiar talent. For as long as Harriet
remains in that harsh and ominous shadow, she cannot really be herself: "'I used to piffle rather well myself,' said Harriet, with tears in her
eyes, 'but it's got knocked out of me. You know—I was really meant to
be a cheerful person—all this gloom and suspicion isn't the real me. But
I've lost my nerve somehow.'" (123–24). In this situation, Peter cannot
be his true self either. He regards it as an obligation to lift the spirits of
the prisoner, but this forces him to be cheerful and light. What could
Harriet learn of him from that? His own real mood was a mix of mel-
ancholy and anxiety verging on terror, but he must carefully mask this
in Harriet's presence. There can be no real chance of love between the
two until the shadow of the noose is lifted.

Unfortunately, even that will not smooth the path. Had Charles Parker found the evidence to save Harriet Vane, Peter's suit might have stood
some more immediate chance. As it was, it is none other than Peter who
saves Harriet's life. Dorothy L. Sayers, a novelist first, mystery writer
second, and romantic a distant third, recognized the difficulty:

I could not marry Peter off to the young woman he had (in the
conventional Perseus manner) rescued from death and infamy,
because I could find no form of words in which she could accept

him without loss of self-respect. I had landed my chief two puppets in a situation where, according to all the conventional rules
of detective fiction, they should have had nothing to do but fall
into one another's arms; but they would not do it, and that for a
very good reason. When I looked at the situation I saw that it was
in every respect false and degrading; and the puppets had somehow got just so much flesh and blood in them that I could not
force them to accept it without shocking myself.[50]

There was no choice. Peter and Harriet would have to build an honest
relationship from scratch after the prison ordeal ended. Sayers understood and accepted this challenge, eventually writing three additional
Wimsey-Vane novels to provide sufficient room for love to bloom properly. But first, Peter had to grow a bit on his own. Sayers gave him the
rest of 1930 to accomplish that, setting two additional novels in the
months following his initial rejection by Harriet Vane.[51]

On the face of the evidence, Dorothy L. Sayers seems to have been
less than anxious to tackle the job. *The Five Red Herrings,* the sixth in
the series of Lord Peter novels, finds a relentlessly cheerful Wimsey on
his yearly pilgrimage to Scotland for fishing and golf. There is no mention of Harriet Vane, almost no sign of the restless and conflicted soul
that Sayers was fashioning for her detective. She finished the novel in
just a few months following completion of *Strong Poison.* Gollancz
published the novel in January 1931.

Only once in the story does Peter give voice to the issues facing the
inner man. One of the six artists suspected of murdering Sandy Campbell is Hugh Farren, a hot-tempered Scotsman married to a cool, pretty,
and astonishingly thick-headed woman named Gilda. Farren has unfortunately run off at just the wrong moment; his actions may be construed
as those of a man guilty of murder. In his determination to find Hugh
Farren, Peter questions Hugh's wife relentlessly, driving her to give the
game away by insulting her sense of self-respect. The interrogation turns
on their differing ideas of proper behavior in marriage.

Gilda Farren claims to be the perfect wife: "'I have been faithful to
him,' said Mrs. Farren, with rising temper. 'I have worked to keep the
house beautiful and—and to make it a place of refreshment and inspiration. I have done all I could to further his ambitions. I have borne my
share of the household expenses—' Here she seemed suddenly to become

aware of a tinge of bathos and went on hurriedly, 'You may think all this is nothing, but it means sacrifice and hard work.'"[52] All well and fine, but the difficulty is that Mrs. Farren is unable to see the world through her husband's eyes. Though she had been faithful, she had opened the refreshing and inspiring doors of her home to Sandy Campbell, not comprehending why this drove Hugh Farren wild with jealousy. To Gilda, this was no more than a hurtful display of mistrust on her husband's part; it is indecent "to believe vile things of other people" (177). Wimsey understands that the jealousy is something profoundly different: a soul-revealing demonstration of how much Farren loves her. Wrapped up in her own narrowly defined virtue, Mrs. Farren is too obtuse to see it that way.

Wimsey drives the point home ruthlessly, stating baldly that he is "not stupid. My wife won't have that to complain of" (177). Gilda is shocked by the notion that Wimsey regards stupidity as a sin as great as infidelity, but Peter is unsympathetic: "The one can cause quite as much upheaval as the other, and the trouble is that it's incurable. One of those things one has to put up with. I shan't necessarily be unfaithful to my wife, but I shall know enough about infidelity to know it when I see it, and not mistake other things for it" (177). Having at last made Gilda Farren understand the position, Peter knows that the worst thing she can do is to absolve her husband. It would be better to battle it out and earn mutual respect. Indeed, Peter has already warned her not to forgive Farren when he returns. "Forgiveness is the one unpardonable sin" (176). Of course the warning will fall on deaf ears. Hugh Farren will come back to his wife's serene composure, the superior virtue that she claims with every action, every breath, and every absolution. Wings clipped, he will never be a completely happy man again.

Peter Wimsey's purpose in this conversation is simply to discover where Hugh Farren has gone. He is almost entirely the detective in this novel, virtually one-dimensional in his role as sleuth. It is this one discussion that suggests the inner turmoil that Sayers was preparing for Lord Peter. What was the key to a happy marriage? How does a person love without trying to possess the other? How does one balance the heart and the intellect? The reader gets the barest clue to Wimsey's inner debate, following the path of his amazing examination of Gilda Farren. The reader can understand only too well why Peter Wimsey's ideal woman, Harriet Vane, is anything but stupid.

This was small stuff, considering what was at stake. As Dorothy L. Sayers continued to enlarge the saga of Peter Wimsey's one great love, it became clear that he was determined to endure a long siege. She reunited Peter and Harriet to solve the murder of a gigolo in *Have His Carcase,* published in April 1932. The investigation proved successful, but Harriet was still too wounded to consider anything approaching romance. Sayers then determined to give the unhappy couple some breathing room, omitting Harriet almost completely from the next two novels. This left Peter to struggle with his emotional balance alone.

Sayers intended to address Lord Peter's emotions, as well as her own, in the next Wimsey story. This was to be a novel like no other in the series, cut off from the familiar haunts of London and separated from the community of supporting characters so integral to Wimsey's cases. Though Charles Parker would appear, lending a very bland and workmanlike assistance to the investigation, Wimsey and his man, Bunter, would go this one on their own. They were transported to another world, less than two hours from London but a century or more removed, spiritually and psychologically. In the treacherous, wild, scarcely populated Fens country of East Anglia, they would confront the memories of their creator.

This was no simple book to plan. Dorothy L. Sayers enlisted not only the recollections of her own childhood but the technical expertise of a range of interested experts. She needed to understand the myriad complexities of the long history of the Fens drainage, a haphazard and piecemeal example of human cooperation if ever there was one. She needed a church—not just any church of England but a centuries' old abbey seat with a Norman foundation, an iron-fisted prelate of the fourteenth century, and a continuous history of architectural modification. Finally, she needed to know a great deal about bells—how to found them, how to ring them. Her imaginary Fenchurch St. Paul possessed a very fine ring of eight bells, the oldest dating back to 1338. The village population she envisioned would take great pride in the ring, devoting themselves to the arcane patterns of campanology with wonderful enthusiasm.[53]

An early notebook for this novel is largely devoted to the ringing of peals; page after page is simply filled with the characteristic plotted numbers. But the notebook further discloses some of the complications Sayers had to confront in construction. At one point, she wondered "if James [Thoday] finds & takes the money? This wd. account for his keeping so quiet about it all." Even the names of characters became a challenge. The infamous Jeff Deacon began existence as Walter Russell, with Russell eventually becoming the maiden name of his wife, Mary. William Thoday was originally to be Robert Thoday. Interestingly, at this early stage, Cranton, perhaps the most lovable of all Sayers's rogues, was not even envisioned.[54]

Creating and mastering the complexities of this rural world took time and devotion, even more than Sayers had anticipated. She had to push in ahead another story, the rapidly written *Murder Must Advertise,* in order to meet contractual obligations. That completed, she turned to complete her labor of love, the story of the bells that killed a brutal thief and murderer.[55]

Sayers placed her imaginary village of Fenchurch St. Paul firmly within the bounds of England's Fens country, north of Cambridge. Though all the places she alludes to in *The Nine Tailors* are fictional, several bear close affinity to the real geography of the region. There is neither a Walbeach nor a Holport in the Fens, but there is a village of Holbeach, scant miles from the sea. No Thirty Foot Drain exists, but the Sixteen Foot Drain originates less than twenty miles from Bluntisham, where Sayers grew up. She was, in fact, molding a most familiar country to her own vision and purposes. The recreation was no mere convenience but rather a deliberate attempt to paint an idealized landscape of her youth. In large part, this new story was to be a vehicle to ponder another of the emotional burdens laid upon her in 1929 and 1930. If *Strong Poison* reflects Dorothy L. Sayers's disappointments in love and marriage, *The Nine Tailors* confronts her great sorrow at the loss of her parents. Among the residents of her tiny Fens village were the Reverend and Mrs. Venables, the devoted and absent-minded High Church cleric and his loving, if far more practical, spouse. These were Sayers's own parents, brought lovingly to life one last time. And, across the way, there lived fifteen-year-old Hilary Thorpe, an awkward girl who would "make a splash" (91) one day. Sayers had placed her own adolescent self in the novel.

The Reverend Theodore Venables is a wonderfully drawn character, a persuasive combination of forgetful impracticality, sincere moral rectitude, attentive responsibility, and childlike enthusiasm. He is the kind of man a person has to love or he will drive you insane. Even at his very advanced age, he is a whirlwind of activity, ferrying parishioners on vital errands, attending the sick, comforting the bereft, and burying the dead. The good reverend putters from one obligation to the next in a fittingly ancient open motor car, blowing the horn at every crossing and every blind spot to warn others of their danger. He and his wife live in threadbare poverty, in part because they have put out so much to help the community, in part because he advances money to members of his flock that they might pay their tithes. If there are sins on his soul, they are negligible—an obvious pride in his church and an overweening passion for the practice of bell ringing. Reverend Venables, like the father of Dorothy L. Sayers, is a decent, God-fearing, unworldly man.

Sayers's mother patiently bore a great deal living with her husband. Though she felt that he had wearied her for years beyond count with his cloistered ways, she missed him painfully when he was gone. They were a true couple, far more intertwined with one another than either could recognize. So it is with Theodore Venables and his wife, Agnes. God knows she suffered. The Reverend could seldom remember where he put anything or when he said anything. With his hectic, unheeding surrender to life as a series of dimly recognized but immediate obligations, there can be no schedule. Meal times come at any hour of the day and sometimes are foregone altogether without warning. Naturally, Agnes Venables finds this distressing; her husband is no longer young. More often than not, she can only bow to the inevitable, doing her best to manage the Reverend's somewhat random approach to life.

Yet Mrs. Venables is a force in her own right. More judgmental than her husband, she is also more politic. She can see the good and bad in people, can size up their character more effectually. This makes her an invaluable peacemaker in the parish and a guiding force in community affairs. If some practical project is afoot to improve village life, Agnes Venables will invariably be found at the bottom of it. She and Theodore are a team, he looking after the spiritual wants of Fenchurch St. Paul, she ministering to the village's material needs.

The story of *The Nine Tailors* is founded on the fabric of the Venables's lives and values. Fenchurch St. Paul is a village isolated from the hustle of the modern world by more than custom and geography. Situated in the Fens country, the village lives in constant danger of flood; the Reverend carefully tracks the changes being made to the drainage system, preparing his flock for the worst. Fenchurch St. Paul is tiny in the scheme of things and must look after itself. Moreover, the village is far removed from city life, little affected by modern convenience and invention. These are mostly people who have never heard live jazz music. But the village is more than a quaint rural outpost stranded in the nineteenth century. It is, for all its bickering neighbors, its complicated and snooty class conventions, and its inbred marriages really a decent, moral community. The presence of the Reverend Venables and his wife make it so. They make an honest difference in the lives of three hundred forty Christian souls. Dorothy L. Sayers has painted an idyll in homage to the values of her parents.

At the same time, Sayers recognizes that she does not belong to this community, that her life will not conform to the idyll. Recalling herself through the character of fifteen-year-old Hilary Thorpe, she is one who loves the village and its people, who is the picture of responsibility and respect for her elders, and who cannot be contained in this tiny enclave. Oxford, notoriety, and the wide world beckon. Hilary's father sincerely wishes there was more money to secure her future, but she is not worried. She will make her own way in the world, as a writer. This surprises her father:

> "Oh? What are you going to write? Poetry?"
>
> "Well, perhaps. But I don't suppose that pays very well. I'll write novels. Best-sellers. The sort that everybody goes potty over. Not just bosh ones, but like *The Constant Nymph*."
>
> "You'll want a bit of experience before you can write novels, old girl."
>
> "Rot, Daddy. You don't want experience for writing novels. People write them at Oxford and they sell like billy-ho. All about how awful everything was at school." (59)

One can easily picture a fifteen-year-old Dorothy L. Sayers having this conversation with her father.

For Hilary Thorpe, Fenchurch St. Paul is a chrysalis, a warm and encompassing home where she will grow her wings and someday soon fly away. Yet, for all its warmth, the village has its troubles, and Hilary comes in for more than her share. Like her creator later in life, young Hilary loses both her parents in a few short months—her mother to influenza, her father to ill health stemming from personal disaster followed by service in the war. It is a sad loss for the community; the Thorpe family, descended from the minor nobility, had long supported and guided the town's fortunes. Now little remains but broken fortunes, heavily

mortgaged properties, and a child with dreams. Shadows of the unfortunate recent past rest heavily on the Thorpe family. The theft of the Wilbraham emeralds on the occasion of the marriage of Hilary's parents
remains an object of speculation sixteen years later. This misfortune is at
the heart of the intricate mystery that Dorothy L. Sayers has in store. The
mystery becomes manifest when the Thorpe family grave is opened to
reveal a strange, unwanted, unidentifiable body.

From the first, it is plain that the Thorpe family tragedy is intimately
connected to the mystery of the man in the grave. Exactly who had been
involved in the theft, and in what capacity, is anyone's guess. So is the
location of the emeralds; they were never recovered. The robbery had
broken the Thorpes. One of the thieves was Jeff Deacon, a trusted family retainer; his wife Mary, a local woman, may have been involved as
well. Hilary's father paid Mrs. Wilbraham the full value of the emeralds,
leaving his family in straitened circumstances.

The dark cloud emanating from the incident persisted through the
years. People remembered, speculated, and whispered. Still, it was the
past, painful in its memories and its effects but dead and gone. Authorities reported Jeff Deacon, the servant turned thief, dead following an
attempted jailbreak in 1918. His wife remarried and returned to live in
Fenchurch St. Paul as Mrs. William Thoday. The parish felt the effects
of the crime; they could no longer rely on the kindness and authority of
the Thorpe family in times of crisis. But life continued restlessly on, for
sixteen years.

The past returned to life in the new year of 1930. Like all shadow
worlds, it was difficult to discern—a dropped cryptogram here, a brief
intrusion by a seedy London ex-convict there, and a mentally impaired
young man witnesses a confrontation in the church that he cannot properly describe or comprehend. The village, gripped by an epidemic of influenza, scarcely notices before returning to its somnolent pace. Then comes
spring and the exposure of the unknown body in Hilary's mother's grave.

The discovery brings the modern era to the village in the person of
Peter Wimsey. Quite by accident, Peter had stayed one night in the village
on New Year's Eve. He was a supplicant then, in need of shelter and aid
following a motor crash. The village, and especially the Reverend Venables, took him in on their terms. He attended New Year's Eve services
(making embarrassing mistakes), took part in nine continuous hours of
bell ringing, shared a community breakfast at the rectory, and had his car

refurbished by a blacksmith. The Reverend and Mrs. Venables did not even recognize him as the famous London detective. When Peter returns in April, invited by the Reverend in the hope of solving the mystery of the grave, he is demonstrably different—a powerful and foreign presence in the village.

The difference is clear at the outset. Arriving just in time for the inquest, Peter is visibly gratified by horrid details of the corpse that the villagers can only find shocking. He plunges immediately into the investigation, cooperating fully with the local authorities but rapidly outdistancing their plodding ways. It is Wimsey who seizes on the significance of the rope that had bound the corpse, Wimsey who unearths a letter from the dead man's wife following an intuitive long shot, and Wimsey who thinks nothing of running over to France to further the inquiry. His is a world of Daimler automobiles, scientific methodologies, and confrontations with news reporters. And it is a large, international world.

Fenchurch St. Paul does its best to go peaceably on. The Venables give Peter a room at the rectory for his investigations, save "on Clothing-Club nights, when I am afraid we shall have to turn you out" (128). It is planting time; farmers must be questioned at the convenience of their demanding work schedules. The two innkeepers are willing enough to talk, but only after they have sold Wimsey a beer. Theodore and Agnes Venables always seem to be caught on the fly; their responsibilities are an endless and unpredictable routine. The rhythms of the village are as always. The church bells—nine tailors for a man, six for a woman—mark the passage of time and mortal flesh.

The village influences Peter in subtle ways, largely for the good. He had failed to win Harriet Vane only three months before (though Sayers does not mention this in *The Nine Tailors);* his mood would be subdued in any case. Yet the presence of this massive and ancient church, this gentle and ancient padre, and this respectful and accepting village folk rob him of his usual careless air. There is essentially no blither in this novel. Peter's touches of humor are attuned to his surroundings, gracious and light. For the greater part, he is simply determined to get on with the job. A gentlemanly and efficient approach is ordained.[56]

For all his ordered method and modern hustle, Peter is stymied until two of the villagers lend assistance. In each case, the aid is accidental, a shot in the dark. Hilary Thorpe sends Peter an odd message picked up in the church belfry; he instantly recognizes the piece to be in code. The

Reverend Venables suggests that Peter's ordered rearrangement of the cryptogram looks like a ringer's peal; this provides the key to read the message. Even this is no immediate help, but Wimsey eventually reads the thing rightly. All falls into place. Peter's hypothetical understanding of the case has been completely in error. Now, a tragedy darker than even he had imagined looms.

The case, looked at as an abstract problem of identification, had seemed to hold such promise at the outset. Peter had been intrigued by the disclosure of mutilations done after death to conceal the body's identity. A most cunning murderer seemed afoot. Then, as the weeks wore on, the components of the problem acquired names, faces, histories, and human lives. Starting out to solve a conundrum, Peter in the end faced the prospect of revealing a tragedy, resurrecting the past in shades of nightmare. Worse still, he could not even provide an absolute solution to the mystery. He knew who was dead, and why, but he could not say how the murder was done or who had done the killing. The shadow of suspicion and guilt would remain forever.

What Peter did was to find the emeralds. Everything fell into place when the green sparklers tumbled from their hiding place in the church. "We've been wrong from start to finish," Peter admitted painfully. "Nobody found them. Nobody killed anybody for them. Nobody deciphered the cryptogram. We're wrong, wrong, out of the hunt and wrong!" (207) All the mysterious business of letters from France, disguised visits by London crooks, codes and beer bottles in the belfry, and all the obfuscation of the dead past suddenly assumed a different hue. With the emeralds in his hand, there is just one possible answer. The unidentifiable body in the grave had to be Jeff Deacon, former servant to the Thorpes and convicted thief. He was finally dead, a dozen years after authorities had thought him so.

The past would have remained the past but for Wimsey's efforts. Jeff Deacon would have remained an unknown corpse, moldering in a soon-forgotten grave. Wholly evil, he had met a much-deserved end. Knowing the extent of his vicious and immoral behaviors, no one would possibly wish to mourn him—let the earth take him. Once again too clever by half, Peter Wimsey unfortunately came to know the actions of every single participant in the whole, sad farce. He knew why the elusive Jean Legros had left France, why Cranton (the London ex-convict) had trekked from London to Fenchurch St. Paul, what Potty Peake had seen in the church, and why William Thoday was so anxious to rise from his sick bed on New Year's Eve. Only the method and hour of Deacon's death eluded him; without those elemental facts, he could not positively say whether Cranton, William Thoday, or William's brother James had done the deed. The village would have been better off left in ignorance. Because of Peter's inspired efforts, Mary and William Thoday were no longer legally married, William and James Thoday were prime murder suspects, and William wanted to die. Peter can only apologize to the much-distressed Reverend Venables: "I rather wish I hadn't come buttin' into this. Some things may be better left alone, don't you think? My sympathies are all in the wrong place and I don't like it. I know all about not doing evil that good may come. It's doin' good that evil may come that is so embarrasin'. . . . I'm sorry to have made so much unpleasantness, anyhow. And I really would rather go away now. I've got all that modern squeamishness that doesn't like watchin' people suffer" (214–15). There is no celebration to conclude the investigation into the mystery of Fenchurch St. Paul's churchyard. There are simply people, bearing up under the evil influences that Jeff Deacon left behind. There is pain and guilt; above all, there is confusion. How did Jeff Deacon die? Wimsey can only feel responsible for the whole, sad, unresolvable mess.

A detective story might have ended here. For Dorothy L. Sayers, however, there was far more at stake than the simple solution of a murder, no matter how puzzling. Wimsey must return to Fenchurch St. Paul, face up to the responsibility for his endeavors, and accept the consequences. It is not that he has sinned, rather that he is a man of action living in a world of moral ambiguities. Ultimate judgment, for his own actions and those of others, does not rest with Peter Wimsey.

Peter returns to the village because of Hilary Thorpe. Old Mrs. Wilbraham has died, leaving the recovered emeralds to Hilary; Lord Peter has been designated trustee of the estate. Hilary will not touch the emeralds "with a barge pole" (238), but the inheritance does make her a wealthy heiress. She insists on returning to the old family house for Christmas and begs Lord Peter to come. With his sole other choice Duke's Denver—where he would endure an eternity of disparaging speculation concerning Harriet Vane—Peter agrees to spend the holidays at Fenchurch St. Paul.

Judgment comes. On the day after Christmas, the old Van Leyden sluice gives way, as the rector had long feared. The country is flooded six feet deep for miles around, with only the ancient church standing clear. The bells toll out their warning. The water claims Will Thoday; he dies heroically, trying to save another man, but he dies with guilt on his soul. The entire village gathers in the church, and Mary Thoday hears the bitter news. Her agonized tears stab at Wimsey, the dregs of the cup he has prepared. He can think only of escape. Dashing for the bell tower, he seeks the roof, only to be confronted by the bells themselves, ringing warning, ringing judgment: "It was not noise—it was brute pain, a grinding, bludgeoning, ran-dan, crazy, intolerable torment. He felt himself screaming, but could not hear his own cry. His eardrums were cracking; his senses swam away. It was infinitely worse than any roar of heavy artillery. That had beaten and deafened, but this unendurable shrill clangour was a raving madness, an assault of devils" (274–75).

Clamboring at last onto the roof, clinging to survival and sanity with his remaining strength, Wimsey knows. Jeff Deacon had been imprisoned in the belfry on the night of the New Year's peal; the bells had killed him. Perhaps this had been God's own justice. Ringing the peal, Lord Peter and eight solid members of the Fenchurch St. Paul community unwittingly had proved the instruments of Deacon's execution.

The solution is truly innovative, a first in the annals of detective fiction, but it is a small thing in the context of this story's final chapters. Lord Peter's explanations to the authorities and Reverend Venables come almost as an afterthought. What matters is that Peter must do his part to protect the lives of the villagers. Life does go on—life must go on—and Peter must subsume his own private remorse for the general good. As the flood waters wash clean the village of Fenchurch St. Paul, Peter organizes the men for games and calisthenics while Bunter directs the common kitchen and provides music hall impressions. Peter Wimsey is a man in the human community; whatever the circumstance, he must do his best and accept what comes. By the close of the novel, he can bow to the ultimate truth: "Nine Tailors Make a Man" (280).

So ended the year 1930 for Lord Peter, the most intensively active year Dorothy L. Sayers ever chronicled for her fictional detective. The process of creating this one year absorbed the author for close to five. Constantly embellishing her craft, Sayers came to use the passage of time in her parallel, imaginary world—"Cloud-Cuckoo Land"—in a variety of intricate and intriguing ways. In the end, she successfully interlayered the full content of two separate novels, splicing to this history portions of two additional novels and a short story. The purpose of this elaborate sequencing of events spread over several works was simple and extraordinarily demanding. Sayers had set out to give Peter Wimsey a lover, a wife. In the process, she discovered that she needed first to provide him a soul.

The Peter Wimsey that emerges from the pages of *The Nine Tailors* is recognizable as the Wimsey of *Whose Body?* As ever, he looks relentlessly forward, embracing the new without utterly rejecting the old. Years have distanced him from the war, but the memories still rise from time to time. Visiting France in search of the mysterious Jean Legros, Peter exhibits painful familiarity with the nightmare events surrounding the third battle of the Marne, June 1918. He remains a skillful, imaginative, innovative investigator who employs all the latest scientific methodology, yet he is curiously reliant on intuition for his most brilliant discoveries. Peter is, as his fictitious surname embodies, still whimsical.

Yet there is now more to the man. His eccentricities have acquired reason, and his studied lightheartedness masks a vulnerable sensitivity. Occasionally the mask will crack: "Oh God! Shall I ever live down this disastrous reputation for tom-foolery?"[57] The care and interest he expresses for others have become genuine; he will do his best to secure the happiness of others, even at his own risk. If he is more virtuous, he is less chivalrous; he is happy to accept women as equal human beings. That process, begun with his recognition that Mrs. Grimethorpe must be her own woman, continued in his encounters with Marjorie Phelps and Ann Dorland and culminated in his surrender to the unhappy fact that Harriet Vane could not marry him on unequal terms. This, undeniably, is the greatest lesson Peter has absorbed through 1930.

Wimsey has by this time become a distant echo of Theodore Venables. No sense of religion will touch him, of course; his duty to the church is mechanically performed. But he is fully aware of a power greater than his own. In the face of that power, Lord Peter Wimsey has reached within himself and found the capacity to be a truly decent human being. Peter has indeed acquired a soul.[58]

Lord Peter Displays His Range

By 1931 DOROTHY L. SAYERS HAD ENTRENCHED HERSELF AS one of the leading detective novelists of her era—the "Queen of Crime."[1] Her reputation rested on the Lord Peter mysteries; she had published six longer works and a collection of short stories, with more to follow soon. Her devotion to the field did not end there. She had another novel, *The Documents in the Case,* to her credit, though she considered it a failure. She had also begun work on a literary biography of Wilkie Collins, a pioneer crime novelist antedating Arthur Conan Doyle and his Sherlock Holmes. (The work was never completed, though she did produce a widely respected bibliography of Collins's works.) 1931 also saw the publication of a new selection of edited mysteries, *Great Short Stories of Detection, Mystery and Horror,* Second Series. As with everything else in her life, Dorothy L. Sayers had thrown herself into a full-time career as detective novelist with unbounded enthusiasm and unparalleled attention to detail. She fully immersed herself in the subject matter.

Much of Sayers's reputation for critical understanding of the detective story rests on the introduction she wrote for her first series of *Great Short Stories.* Even after World War II, critics regarded the essay as "the finest single piece of analytical writing about the detective story," containing "all that was to be said about the detective story up to the date of its composition." The introduction reflects both her devotion to thorough background research for any project she chose and her critical perspective on the mystery story as literature.[2]

Sayers regarded the popularity of the detective story as one more example of the strange human predilection for "puzzles and bugaboos" ranging from crossword puzzles to mathematical conundrums. Perhaps it was an expression of the inquiring intellect, perhaps mere perversity. In any case, she traces the roots of the mystery story to the tales of horrors and the supernatural that delighted the ancients, but she acknowledges that credit for the modern form of detective fiction belongs to "the wayward genius of Edgar Allen Poe." Two elements were necessary in society for the mystery to flourish: the presence of an organized and effective force of police, and popular sympathy for the cause of law and order in conflicts with the exotic criminal. When these conditions came to exist in the nineteenth century, Poe seized the opportunity to combine the chilling horror of some terrible crime with the studied efforts of the detective to expose the perpetrator. The mystery story was born.[3]

In Sayers's analysis, the five detective stories of Edgar Allen Poe stand as the source for two critical forms of development, which she labels the "intellectual" and the "sensational." In the intellectual story, the plot hinges not so much on the crime as its detection: the puzzle is intricate, the clues for a proper solution present but cunningly disguised, and action, such as it is, focuses on the investigator. As Sayers noted, "The strength of this school is its analytical ingenuity; its weakness is its liability to dullness and pomposity, its mouthing over the infinitely little, and its lack of movement and emotion." The sensational, on the other hand, sacrifices intricacy for adventure; the detective (and the reader) may have little to go on, but the threat of danger is a constant. "This school is strong in dramatic incident and atmosphere; its weakness is a tendency to confusion and a dropping of links—its explanations do not always explain; it is never dull, but it is sometimes nonsense." The intellectual and the sensational, therefore, defined the range of the detective story genre, while a third category, the combined puzzle-thriller, represented a kind of golden mean.[4]

Sayers traces the evolution of the detective story following Poe by tracking two separate but integral lines of development: the plot of the mystery, and the growth of the investigator as a standard character. She emphasizes the work of two nineteenth-century English writers, Sheridan Le Fanu and Wilkie Collins, both of whom made critical contributions to plot development. Le Fanu, she argued, had a better eye for the sensational—the weird and horrible—but Collins was the truer mystery writer, a master of posing the mystery as a puzzle for the reader to solve along with the participants. At the same time, Collins's characters exhibited wonderful variety and a sense of genuine presence. Without hesitation, Sayers pronounced Wilkie Collins's *The Moonstone* "the very finest detective story ever written." Small wonder she chose Collins as her subject for critical study in 1931.[5]

If Poe invented and Collins perfected (at least once), Arthur Conan Doyle crystallized the detective story. Beginning with his introduction in 1887, Doyle's Sherlock Holmes became the master by which all other fictional detectives would be measured forever. Sayers maintains that the reason for this lies less with the genius of Holmes than that of his creator. In many ways, Holmes is the mirror image of Poe's Inspector Dupin. What makes the Holmes stories come alive, Sayers argues, is the effective interaction between the investigator and the narrator, Doctor Watson. In Watson, Doyle has created a multilayered and sympathetic character who shares the reader's mystification over Holmes's latest challenge. He makes the wildly eccentric Holmes an approachable and believable entity.

Ironically, while the characters of Holmes and Watson are perhaps the most recognizable in all of English literature, the immense popularity of Doyle's stories actually had the effect of promoting plot at the expense of characterization in the detective story. Holmes is the ultimate logician; the people who consult his practice are simply elements in a puzzle that Holmes must reconstruct. Apart from Sherlock Holmes and John (or is it James?) Watson, Doyle's characters are largely interchangeable cutouts. The plot is everything.[6]

Worse, Doyle's followers and imitators fastened on just one of Holmes's salient characteristics: his scientific methodology. Great though the Holmes stories were, Sayers was dismayed by the manner in which "the detective story became swept away on a single current of development." The difficulty was that Doyle did not consistently "play fair" with the reader—too often Holmes would seize on some clue, receive some important telegram, or hold some critical conversation outside Watson's hearing. For all the logic of Holmes, there is no chance that readers can exercise their own logic; they do not have the complete information. As time went on, fiction writers in the Doyle tradition became more adept at providing readers the necessary clues, but their detectives grew correspondingly more cold and analytical. The stories became exercises in logic, devoid of any real human element. The potential recognized by Wilkie Collins was left unfulfilled. This, Sayers maintained, was pretty much the way matters stood in the years just before the Great War.[7]

The introduction to *Great Short Stories of Detection, Mystery and Horror,* First Series, next takes up the trends of the modern era. Though it is implicit in every word she writes, Sayers does not actually mention the fact that she is herself a leading practitioner of the art during the twenties. She considers modern developments in the genre from several perspectives, including viewpoint, love interest, methods of murder, and identification of suspects. Sayers is at pains to emphasize that while mystery writers were exploring several intriguing new avenues, the basic concept remained firmly imbedded in the traditions of Poe, Collins, and Doyle. What she did not explore was the influence of recent developments on her own work. She also did not consider her own position with respect to the various categories of mystery writing that she had constructed.[8]

Sayers, in fact, was one of the great experimenters with the potentials inherent in detective fiction. She had modelled her great detective in reaction to Sherlock Holmes, but she placed him in situations worthy of Wilkie Collins's imagination. Like Collins, she was capable of producing a tight, intellectual (and dull) detective puzzle or exploring the sensational. Sayers surveyed the full range of possibilities. At the same time, she was careful to make her audience understand that they were reading mystery stories, that they were indulging in a species of literary sleight of hand.

Though Dorothy L. Sayers worked hard to create a sense of the real in her novels, mirroring the England she knew and incorporating news items of the current moment, she employed several devices to remind readers that they were reading a story, that none of these horrible, murdering people were real. The most obvious of her tricks was the naming of places and characters. No one would conceive that places with names such as Riddlesdale, Little Dorking, or Little Doddering could actually exist. What better name for a psychotic villain than Freke? For a slow and cautious police superintendent: Mr. Glaisher. Vera Findlater, Bertha Gotobed—who would believe that these were the names of real people? Even the names of some of the stock characters—Murbles, Sir Impey Biggs—are patently ludicrous. And of course, the most blatant of all is the name of her hero, Peter Wimsey. Sayers had selected the name to suggest the essence of his character: an excessively playful if capricious disposition. Sayers was much surprised to discover that there actually were English people bearing the surname Wimsey; she occasionally received actual obituary notices for Peter Wimseys in the mail.[9]

If the names of places and characters did not serve as sufficient reminder, Sayers planted occasional reminders in the text, conversations that pointed up the fictional context of the action. In *Whose Body?* Parker remarks that "If this were a detective story, there'd have been a convenient shower exactly an hour before the crime and a beautiful set of marks which could only have come there between two and three in the morning, but this being real life in a London November, you might as well expect footprints in Niagara" (59). Of course, this is a detective story and in no way real life in a London November. Sayers is simply pointing up the fact that she is making things difficult for her characters—and her readers.

Sayers employed similar devices in subsequent stories. In *Unnatural Death,* she promises the reader that she will not lower herself to employ the most unfair of murder methods, the "native poisons which slay in a split second and defy the skill of the analyst." Such things might have passed muster in Arthur Conan Doyle's heyday, but they were now "familiar to the meanest writer of detective stories." At the same time, Sayers revealed in this story her ultimate goal as a writer, one she shared with all mystery writers and with all fictional detectives. The strange death of Agatha Dawson was meant to be "The case of cases. The murder without discernable means, or motive, or clue" (97, 131).

By the 1930s, Sayers had raised the reversal of fact and fiction to a real art, placing the fictional fiction writer Harriet Vane in the text to point up the differences between standard fictional convention and the actions taking place before her eyes. Even in *Strong Poison,* Harriet Vane the mystery writer becomes a fulcrum for commentary on the craft of writing mysteries. While Peter's mother wonders if Harriet's arraignment for murder is perhaps "a judgement" for Harriet's vocation of writing murder mysteries, Peter is willing to argue that "in detective stories virtue is always triumphant. They're the purest literature we have." Early on in *Strong Poison,* Peter tests a scenario intimating that Harriet might be the murderer by suggesting she write it up as a new detective novel. Harriet hears him out with great interest, and is duly impressed. "That's really ingenious," she admits. "An entirely new motive for murder—the thing I've been looking for for years." When Harriet is at last freed from prison and able to take an active part in Peter's investigations, the mystery writer's perspective will become integral to the action on the page. Essentially, Sayers is able to insinuate her own commentary on the plot into the weave of the dialogue. And that really is ingenious (30, 127, 70).

Sayers further reminds the reader that the novels are the purest fiction by implanting references to other mystery writers into the texts. Again, this is a form of reverse psychology—the characters in Sayers's books argue that the tale they experience differs sharply from recognized fictions; therefore it has to be real. Beneath it all is Sayers, gently pulling the reader's leg.

Arthur Conan Doyle's great detective is the most obvious target for this kind of play. The repeated use of the name Sherlock Holmes was meant to summon images of a legacy—every detective, fictional or real, is to some extent the embodiment of Doyle's creation. To call someone a "Sherlock" is to conjure up an image, real or ironic, of investigative genius. Sayers was laboring in a tradition largely shaped by Doyle— better to acknowledge this openly and have done with it. In addition to the references to Holmes found in *Whose Body?* they litter the text of *Clouds of Witness,* Sayers's second novel. Newspapers refer to Peter as "the Sherlock Holmes of the West End"; Wimsey and Parker deride one another with such comments as "Holmes, how do you do it?" (191, 223) Similar tokens of respect appear in each subsequent novel, gaining renewed emphasis when Peter and Harriet invoke the name of Holmes to mock one another's obvious deductions. They are treading in the footsteps of the master.

References to additional mystery writers—more specific and more pointed—abound in the works of Dorothy L. Sayers. The practice began, in a modest fashion, with the publication of *Whose Body?* In Julian Freke's written confession addressed to Lord Peter, he acknowledges the attention to detail emphasized in "that well-thought-out little work of Mr. Bentley's."[10] Freke is referring to *Trent's Last Case,* published by E. C. Bentley in 1912. Sayers felt enormous respect for this book, a work that ran contrary to the Doyle-inspired fashion in detective literature by emphasizing character development and introducing a love element involving the detective. In her 1928 essay on the development of the detective story, Sayers argued that "E. C. Bentley, in *Trent's Last Case,* has dealt finely with the still harder problem of the detective in love. Trent's love for Mrs. Manderson is a legitimate part of the plot; while it does not prevent him from drawing the proper conclusion from the evidence before him, it does prevent him from acting upon his conclusions, and so prepares the way for the real explanation. Incidentally, the love-story is handled artistically and with persuasive emotion."[11]

Bentley wrote the book in response to a bet with fellow author Gilbert Keith Chesterton, to whom *Trent's Last Case* is dedicated. The goal was to write a successful detective story in which the detective was logically brilliant and totally wrong in his deductions. Bentley succeeded beyond imagination; the book sold out four editions in just five months. As Sayers wrote in the introduction to a 1930 edition, the work "welled up in the desiccated desert of mystery fiction like a spring of living water. No other writer had ever handled that kind of theme with so light and sure a hand."[12] Certainly the book—the supreme model of a detective story that was a novel in the truest sense—stood as a beacon for Sayers herself.

Dorothy L. Sayers was not always so kind. In *Unnatural Death,* she began the practice of mentioning the work of other detective authors for the general purpose of illustrating and criticizing their shortcomings. Her first target is "the works of Mr. Austin Freeman," author of a long series of modern scientific police procedurals featuring his investigative logician, Doctor Thorndyke. Freeman's works, which began to appear in 1907, were rigidly logical puzzles involving the carefully crafted criminal plots of most inventive ne'er-do-wells. The puzzle is everything, as there is little character development; even Thorndyke is flat and uninteresting as a human being. In *Unnatural Death,* Sayers suggests the essence of Freeman's ideas of proper mystery: Mary Whittaker has faked an elaborate kidnapping by superimposing several sets of footprints—all her own wearing different shoes. Inventive but altogether obvious—and tedious.

In her 1928 essay, Sayers is at pains to explain the problem with the Doctor Thorndyke stories. The reader "knows that, when Mr. Austin Freeman drowns somebody in a pond full of water-snails, there will be something odd and localised about those snails." The solution to every story is logical, yes, but overreliant on knowledge of arcane minutiae. After reading two or three Thorndykes, the reader will have the method down pat; instead of detecting with the detective, the reader is detecting the author.[13]

Sayers also complained that Freeman succumbed monotonously to the temptation to place impertinent romance in his stories: "Some of the finest detective-stories are marred by a conventional love-story, irrelevant to the action and perfunctorily worked in. The most harmless form of that disease is that taken, for example, in the works of Mr. Austin Freeman. His secondary characters fall in love with distressing regularity, and perform a number of antics suitable to persons in their condition, but they do not interfere with the course of the story. You can skip the love-passages if you like, and nothing is lost."[14] Whatever else could be said of Austin Freeman, his stories did not equate with Dorothy L. Sayers's idea of a true crime novel in the Wilkie Collins tradition.

The carefully camouflaged barb directed at Freeman was simply an opening salvo. She broadened the scope of her intent in the fourth Wimsey novel, *The Unpleasantness at the Bellona Club*. This time the attention to other writers is most plain: Peter discovers a shelf of mysteries in Ann Dorland's studio and proceeds to read the titles aloud for the reader's benefit: "Austin Freeman, Austin Freeman, Austin Freeman—bless me! she must have ordered him in wholesale. *Through the Wall*—that's a good 'tec story, Charles—all about the third degree—Isabel Ostrander—three Edgar Wallaces—the girl's been indulging in an orgy of crime!" (277) Again Sayers has singled out authors she does not really like. She offers another take on Freeman, as Charles Parker finds one of his plots "a bit elaborate for the ordinary criminal" (278). There is no further comment in the book regarding Isabel Ostrander, as Sayers had some small respect for this author. In her 1928 essay she condemns her with faint praise, writing in a footnote that her *Ashes to Ashes* "is a very excellent piece of work which, in the hands of a writer of a little more distinction, might have been a powerful masterpiece."[15] She had almost nothing at all to say about Edgar Wallace in the essay, regarding him as the author of commonplace "sensational thrillers." She does mention him again in the Bellona Club affair. Ann Dorland and Peter discuss the fact that "When Crippen and La Neve were taken on the steamer, they were reading Edgar Wallace." Probably Sayers agreed with the summation provided by contemporary American critic Willard Huntington Wright, who argued in 1927 that "Wallace has written too much and too rapidly, with too little attention to his problems and too great an insistence on inexpensive 'thrills.'" The man published one hundred seventy books between

1905 and 1932. It is more this volume of accomplishment rather than the content of any one book that makes him remembered at all.[16]

Presumably having had her full say in the introduction published in 1928, Sayers restrains herself in the next Wimsey novel, *Strong Poison*. There is just one reference to other mystery authors. Contemplating the role of the detective-fiction writer in real life, Peter's mother cites two examples by name to contradict her own contention that writers are not much for investigation in real life. There is "Edgar Wallace of course, who always seems to be everywhere and dear Conan Doyle" (30). Doyle seems to have gotten the better of the assessment.

Following the heady and intimidating complications introduced with Harriet Vane, Sayers felt the need for a break, both for herself and for Lord Peter. Writing to a close friend, she confessed that she was "getting a bit weary of Lord Peter, but I suppose he must be kept going, as he still seems to pay pretty well. But, as you may have noticed, he is growing older and more staid. There are times when I wish him the victim of one of his own plots!"[17]

Sayers composed much of her next book while on vacation in Scotland in 1930, staying at the hotel to write through most of the summer while Mac Fleming fished and dabbled at landscape art. The result was an almost total change of pace for the Wimsey series. Virtually devoid of complicating love angles, anguished guilt complexes, or moral dilemmas, *The Five Red Herrings* emerged as a detective story almost purely in the puzzle tradition.

Sayers had determined to try her hand at an old-fashioned pure detective puzzle in the conventions of Doyle-Freeman-Chesterton. As she confessed in a letter to Victor Gollancz, she liked "each book to have a slightly different idea behind it. I have also been annoyed (stupidly enough) by a lot of reviewers who observe the identity of the murderer was obvious from the start. . . . Personally, I feel that it is only when the identity of the murderer *is* obvious that the reader can really concentrate on the question (much more interesting) *How* did he do it? But if people really *want* to play 'spot the murderer,' I don't mind obliging them—for once!"[18]

Dorothy L. Sayers carried the concept of the puzzle to the extreme of arranging that a page be left blank in the published story. This missing page ostensibly recorded a conversation between Lord Peter and the official police investigator, Sergeant Dalziel. Examining Sandy Campbell's death scene, Peter has noticed a critical accoutrement missing. If the object is really not there, it can only mean that Campbell was murdered. On the missing page, Peter went on to identify the object. Sayers has carried the puzzle game another step forward.

She more freely acknowledges the existence of fellow mystery writers in this book than in any other. Allusions and direct quotations are sprinkled liberally throughout the work, a kind of Greek chorus commenting on the investigation at hand. Again, the authors are often those with whom Sayers has some quarrel.

Not quite halfway through the work, Lord Peter listens to Bunter's report of a conversation with Betty, maidservant to Gowan, one of the six murder suspects in the case. Betty has glimpsed what she first thought a corpse but now believes to be a sick and bandaged man. Peter's response is to observe that "As G. K. C. says, 'I'd rather be alive than not'" (142). It is an amusing enough reaction, even if the reader does not recognize the source.

Sayers was probably correct in assuming that most of her readers would instantly recognize G. K. C. as none other than Gilbert Keith Chesterton, Roman Catholic apologist and author of the Father Brown detective stories produced between 1911 and 1935. Chesterton was the first to use popular mystery as a vehicle to promote his views on a serious subject, namely proper Christian behavior. Respect for this kind of fiction, which attracted a large international audience, grew as a consequence of his efforts. Still, Sayers was a little skeptical. She became a friend of Chesterton, joining him as a founding member of the Detection Club, but in her 1928 essay she takes him to task for refusing to acknowledge the consequences of a successful criminal investigation: "It is especially hard when the murderer has been made human and sympathetic. A real person has then to be brought to the gallows, and this must not be done too lightheartedly. Mr. G. K. Chesterton deals with this problem by merely refusing to face it. His Father Brown (who looks at sin and crime from the religious point of view) retires from the problem before the arrest is reached. He is satisfied with a confession. The sordid details take place 'off.'"[19] Obviously this was a solution that Sayers strenuously sought to avoid in her own work.[20]

Fifty-some pages following the homage to Chesterton, the reader encounters a specific reference to Freeman Wills Crofts. The reason is quite simple and direct. As Strachan, another of the artist-suspects, explains, "I had a book—a very nice book, all about a murder committed in this part of the country. *Sir John Magill's Last Journey*, by one Mr. Crofts. You should read it. The police in that book called in Scotland Yard to solve all their problems for them." Sayers had discovered, as she neared completion of her own book, that by some bizarre coincidence Crofts had set this book, published in 1930, in exactly the same real location as her own. What was more, his book turned "on real distances and time-tables," exactly like *The Five Red Herrings*. Fortunately, the plots of the two stories were vastly different.[21]

Sayers also had her doubts about Crofts's approach to the craft of mystery writing. His principal character was Inspector Joseph French, who emphasized "reconstructing his cases from the point of view of time." Beginning in 1925 Crofts had produced a new French novel every year through 1931, each written to a rigid formula that Sayers disdained. "When one of Mr. Wills Crofts's characters has a cast-iron alibi, the alibi will turn out to have holes in it," she warned in her 1928 introduction.[22] She used the trick sparingly herself. *The Five Red Herrings* abounds in alibis, satisfactory and unsatisfactory. And a clever and ironclad alibi is critical to the plot of *Have His Carcase*, published the year after. Even then, Sayers provided a unique and ingenious twist: the alibi seemingly is for the wrong time.

As matters turn out, the murderer in *The Five Red Herrings* possesses a small library of detective stories. There is the much-maligned Austin Freeman again ("He's always sound and informative"), J. J. Connington, whose *Two Tickets Puzzle* made the murderer uncomfortable because it too closely paralleled the murder plot at hand, and G. D. H. Cole and Margaret Cole, early but not terribly effective pioneers in introducing a female sleuth. ("But the really brilliant woman detective has yet to be created," Sayers wrote.) All amusing entertainment, Wimsey intimates, but not good for much more.[23]

What positive models did Dorothy L. Sayers have in mind as she wrote? There was Arthur Conan Doyle, of course—Sayers became a charter member of the Sherlock Holmes Society in 1934. At his moment of investigative triumph, Peter could only say that "At last I really feel like Sherlock Holmes." But *The Five Red Herrings* is not a Holmes story, any more than it is an austere Austin Freeman knockoff. Sayers pays tribute to her truest inspiration at mid-story, when Lord Peter shares a perspective with his manservant:

"Bunter," said Wimsey, "this case resembles the plot of a Wilkie Collins novel, in which everything happens just too late to prevent the story from coming to a premature happy ending."

"Yes, my lord." (95)

Writing of *The Moonstone* in 1928, Sayers stated baldly that "By comparison with its wide scope, its dove-tailed completeness and the marvellous variety and soundness of its characterization, modern mystery fiction looks thin and mechanical. Nothing human is perfect, but *The Moonstone* comes about as near perfection as anything of its kind can be."[24] For all her intention to produce a story in the Austin Freeman tradition in 1931, it is Wilkie Collins and E. C. Bentley who remain her most important models, her writing icons. (Instructively, both authors wove love stories into their detective novels.) Sayers simply could not resist the manifold attractions of really good writing, no matter the venue.

Nonetheless, *The Five Red Herrings* is a most curious Peter Wimsey story, a definite break from the tendencies evidenced in the preceding novels. The reader senses from the first that something is odd, as the book opens with a confrontation at the McClellan Arms, a tavern in Kircudbright, Galloway. Lord Peter is a bystander, a witness to the dustup, but it is made plain that he is a stranger in this community, though "received on friendly and even affectionate terms" (2).

The community is decidedly unfamiliar territory for Lord Peter's regular readers. Far removed from London and 110A Piccadilly, this is a foreign locale, in the most eloquent sense of the term. English is spoken after a fashion, but the laws and customs are passing strange. Even law enforcement operates under a different set of procedures. Wimsey is emphatically a visitor to these surroundings, a vacationer accepted despite his eccentric ways. He is cut off, not only from the familiar haunts of London, but from the large and varied community of stock characters that Sayers had created to assist him over the years. Charles Parker makes a brief appearance to assist the Scots investigators, but he and Wimsey do not interact. Peter must work this one out on his own.

The Galloway artistic colony that accepts Lord Peter as a harmless visitor is far removed from London by more than geography. After providing her readers an intriguing (and appalling) glimpse of the Bloomsbury artists in *Strong Poison,* Sayers now sought to capture a different kind of artistic community. The painters inhabiting the environs of Kircudbright are an outdoorsy lot, drawn to Scotland by the long hours of steady and suffused daylight, the spectacular scenery, and the variety of happy distractions. If these people are not painting—and it seems that much of their time is spent far from brush and canvas—they are poaching trout from some private stream, playing a highly competitive round of golf, sailing small boats on the Irish Sea, or doing some serious drinking at one of the local pubs. These are artists content with the conventions of northern life, though they are inventive as landscape painters go.

An uneasy bond exists among the males of this contingent. Sayers concentrates the bulk of her attention on seven artists: Sandy Campbell, who is dead by the second chapter, and six fellow painters who possessed sufficient motive to do him in. These are manly men, taking pleasure in outdoor pursuits, keeping their women in their places to the extent they can, and resorting to violence all too easily. Campbell gets into four separate fights on the night of his murder. True, he was an unusually quarrelsome type, but the others are not much better. The Englishman, Waters, is more than ready to duke it out with Campbell, Strachan and Farren mix it up out in the hills near the old mine pits, and Ferguson and Campbell have wasted breath over next to nothing on more than one occasion. Jock Graham had a reputation for tweaking anyone who took things too seriously, and even the staid and reserved Mr. Gowan harbored an itch for a good fight. Worse, several of them drank altogether too much. But they were good painters, presumably because their many outlets freed them from the self-absorption characteristic of their Bloomsbury brethren. This was a more traditional British community, full of hard-drinking, hard-playing, fist-waving, overgrown boys. Small wonder that inane jealousies broke out at the least provocation.

Though the group shares several important attributes, as they must if they are to pose a puzzle of identity to the reader, Dorothy L. Sayers is at pains to furnish each painter a distinct personality. In the Wilkie Collins tradition, each player must remain a distinct and believable character with values and motivations peculiar to himself. Sayers takes special delight in this, creating through the merest suggestion the idea that Strachan is a domestic tyrant with a temper, that Waters is a fiery and none-too-practical whelp, and that Farren is a hen-pecked victim of domestic bliss. Jock Graham is a very bright and very childish imp. Sparring words with Wimsey, Graham imitates the artistic styles of each of his fellow artists in turn, re-emphasizing the individuality of each. These are six men of mixed character, likeable in some ways, repellent in others. Sayers will not make Chesterton's mistake. These are human beings, and one of them may indeed go to the gallows.

Or will he? In *The Five Red Herrings,* for the first time in any Peter Wimsey novel, Sayers creates a situation in which the reader's sympathies are fully with the murderer rather than the victim. Sandy Campbell is a bad man. He drinks too much, he argues too loud and violently, he has a chip on his shoulder, and he simply itches for trouble. He does not deserve to die by violence, but no one in the novel is very sorry to see him gone. Not even Wimsey can work up much sympathy for the dead man.

This puts Peter in a particularly awkward position. Though none of the six suspects is an especially noble human being, each is far more likeable than Campbell. This fact in an odd way serves to emphasize the lighthearted nature of the puzzle that Sayers has prepared. Even as Wimsey unravels the whole complex murder plot, the shrewd reader can guess that the culprit, though exposed, will get off lightly. The oppressive weight of Campbell's ugly personality demands such a resolution.

But "who done it"? That really is the question in this novel, more so than in any other Wimsey story. Sayers provides the reader more than one avenue to get at the answer. For those who, along with Inspector MacPherson of Kircudbright, take special joy in material clues, there is the matter of the item missing at the falls where Campbell's body is found. For those with enough artistic knowledge to recognize what has to be missing, the solution may be relatively simple. Wimsey tantalizingly handles the object—in Ferguson's studio—very early in his investigation. In the meanwhile, those who share a belief in Dorothy L. Sayers's own dictum—what matters is not so much who but how—can solve the mystery by focusing on method.

From the outset Sayers goes out of her way to isolate the culprit. Ferguson's name appears by itself on Peter's list of suspects as an afterthought to the five possibles clustered on the preceding page. She furnishes telling phrases for the reader's benefit and emphasizes these by attaching a pointed disclaimer: "Somebody had breakfasted in Campbell's cottage, and the person who could do that most easily was Ferguson. Alternatively, if it was not Ferguson, Ferguson might have seen whoever it was" (64). There is a fair amount of obfuscation, of course.

To really mimic the inductive feat performed by Peter Wimsey, the reader must recognize the existence of a consistent pattern in the midst of much conflicting information. Just about everybody in Scotland had a quarrel with Sandy Campbell; his wake is a trail of bruised egos and angry, offended men. Then there are mysterious bicycles that end up in London, train tickets that should not add up but do, and a Campbell landscape—"thoroughly Campbellish" (219)—that Sandy Campbell did not paint. Finally, the plot is littered with alibis in the tradition of Freeman Wills Crofts. Most of them are genuine and do not matter; Lord Peter breaks the false one with astonishing ease.[25]

In a puzzle story such as this one, the skeletal structure of the plot is far more visible and obvious than is usually the case in a Wimsey novel. *The Five Red Herrings* has a contrived feel—would (or could) anyone really go to this much trouble to disguise an unpremeditated killing? When Campbell falls dead, the plot dictates that his murderer invent and carry out a highly public false alibi, drive the body several miles through the countryside, perpetrate an elaborate fake accident, catch a train at the last second after a cross-country rush on a bicycle, and then complete the falsification of his alibi in Glasgow. How much easier to shove the body in the nearest burn, "discover" it the next morning, and hope for the best. Of course, then there would not have been much of a puzzle for the reader to solve. It seems that the more intricate the puzzle mystery becomes, the more removed from believable reality will be the result.

The story is hampered as well by Sayers's conscious decision to avoid complications of emotion. The book is a stark contrast to *Strong Poison,* where intense emotional reactions to the human drama are integral to the success of the novel. This is best illustrated by the behavior of Wimsey himself. In *Strong Poison,* he is gnawed by doubt, hampered by the emotional burden of the task he has set himself. In *The Five Red Herrings* such feelings are nowhere in evidence. This time the entire investigation is essentially a game. Peter baits each of the artists in turn, nonchalantly pushing them to the edge with an endless chatter barbed with calculated insult to the intelligence. His blither is as brisk as ever ("Put on your nightgown, look not so pale. I tell you yet again, Campbell's dead; 'a cannot come out on's grave" [210].) He is, in short, relentlessly light. Not even the prospect of hanging a man seems to affect him in any serious way. At story's end, he sets himself the task of reenacting the entire murder plot and tying up half the police in Galloway for a full day rather than simply setting them straight with a half hour's conversation. They are all wrong, and Peter wants to enjoy every minute of his triumph. He has no regrets.

Though the characters supporting Wimsey are drawn with Sayers's usual attention to human detail, they do little to increase the work's human dimensions. These people have real lives—in some ways happy, in some ways painful—but their conditions do not in any way entangle the plot. Strachan's wife may walk in fear of her husband's anger, but his king-of-the-castle approach to marriage in no way affects the action of the story. Gilda Farren's clinging stupidity is merely something Peter must see through to get at Hugh Farren's whereabouts. The Smith-Lemesurier woman may have falsely sacrificed her reputation to entrap Jock Graham, but this is an embarrassment rather than a complication. Graham needs merely to own up to his real activities on the night of the murder to defeat Mrs. Smith-Lemesurier's designs. The book is a straight murder puzzle. Human dramas do not much get in the way.

There are some delicious moments. Early in the story, Peter packs Strachan's young daughter, Myra, and her nurse into his Daimler for a ride home. Myra is delighted as Peter pushes the speedometer to eighty-five and nearly hits some cows. She is a modern young woman who would like to make the cows run. Peter suspects that "One of these days you'll be a menace to society." "How lovely!" she responds. "I could have a pistol and a beautiful evening dress, and lure people to opium-dens and stick them up. I think I'd better marry you, because you've got such a fast car. That would be useful, you see" (36). She is indeed a modern woman.

At the other end of the scale is wee Helen McGregor, farmer's child and witness to the fight between Campbell and Gowan. Frightened nearly out of her wits by the violence of the altercation, she hides under the bedcovers when her parents come home, only to wake up three times crying in the night. Poor Helen's father finally gets the truth out of her, but it is her mother who hauls her down to the police station, threatening to "skelp her ower the lug" if she refuses to tell her story. Inspector MacPherson bribes the child with "a bag of sweeties, which a constable was sent out to procure." She is perhaps a not-so-modern young woman (95–96).

Still, *The Five Red Herrings* is the one long Peter Wimsey story that cannot be called a novel. The characters are sure, the plot intricate. It is just that one has very little to do with the other. Sayers succeeded in her stated goal of producing a traditional detective puzzle. The puzzle is a good one, with enough fully developed red herrings (five of them!) to keep the solution from becoming obvious. But it is the essential humanity of the Wimsey series as a whole that separates the work of Dorothy L. Sayers from that of the other mystery writers of her time. Thankfully, this was the sole story to deviate from that rich and varied humanist approach.

Victor Gollancz brought out *The Five Red Herrings* in January 1931, following this with *Great Short Stories of Detection, Mystery, and Terror,* Second Series, in July of that year. In addition to selecting and editing this second set of short stories, Sayers again wrote an introduction, this time focusing on the future of the detective story. Noting a trend toward greater character development and a fuller recognition of the psychological motivations to crime, she cannily predicted that these were the factors that would shape the mystery novel of the thirties and forties. Of course her own novels proved a key element in the development of the style.

Having given Lord Peter his vacation in Scotland, Sayers spent much of 1931 plotting and writing the first Wimsey novel to fully incorporate the character of Harriet Vane. A victimized bystander in *Strong Poison,* Harriet emerges from prison to assume a full role as Peter's investigative partner in *Have His Carcase.* Writing to Victor Gollancz in January 1931, Sayers promised that she was finished with the mystery-as-puzzle format:

> I will return to a less rigidly intellectual formula in HAVE-HIS-CARCASE which will turn on an alibi and a point of medicine, but will, I trust, contain a certain amount of human interest and a more or less obvious murderer. But I haven't made up the plot yet.[26]

Much of the human interest, of course, would lie in the development of the relationship between Peter and Harriet.

The full presence of Harriet Vane in the novel—Sayers builds as much narration on Harriet's activities as she does on Lord Peter's—provides her creator an irresistible opportunity to weave the mystery writer's perspective into the story. By allowing Harriet Vane to continually comment as a mystery writer on the murder scene, the conditions of material evidence, the reliability of alibis, and the relative truthfulness of suspects' explanations, Sayers is able to deliver her criticisms of mystery structure and content without intruding unduly into the narrative.

Harriet Vane's running observations are an elemental part of her character. When Peter and Harriet consider the well-disguised activities of the mysterious Haviland Martin, Harriet suspects "that if I had been inventing a way for a murderer to reach an appointed spot and leave it again, complete with bag and baggage, and without leaving more trail than was absolutely unavoidable, I should have made him act very much as Mr. Martin has acted" (125). Again, when the pair face the daunting task of deciphering the coded letter found in the murder victim's possession, Harriet notes that in her own books, "I usually make the villain end up by saying 'Bring this letter with you.' The idea is, from the villain's point of view, that he can then make certain that the paper is destroyed. From *my* point of view, of course, I put it in so that the villain can leave a fragment of paper clutched in the victim's stiffened hand to assist Robert Templeton" (364).

In *Have His Carcase,* such comments carry a dual purpose. They offer a window into Harriet Vane's thought processes and life work and, at the same time, point the way to the proper solution of the murder. The reason that so much of the activity of the perpetrators sounds to Harriet as if it had been plotted out—essentially written—beforehand is that it *was* scripted in advance by the conspirators. It is a cunning and multilayered device, this business of writer-as-character participating in a murder mystery.

On the very first page of *Have His Carcase,* the reader discovers that Harriet Vane is the author of detective thrillers. She had completed *Murder in the Pot* while in prison and had since delivered *Murder by Degrees.* Due to the publicity resulting from her false arrest for murder, sales of these and previous works have boomed, making Harriet comfortably well off. Feeling that she has earned a vacation, she is on a walking tour of the southwest coast of England while developing her next project, *The Fountain Pen Mystery.* Serial and publication rights are already contracted.

By intimation, the reader comes to understand the nature of Harriet Vane's works. They are much closer to those of Edgar Wallace, or perhaps even to the Sexton Blakes, than they are to Austin Freeman's (she mocks Dr. Thorndyke) or, for that matter, Dorothy L. Sayers's. This is suggested by the idealized portrait of Harriet's fictional detective, which she brings to mind whenever she has to do any investigating of her own: "Robert Templeton would examine the body. He was, indeed, notorious for the sang-froid with which he examined bodies of the most repulsive description. Bodies reduced to jelly by falling from aeroplanes; bodies charred into 'unrecognizable lumps' by fire; bodies run over by heavy vehicles, and needing to be scraped from the road with shovels—Robert Templeton was accustomed to examine them all, without turning a hair" (15). Generally speaking, bodies do not show up in these kinds of conditions in the puzzle-oriented mystery stories, at least not with appalling regularity. Plainly, some serious adventure was taking place in Harriet's stories.

Robert Templeton was a man designed for the rigors of strenuous adventure, "a gentleman of extraordinary scientific skill, combined with almost fabulous muscular development." The reader soon learns that Templeton is a thorough and determined detective; he has undertaken a full study of medicine to assist him in examining bodies. He is altruistic as well, doing all the hard investigating while secondary characters fall cozily in love. Almost his only failing is his inability to dress with any taste. Knowing nothing about men's clothing herself, Harriet has avoided the problem by making Templeton a man who does not care about his dress. Lord Peter can only remark with exasperation that "Robert Templeton's clothes have always pained me." One can only wonder, has Harriet Vane followed the career of Peter Wimsey through the novels of Dorothy L. Sayers? After all, the alias that Peter assumed to fool Mrs. Forrest in *Unnatural Death* was none other than Mr. Templeton.[27]

All of this is great fun and more than a little mischievous. Harriet spends her spare moments in *Have His Carcase* working out the plot for her own *Fountain Pen Mystery*. On her first night in the seaside resort town of Wilvercombe, she divides her time between contemplating the body she has discovered on the beach and puzzling on the thorny problems posed by her own imagination:

> The villain was at the moment engaged in committing a crime in Edinburgh, while constructing an ingenious alibi involving a steam-yacht, a wireless time-signal, five clocks and the change from summer to winter time. . . . The town clock was the great difficulty. How could that be altered. And altered it must be, for the whole alibi depended on its being heard to strike midnight at the appropriate moment. (42)

The painful thing is that the reader will never discover how all of this turns out. Harriet Vane is a fictional character inventing a twice-removed fictional story—none of this, nor any of her internationally famous bestsellers, will ever see the light of a genuine day. Sayers has created a writer creating a story for the purpose of giving the reader entrance into the mechanics of the detective story. As Harriet works, so too has Sayers worked; the reader must understand this to appreciate the novel to its fullest extent.

Still, Harriet Vane and Dorothy L. Sayers are not one and the same person, no matter the parallels in their biographies. Sayers has not simply written her own perception of herself into the story. Though both Sayers and Vane have been wounded by life and love, they have chosen to deal with their sorrows in different fashions. This may be a product of the kinds of mysteries each prefers to write. Harriet Vane pens thrillers with little emphasis on character development. In *The Fountain Pen Mystery,* Harriet confronts her serial editor's request that her heroine and Robert Templeton's friend "indulge in a spot of lovemaking"[28] by refusing to write it. Peter will take Harriet to task for this pointed avoidance of the human element in *Gaudy Night,* challenging her "to abandon the jig-saw kind of story and write a book about human beings for a change" (311).

For Sayers, on the other hand, careful and deliberate characterization is at the heart of her work. When people fall in love, as Flora Weldon so pathetically falls for Paul Alexis or as Peter Wimsey falls for Harriet Vane, the emotional pain is critical to the plot development. Sayers has chosen to wear her wounds on her sleeve.

One thing that Sayers and Vane did share in common was their approach to the business of writing. While attempting to solve the murder of Paul Alexis, Harriet suffered continual difficulties working out the plot of the latest Robert Templeton story. She fell into habits reminiscent of Sayers attempting to write from the comfort of her automatic chair:

Harriet continually found herself putting her work aside—"to clear" (as though it were coffee). Novelists who have struck a sag in the working-out of the plot are rather given to handing the problem over in this way to the clarifying action of the sub-conscious. Unhappily, Harriet's sub-conscious had other coffee to clear and refused quite definitely to deal with the matter of the town-clock. Under such circumstances it is admittedly useless to ask the conscious to take any further steps. When she ought to have been writing, Harriet would sit comfortably in an armchair, reading.[29]

Harriet's largest problem was that Robert Templeton had begun to talk like Lord Peter Wimsey.

By this time, Lord Peter had been a part of Dorothy L. Sayers's subconscious for about a dozen years. He had assumed a strange kind of separate reality, shaping action in his novels to suit his own convenience as much as his creator's needs. He has already refused to marry Harriet, as much as he and Sayers would have liked him to; he cannot change himself to fit the demands of the author's moment. He is a character whose attributes have been shaped by six previous novels; he cannot allow himself to be altered. Sayers can only add to him. At times, he even mocks her plans for him. This is most plain when Peter and Harriet get to arguing about her books. It is as if Lord Peter is quarreling with his creator, or, more precisely, as if Sayers was debating with herself: "'And that reminds me, in one of your books—' 'Bother my books! I quite see what you mean.'"[30]

The Peter Wimsey of *Have His Carcase* largely returns to the form exhibited in *Strong Poison* and the two previous novels. He exhibits a far greater range of emotions, beginning, of course, with his painfully awkward approach to gaining Harriet's love. He is reduced to treating his own "sincerest feelings like something out of a comic opera" (175), a condition that somewhat handicaps but does not negate his abilities as an investigating detective. In fact, working in tandem with Harriet seems to inspire him to greater efforts.

In the early cases, Charles Parker was apt to complain that he did all the hard, grinding work while Peter blithely examined the results and spun theories to fit the facts. In *Strong Poison,* this tendency reached a dramatic pass when Peter was unable to act, having to rely desperately instead on his confederates to find the necessary evidence to clear Harriet. As Peter moved into the 1930s, he began to show a disposition to undertake a little legwork. This tendency is demonstrated time and again in *Have His Carcase.* Peter first exerts himself in the matter of tracking the straight razor that cut Paul Alexis's throat. He follows this with a house-to-house examination of the residents of the village of Darley, closest to the crime scene. (In the old days, this would have been Parker's job, or Bunter's.) Peter then proceeds to Haviland Martin's campsite at Hinks's Lane, where he studies the ground with exquisite care, even unfolding the "distasteful sheets" of a "greasy newspaper." Peter has become a meticulous seeker after material clues. His determination will pay off; the discovery of "a piece of thinnish rope about three inches long" will provide the key to how the murder was done (147).

If Peter Wimsey has become more meticulous, he is not, at least in this case, self-sufficient. Armed with the unique perspective acquired as a novelist and an advanced woman, Harriet Vane works several angles that Peter cannot. The process begins with her discovery of Paul Alexis dead on the beach. Truly alone, Harriet can only investigate in her best Robert Templeton manner, with the strengths and weaknesses such an approach implies. She does an excellent job of gathering clues for identification and scouts the scene for evidence of other visitors quite thoroughly. But she fails to grasp the implication of the freely flowing blood; Wimsey must explain its significance.

There are, in fact, several important gaps in Harriet's knowledge, products of her upbringing and her life experiences to date. Her parents had died when she was young; her (presumably) one serious opportunity to observe a man's personal habits was the year she spent living with the self-absorbed Philip Boyes. She knows nothing about men's clothing, nothing about the esoteric process of shaving with a straight razor; as a town woman, she knows nothing about horses. This is by way of pointing up the odd bits of information that the mystery writer must pick up to produce a believable mystery. Sayers does know about shaving, if Harriet does not.

Still, Harriet Vane is a capable and inspired investigator on her own ground. In a series of woman-to-woman chats with Flora Weldon, Harriet extracts a wealth of valuable information regarding Flora's proposed marriage with Paul Alexis, the disposition of her money, and her relationship with her most unsatisfactory son, Henry. In turn, Harriet becomes extravagantly feminine in "a slinky garment, composed of what male writers call 'some soft, clinging material,' with a corsage which outlined the figure and a skirt which waved tempestuously about her ankles" (235). An oversize hat completes the outfit, making her into a femme fatale to prise information from an overconfident Henry Weldon. Vamping him perhaps a little too successfully, Harriet discovers that Henry and the mysterious Haviland Martin, the camper at Hinks's Lane, are one and the same person.

Harriet Vane and Peter Wimsey are a true team, each collecting and interpreting information in a manner beyond the reach of the other. Peter knows the arcane habits of men and horses; he also has a rich and varied experience investigating actual crimes. Harriet knows the ways of women and the womanly woman; she can, in addition, analyze the stories provided by suspects from a fiction writer's perspective. The team-work necessary to gaining a solution is emphasized when the two sit down together to decipher the cryptogram found on Alexis's body. Peter is the experienced former intelligence officer, Harriet the wordsmith. Together, they break the thing in an evening; if only the path of love had been so smooth.

As Sayers had promised Victor Gollancz, *Have His Carcase* turns on a curious alibi and an obscure bit of medical knowledge. In consequence, both rational planning and pure chance play critical roles in obscuring how the murder was done; this makes the crime doubly hard to bring home. The three conspirators, Weldon/Martin, Morecambe/Bright, and Mrs. Morecambe, have carefully scripted an elaborate, fully orchestrated brutality designed to provide multiple layers of defense. When Harriet penetrates Haviland Martin's disguise to reveal Henry Weldon, she and Peter encounter only a new fiction. Henry supposedly concealed his identity merely to better investigate the activities of Paul Alexis; he still has a perfect alibi for the time of the murder, thanks to Mrs. Morecambe. When Bunter discovers that the itinerant hairdresser Bright is actually a commission agent named Morecambe, the explanation is ready: Morecambe had adopted the role to gain local atmosphere for a play he is writing for his wife, an actress. Every word of his tale about giving the razor to Alexis is still true, he swears. Peter, Harriet, and the police must peel away layer after layer to get at the real truth. Harriet's experience as a writer is unusually invaluable for just this reason. The investigators must see through the layers of long-prepared fictional invention.

Yet even when the last stories are stripped away, when the police have established a long and intimate connection among the perpetrators, there is still no solution. Nothing any of the three has claimed is true; there is nothing to show where Henry Weldon really was on the morning of Thursday, June 18, 1931. It does not matter. The medical evidence clearly demonstrates that Paul Alexis did not die until 2 o'clock that afternoon. The alibis for all three conspirators for that hour really are watertight. Chance has intervened and almost saves them.

Sayers begins dropping hints as to Paul Alexis's medical condition early on in the narrative. In reconstructing his life as a gigolo, Peter and Harriet quickly discover that he was sickly as a boy—a playground accident had left him prostrate for some time—that he had trouble with his joints, that he feared any kind of rough physical encounter, and that he kept a neat beard primarily to avoid the necessity of his shaving. Combine this with the many pointed references to his Russian heritage, especially his claim to "the blood of the czars"; hemophilia becomes obvious. As Peter explains, "It's a condition in which the blood doesn't clot properly; if you get even a tiny little scratch, you may bleed to death from it" (444). The medical evidence was worthless. Cut at eleven in the morning, the dead Alexis would continue to bleed until his body was utterly emptied; the slash would continue to appear fresh three hours later. Grasping the significance of the hemophilia, the investigators finally arrive at the real time of death—the time for which the three conspirators could furnish Henry Weldon no real alibi.

Following on the heels of the one-dimensional *Five Red Herrings*, *Have His Carcase* stands as an elegant and multifaceted work. Sayers has continued to employ the elements of puzzle making in this second Harriet Vane novel, this time posing a criminal investigation in which the reader must perceive both planning and happenstance. Though it is relatively simple to finger Henry Weldon as the murderer, it is very difficult to grasp the nature or extent of the conspiracy behind him. More difficult still is the boggling combination of perfection and ineptitude in Weldon's alibi; why is it so plainly manufactured, yet so perfect? The addition of a fluke of fate gives the narrative an artful and inventive twist; no matter how cleverly the conspirators plan, it is chance that makes their paper-thin fables at all palpable.

But this is not a simple puzzle, as Harriet reminds the reader with her caustic remarks about Dr. Thorndyke. For all its convoluted structure of plot, this is a plainly brutal human tragedy. Flora Weldon wished to marry Paul Alexis because he gave her the illusion of perpetual youth; her wretched desires got him killed. Alexis, scrupulous though he was, agreed to marry Flora for her money; he could not last much longer as a dancer. Still, he harbored dreams of greatness and was foolish enough to believe in them. That was his doom. The Morecambes and Henry Weldon used Alexis's dreams to ensnare him. Alexis travelled to the Flatiron Rock expecting to reclaim the throne of the czars. Instead, he got his throat cut with a razor. The motive was money, the weapon cold, sharp steel. What could be more elemental?

The plot turns not on the convolutions of alibi but on the personalities of all concerned. For all his machination, Henry Weldon quickly reveals himself a rude and brutish bully, a thick-headed masher at best. His mother is vain and stupid, without interests or purpose, wandering a forlorn life made possible by an inheritance—a sorry waste to everyone, most especially herself. Probably she and Alexis deserved one another; both were equally self-deluding. The other principals in the story, the Morecambes, are marginally more intelligent, but they richly deserve what they get. They have concocted a fabulous story and then relied on a witless amateur to help them carry it out. Their only excuse is desperation; business reversals have driven them to the wall.

The smaller fry are equally vivid. Alexis's fellow gigolo, Antoine, is a memorable and sympathetic character despite his loathsome profession. His realistic fatalism, combined with the fact that he willingly supports his aging mother and imbecile brother, make him human. Readers may wish him well—even as they shudder—as he plays on Flora Weldon's affections at story's end. The professional dancing women, in invigorating youth and disparaging the predatory hags, are equally believable, as is Mrs. Lefranc, Alexis's discrete and motherly landlady. Why shouldn't she be a former circus acrobat?

Finally, there are Harriet Vane and Peter Wimsey, the most vivid characters of all. *Have His Carcase* was Dorothy L. Sayers's first opportunity to explore Harriet's character. She rounds into a full human being, an articulate and ingenious self-supporting modern woman. She has been hurt, bruised in the heart by betrayed love and false accusations of murder, but she is determined to look only forward. Still, she protects herself, choosing a relentlessly self-directed, solitary life as the best answer to her sorrow.

And Peter is still Peter, past age forty now. If ever he thought a noble birth and untold riches could bring whatever he wanted, he now has discovered otherwise. Fate has been unkind. The one woman for him is a woman wounded; all he can do is stand patiently by, hoping she will heal. And there is detection still, to give his life some meaning. Sadly, the meaning comes with pain. Peter sums up the Alexis murder for what it was: "'Well,' said Wimsey, 'isn't that a damned awful, bitter, bloody farce? The old fool who wanted a lover and the young fool who wanted an empire. One throat cut and three people hanged, and £130,000 going for the next man who likes to sell his body and soul for it. God! What a jape. King death has asses' ears with a vengeance'" (448). Harriet can only echo his fervent desire to escape from it all. It is a page out of Wilkie Collins.

Gollancz published *Have His Carcase* in April 1932, ten months after the events related in the story ostensibly took place. Sayers by that time had begun work on two additional Wimsey stories, neither of which would feature Harriet Vane. She planned originally to push *The Nine Tailors* to completion first, thereby putting the finishing touches on the process of giving Wimsey a soul. When technical problems intervened, she turned her attention to the second project in order to meet contractual obligations. In this new novel, *Murder Must Advertise,* Sayers stretched her limits as a detective novelist as far as she could toward the other end of the scale.

Dorothy L. Sayers found *Murder Must Advertise* the most unsatisfactory of her Wimsey novels, both at the time of writing and in retrospect. Writing to Victor Gollancz in September 1932, she could only say, "The new book is nearly done. I hate it because it isn't the one I wanted to write, but I had to shove it in because I couldn't get the technical dope on *The Nine Tailors* in time."[31] Forced to turn something out in a hurry, she chose to center the novel in a London advertising agency—something she knew intimately. Unfortunately, the plot turned on drug trafficking—something she did not know at all. In a letter to Harold Bell written in March 1933, she admitted that the "plot is rather hasty and conventional, because I wrote against time and rather against the grain."[32]

Sayers re-examined the story for an essay published in 1937, but remained unhappy with it. She regarded *Murder Must Advertise* as her first real attempt to produce a combined detective story and novel of manners. Looking back over the previous dozen years, she saw herself growing as a writer in the Wilkie Collins tradition; each novel after *Whose Body?* was a little less conventional, a little more human than its predecessors. By the time she reached her eighth novel, she should have been fully prepared to write the true work of her dreams. In her own estimation, she made a hash of it:

I think the first real attempt at fusing the two kinds of novel was made in *Murder Must Advertise,* in which, for the first time, the criticism of life was not relegated to incidental observations and character sketches, but was actually part of the plot, as it ought to be. It was not quite successful; the idea of symbolically opposing two cardboard worlds—that of the advertiser and the drug-taker—was all right; and it was suitable that Peter, who stands for reality, should never appear in either except disguised; but the working-out was a little too melodramatic, and the handling rather uneven.[33]

Melodramatic was certainly the right word for what happened. The sad fact of the matter was that Sayers allowed Lord Peter to slip his leash.

If Peter Wimsey had grown as a human being through seven novels, the list of his talents also had grown enormously. He started off rich, possessed of a sumptuous London flat and a really valuable library of rare volumes; he was something of an expert on book collecting. By 1923 he was an experienced international traveler, by 1926 a sometime agent for the foreign office. 1927 brought him a brand new, sleek, black, twelve-cylinder Daimler-Benz, custom made to purr along at heart-arresting speed without racket. Naturally, an exquisite driving skill accompanied the car. By the close of the decade he was an expert on art, a gifted musician, a connoisseur of fine food and finer wines, and an expert (if sensitive) lover. About the only thing he openly admitted he could not do is play chess.

Presumably, Sayers did not set out to make Wimsey some sort of superman. He just gradually accrued more aptitudes as the series moved along, as more and different talents were required of him. Still, she had succeeded in making Wimsey believable. There is no ongoing display of natural superiority, no endless exhibition of skill after skill. The impression delivered through the first seven novels is that of a sensitive man, one who is willing to experiment with life and generally make good at what he tries. If Peter exudes a general quality with respect to his gifts, that quality has to be quiet self-confidence. This multiplicity of talents is, after all, merely a collection of things; they do not make him a superior, or even a better, human being.

The Peter Wimsey of *Murder Must Advertise* is a disturbing departure from that carefully nourished approach. In many ways, Sayers has allowed him to return to the character he displayed in *Clouds of Witness*. Once again, Lord Peter has become intrepid. In fact, for the first time since the day he broke it, Peter refers in this novel to the collarbone damaged during the investigation that freed his brother.

A couple of early references to Edgar Wallace intimate that Sayers intends to slide to the sensational side of the mystery story in this novel. The model closest to her heart, however, is one rooted in the earliest days of Lord Peter: Sexton Blake. Sayers pays tribute to the most sensational of all detective heroes not once, but twice, at great length. Early on, Ginger Joe Potts, Peter's young assistant at the advertising agency, lends him a Blake adventure. Peter reads it avidly, sharing a description of the action with his sister Mary and (finally) brother-in-law, Charles Parker. Not much later, the reader discovers that Ginger Joe imagines his own life as a sort of Sexton Blake adventure. After fighting with his brother to keep secret a report that Wimsey has asked him to write, Ginger Joe curls under the bed covers and summarizes the day's activities: "Bruised and battered, but unshaken in his courage, the famous detective sank back on the straw pallet in the rat-ridden dungeon. In spite of the pain of his wounds, he was happy, knowing that the precious documents were safe. He laughed to think of the baffled Crime King, gnashing his teeth in his gilded oriental saloon. 'Foiled yet again, Hawkeye!' growled the villainous doctor, 'but it will be my turn next!' Meanwhile . . ." Sayers's comment: "The life of a detective is a hard one."[34]

Peter's life never becomes quite this adventurous (or arduous) in *Murder Must Advertise,* but the novel, and Peter's actions especially, convey a decidedly sensational air. By day Peter Wimsey lives as Death Bredon (a name he derives by taking his own two middle names), a clever, impish, and gifted writer of advertising copy (still another talent). By night he transforms into the masked and mysterious harlequin, a drug addict's nightmare. Peter is not mentioned by his real name until the fifth chapter, when he emerges momentarily in his true persona to comment on the action. In both disguises, he is required to perform feats of physical daring beyond the reach of the average human being. Wimsey has become a kind of Sexton Blake or maybe a Robert Templeton.

As Death Bredon, Wimsey seizes the opportunity to play an undercover role, posing as a copywriter while investigating some unspecified irregularity at Pym's Publicity, a staid old advertising firm. The mystery is in some obscure way connected to the death of Bredon's predecessor at the office, one Victor Dean. While Bredon idles, frivols, and somehow produces some priceless copy, Wimsey determines that Dean's "accidental" death was actually murder. Grasping at straws, he can only suspect that the death was somehow connected to blackmail and that the blackmail was somehow connected to drug trafficking. His one tenuous connection is that Victor Dean had spent considerable time partying with the sad remnants of the Bright Young Things, a fast crowd now doomed by drug abuse.

In the role of Bredon, Peter returns to the blithering lightness that characterized his makeup through the twenties. As Wimsey, the trait peeked out only at rare moments in the later books. As Bredon, it runs wild. He plays a Jew's harp while leaning on his door jamb, does handsprings down the hallway, recites juicy limericks, and spends too much time with the typists. In a truly inspired moment, he prises confidences from a colleague by assuring him that "In all social difficulties . . . ask Uncle Ugly." The assurances continue: "Say on, Tompkin. We will be as silent as a pre-talkie movie. Any sum from £5 to £5,000 advanced on your note of hand alone. No embarrassing investigations. No security required—or offered. What's your trouble?" (214)

At Pym's, this kind of breezy dialogue passes as normal. None of the copywriters, particularly those graduated from university, take anything any more seriously than they can help. Peter admits that a colleague "has put his finger on the real offensiveness of the educated Englishman—that he will not even trouble to be angry" (279). Whatever happens, these men and women will maintain their equanimous facade.

The facade is in some ways a product of their culture and their education, but at Pym's it serves the additional purpose of lending a measure of defense against the essential immorality of their occupation. Though the general public does not genuinely recognize the hand or even the existence of the advertising agency, its influence is everywhere and personal. It aims its appeal not at the rich but at the working poor, the class with so little to spend. The struggle to steal those pennies from rivals creates the need for delusion and deceit. The poor must be convinced that their life is no good, their health threatened, their simple pleasures empty, their attractions insufficient, and their food and shelter not up to snuff. Left in an agony of doubt, the advertiser then convinces the poor consumer to part with his (or, more likely, her) pennies for some cosmetic illusion that will not deliver of its promise. It is conscience-sapping work, as Wimsey soon comes to realize:

"I think that this is an awfully immoral job of ours. I do, really. Think how we spoil the digestions of the public."

"Ah, yes—but think how earnestly we strive to put them right again. We undermine 'em with one hand and build 'em up with the other. The vitamins we destroy in the canning, we restore in Revito, the roughage we remove from Peabody's Piper Parritch we make up into a package and market as Bunbury's Breakfast Bran; the stomachs we ruin with Pompayne, we re-line with Peplets to aid digestion. And by forcing the damn-fool public to pay twice-over—once to have its food emasculated and once to have the vitality put back again, we keep the wheels of commerce turning and give employment to thousands—including you and me."

"This wonderful world!" Bredon sighed ecstatically. (52–53)

It is a world of facades, not unlike Death Bredon himself.

This was an immorality so deeply bred into the culture by the 1930s that no one even thought to question the validity of its practices. Parliament passed laws to prevent flagrant misleading and lying, but the essentials of the system went unchallenged. Sayers knew this well; she had written advertising copy for Benson's for more than seven years. Peter's brief career is in fact modeled on that of his creator. Pym's was Benson's, right down to the circular iron staircase that did in Victor Dean; Peter's blanket advertising campaign to promote Whifflets mirrored Sayers's own great success.[35] As Sayers advised in concluding the book, "Advertise, or go under" (344).

Wimsey's classical education and his long-exercised penchant for irresponsible lightness made him a natural copywriter. Though it is painful to watch Peter employ his impressive familiarity with Dickens to produce lines such as "It's a far, far butter thing" (27), this is small stuff when considered next to his real purpose at Pym's: to expose some bona fide criminal activity. He knows only that Victor Dean had uncovered some such activity among the staff, had begun a letter to Mr. Pym, and had met a fatal "accident" before he could finish or send it. Peter, assisted by his junior colleague, Ginger Joe, undertakes the long and trying task of investigating Pym's employees. Soon armed with suggestive clues to Dean's murder, Peter relentlessly seizes every opportunity to surprise employees with this knowledge and observe their reactions. Recognizing that Dean was killed with a catapult, Peter carries one around with him, spurring conversations about the weapon's use. Sooner or later, someone is bound to crack.

The only other handle to the mystery is Dean's brief association with the "Bright Young Things," notably the black-sheep daughter of the gentry, Dian de Momerie. Peter gains access to the doings of this crowd through Dean's sister, Pamela. She is an innocent as far as the Bright Young Things are concerned, but she has contacts among them, thanks to her late brother. Together, she and Peter attend one orgy of a costume party, where Peter latches on to the notorious Dian.

Historically speaking, the heyday of the Bright Young Things was largely past by the time Sayers wrote *Murder Must Advertise*. Never a large coterie, these were young people who snatched at the extremes of possibility inherent in the freedoms of the twenties. The men were largely too young to have fought in the war, the women too youthful to comprehend the extremes of sexual discrimination that their mothers and sisters had suffered. Of the upper and upper-middle classes, they had too much time and money on their hands and lived for naughty thrills. They frequented the jazzy nightclubs, drank cocktails, sniffed cocaine, indulged in frequent and meaningless love affairs, and sought above all to mortify staid traditional society. By 1930 those not dead or ruined in health, destroyed by the financial crash, or utterly burned out had largely sobered up and wised up. In *Strong Poison,* Sayers mentions that a couple of Bright Young Things had joined Miss Climpson's typing bureau, seeking a more substantive kind of thrill.[36]

The few remaining thrill seekers sought out the wild parties such as the one attended by Peter Wimsey and Pamela Dean, where they were greeted by "the strains of a saxophone" (68). Different doors opened to reveal gambling, drinking, nude dancing, and orgies. At the bottom of it all, the attraction was cocaine—this was a gathering of the addicted. Faced with this hedonistic tumult, Peter takes steps to assure Pamela Dean's safety and then metamorphoses into the harlequin, denizen of the night.

Peter's masquerade as the harlequin plunges him into the world of the sensational novel. There are no clues here, only the dimmest notion of what exactly is being detected. Peter understands instinctively that he must get hold of Dian de Momerie and pry what he can from her drug-addled brain to shed light on the mystery at Pym's. In the process, he becomes superhuman.

The charade begins at the party, when Peter, dressed in harlequin costume and mask, climbs atop the statues in the center of a pool:

> Up and up went the slim chequered figure, dripping and glittering like a fantastic water creature. . . . It was the easy, unfretted motion of the athlete, a display of muscular strength without jerk or effort. Then his knee was on the basin. He was up and climbing upon the bronze cupid. Yet another moment and he was kneeling upon the figure's stooped shoulders—standing upright upon them, the spray of the fountain blowing about them. . . . The black and white figure raised its arms above its fantastic head and stood

poised. . . . The slim body shot down through the spray, struck the surface with scarcely a splash, and slid through the water like a fish. . . . It was perfectly done. It was magnificent. (70)

Dian de Momerie was among those yelling for the harlequin to dive. He now ran off with her, defying all within earshot to catch them. Fortunately, the infamous Dian was stone drunk, or Peter would have had to add debauchery to his list of accomplishments.

As it was, Wimsey had crossed the line into the fantastic. In the next few weeks, he became a near demon, capable of astonishing physical feats, taunting and tantalizing psychological cruelty, and reckless abandon. Dian is drawn to him because, as the harlequin, he *is* a thrill, a deadly nightmare embodied. She does not love him nor want to be loved by him; she in fact dreads the tinny sound of the pennywhistle that signals his approach. But she is drawn to him. Wimsey preys upon her amoral and drug-debilitated character for all she is worth. In the end, she provides him, serendipitously, with the key to the Pym's mystery.

Lord Peter stretches himself to the limits of the humanly possible in this novel. Perhaps he exceeds the limits. Copywriter by day, harlequin by night, Peter has become the Sexton Blake of Ginger Joe's imagination:

> Death Bredon, driving his pen across reams of office foolscap, was a phantasm too, emerging from [his] nightmare toil to a still more fantastical existence amid people whose aspirations, rivalries, and modes of thought were alien, and earnest beyond anything in his waking experience. Nor, when the Greenwich-driven clocks had jerked on to half-past five, had he any world of reality to which to return; for then the illusionary Mr. Bredon dislimned and became the still more illusionary Harlequin of a dope-addict's dream; an advertising figure more crude and fanciful than any that postured in the columns of the *Morning Star*, a thing bodiless and absurd, a mouthpiece of stale cliches shouting in dull ears without a brain. From this abominable impersonation he could not free himself. (180–81)

Certainly the life of a detective is a hard one.

At the end, the superhuman aspects of Peter's character permeate even the persona of Death Bredon, supercilious copyeditor. Demonstrating his ingratiating approach to women, he soothes the ruffled feathers of a gold digger ("a tough Jane" [215]) who has come to confront one of the group managers, Mr. Tallboy. Wimsey warns Tallboy not to thank him; in fact, Peter has pretty much identified the man as Victor Dean's murderer. All that remains is to figure out how Tallboy fits into the operations of the dope gang.

Peter demonstrates his physical prowess even as a Pym's employee. At the annual cricket match between Pym's and one of the firm's clients, he forgets himself. Striving for a steady mediocrity, he is stung by a ball running up his arm and sees red. The Wimsey of Balliol days at Oxford emerges; he punishes the opposition to the incredible tune of eighty-three runs. Naturally, Peter is not just a good cricket player; he is a batsman whose university performances are eagerly recalled more than twenty years later. Is there anything this man cannot do?

Both Death Bredon and the harlequin must dissolve before novel's end. Peter succeeds in piercing the mystery surrounding Pym's; drug smugglers are relying on Tallboy to give them advance notice of the first letter of a weekly advertisement, which is used to signal the gang where the drugs will be distributed that week. In making the discovery, Peter foolishly exposes himself to danger. The gang frames him for the murder of Dian de Momerie; he and Parker must now stage the arrest of Death Bredon. More intrepid behavior follows. Bredon leads the police a merry chase around the cenotaph; Wimsey contrives to appear in the newspapers as himself by a display of consummate horsemanship (of course). It is all very convoluted, more than a little fantastic, and altogether too sensational.

Sayers ends this sordid tale with a bump. No longer Bredon, no longer the harlequin, Peter reclines in his flat at 110A Piccadilly, reassuring the reader that for all his sensational behavior, he is still the same character. Tallboy comes to him there, confessing his pathetic and greedy sins in that place of shelter where so many mysteries have been unravelled. Peter cannot help him; he can only suggest the most direct way out of the intolerable situation. As he watches Tallboy leave, knowing he will be killed by the gang, he intones the words of judgment: " —and from thence to the place of execution . . . and may the Lord have mercy on your soul" (337). When Parker calls soon after to announce the arrest of the whole dope gang, Peter feels too bitter to celebrate. He is still Wimsey, still cognizant of what it means to be the agent of justice.

The root of the difficulty Sayers sensed in this book seems to lie in the nature of the crime that Lord Peter is asked to solve. His task is at once very simple—find out what is wrong at Pym's—and fearfully complex: bring a huge dope gang to heel. The first is within the scope of Peter Wimsey, a specific crime demanding a specific resolution. But the second is really beyond his reach. He may be able to turn up the key that exposes the gang, but actually breaking the ring necessitates the full involvement of the official police. For Peter to achieve as much as he does, he is called upon to display physical, mental, and emotional powers beyond the scope of any human individual. In writing a sensational tale, Sayers allowed Peter to become sensational. It was a mistake she would not repeat.

This was the first book Sayers set in London since *Strong Poison,* and it was also the last. In removing Wimsey from town, she sought to establish his presence on a different footing, free from the steadily grow-ing community of stock characters she had established. Returning him to London for *Murder Must Advertise,* she firmly held the line against the intrusion of this community. The only familiar characters to fully participate in this drama are Peter's sister Mary, now married to Charles Parker, and Chief Inspector Parker himself. Helen, Duchess of Denver, appears briefly, but Peter absents himself readily enough.

The novel provides the reader's first real look at Lady Mary since *Clouds of Witness.* She made brief appearances in *Strong Poison,* but only in *Murder Must Advertise* is she fleshed out as a character. Mary has now become a modern married woman, straightforward, practical, and capable of real affection for her husband and children. She chooses for the moment to be domestic, taking pleasure in managing the house-hold and doing without servants. To emphasize her equality with Park-er, Sayers has invented a unique manner of trust fund for her. Being a Wimsey, she is actually quite wealthy, but she has access only to an amount of money equal to her husband's income. On this she must, and does, manage comfortably. She does retain some attributes of the wealthy: she never reads advertisements. Her copywriting brother can only reply that she "should have been smothered at birth" (292).

Mary becomes a welcome addition to the detecting team of Wimsey and Parker, offering careful analysis of information and sound advice. Often she anticipates Peter and Charles, urging them to "step on the gas" (83) when they mull the possibility that Victor Dean was blackmailing somebody. At each succeeding stage of the investigation, Mary proves an adept and critical sounding board. Here is suggested the possibility that a woman can marry, maintain her equality in the face of her man and society, and sustain her modern outlook.

The Charles Parker of this case is remarkably consistent with the Parker of every Wimsey story to date. Happily married to Mary, he is relieved of the necessity of making the foolish displays characteristic of the Riddlesdale investigation—his one lapse from steady dependability. Given something substantive to do for the first time since *The Unpleasantness at the Bellona Club,* he is his usual disciplined, cautious, determined self. Responsible for the official investigation into the drug smuggling, he falls back once again on his interest in theological debate to help him through. "Fear not him that killeth, but him that hath power to cast into hell" (243), he intones, comparing the common murderer to the drug peddler. Even Peter is impressed by the enlightened sentiment in that observation.

Though in no way intrepid himself, Parker comes in for more than his share of sensational adventure, thanks to his association with Wimsey. This time Charles breaks his collarbone, in an attack meant to kill Peter. His reaction is far more realistic than Peter's had been ten years before. Suffering from debilitating pain and nagging headache, he is in a foul temper for days afterward. Charles apparently is not cut out for the adventurous life.

One stock character conspicuously missing from *Murder Must Advertise* is Peter's manservant, Mervyn Bunter. Sayers does not mention Bunter at all until the next-to-last chapter, when he opens the door to Mr. Tallboy and later sees him out. Bunter has no role to play in the resolution of this case.

Until the writing of this novel, Bunter had been the fixed point in Peter Wimsey's universe. He has a critical function in *Strong Poison* and equally strong investigative parts in each of the two novels directly following. In the Philip Boyes murder investigation, his station and his talents dictate that he cultivate a relationship with the maid Hannah Westlock "almost to breech of promise point." [37] The evidence he gathers is critical in bringing the murder home to Norman Urquhart. In *The Five Red Herrings,* Bunter performs a similar service, taking it upon himself to escort young Betty, one of the Gowan household domestic staff, to the cinema. Here the information Bunter derives does not point to the murderer, though it does clear up several important points. And, in *Have His Carcase,* Bunter steps beyond the stereotypical task of dating housemaids to undertake truly yeoman detective work. After investigating the deplorable conditions at the Weldon farm and determining that its owner was up against the wall, he undertakes to trail the elusive William Bright, itinerant hairdresser, following the Alexis inquest. Doggedly trailing Bright's wandering path through London over four days, Bunter discovers that the quarry is actually Alfred Morecambe. This furnishes the final link in the conspiracy to kill Paul Alexis. It is also Bunter's greatest moment as a criminal investigator. Having exercised the butler's talents to the fullest, Sayers chose to let him rest through *Murder Must Advertise.*

After completing her sensational tale of dope and advertising, Sayers returned to her labor of love, *The Nine Tailors,* where once again Peter and Bunter must work on their own. Bunter's return to action in this novel marks the culmination of a development of character paralleling that of Lord Peter. If Peter acquired a soul in the 1930s, Bunter became, for the first time, a truly fallible human being. In grasping the nature of this small but arresting accomplishment, the reader comes to appreciate more fully the depth of Dorothy L. Sayers's wonderful triumph.

In *The Nine Tailors,* Sayers achieved the perfect balance between the puzzle—who is the body in the grave? why did he die?—and the sensational—why cut off his hands? smash his face? More important, she created a novel in its truest form, set in a sympathetic and persuasive community peopled by characters possessing the range of absorbing human qualities. The detective and his assistant descend on this community, not as experts or officials but as outsiders of unfamiliar habit and uncomfortable ideas. As the community suffers the anguish of this most hideous and disquieting case, the detective and his man suffer alongside. *The Nine Tailors* is about a bizarre series of contingent crimes witnessed by God and humanity. No one escapes unscathed.

Bunter's ordeal in Fenchurch St. Paul illustrates the gravity of the episode as much as does Lord Peter's experience. Sayers sees fit to expand Bunter's character somewhat, providing him a talent for music-hall impressions to go with his usual qualities: a fierce correctness in all matters of service, an untouchable knowledge of fashion and dress, an adept's skill in the science of criminology, and a decided way with women. In the past, such a formidable array of attributes has made Bunter unerring on his own ground. At Fenchurch St. Paul, he comes to grief.

Entrusted with a beer bottle found in the church belfry, Bunter places this clue safely in a cabinet until fingerprinting can be carried out. Before Bunter can see to this process in his usual capable fashion, the Venables's maid, Emily, dusts the bottle. Helpless and enraged, Bunter forgets himself and his place, turning against Emily. Mrs. Venables is forced to step in; Bunter is mortified, both for his failure and his lapse. The episode is a small one but important. In the life made real by the craft of Dorothy L. Sayers, no one is faultless.

Like Lord Peter, Bunter achieves a measure of redemption in the flooding of Fenchurch St. Paul. Faced with a life-threatening crisis, Bunter applies his talents to their fullest extent, not simply for the comfort of his master but for the good of all. It is Bunter who organizes the kitchen and oversees the preparation of meals. And again it is Bunter who lends much-needed assistance to the thrice-weekly series of concerts and lectures that sustain community morale. His unsuspected gift for musical comedy assumes the quality of a blessing in this desperate surrounding.

Sayers wrote *Murder Must Advertise* and *The Nine Tailors* more or less in tandem, publishing the former in February 1933, the latter in January 1934. This made a total of four books in four years following her decision not to marry off Peter at the conclusion of *Strong Poison*. These four books may be regarded as the fruits of her status as an independent author, fully freed from the worry and necessity of having to work outside to support her writing. Sayers now identified herself wholly as a mystery writer, a devoted and fully-informed expert in her craft. The definition encompassed not only her own tales but also her reflections in critical essays and the editing of anthologies. She is fully aware of the history and the potential of the detective story, and she is quite prepared to employ that knowledge in an array of ingenious (and sometimes devastating) manners. If life determines that she is best cut out to write detective fiction, she will attack the demands of this calling with her full faculties. The mysteries written between 1931 and 1934 reflect the range of the possibilities as she understood them. She explored that range fully and consciously, producing a traditional puzzle, a combined puzzle-thriller coupled with the exploration of a love interest, a sensational thriller, and finally her ultimate achievement: a rich and varied mystery novel, incorporating all the elements she had defined. Another daunting task now stood on the horizon: the tantalizing possibility of marrying the mystery story to the novel of manners.

Lord Peter Achieves a Balance

THE WESTERN WORLD HAD BECOME A DESPERATE AND FRENETIC place in which to live by the middle of the 1930s. If Dorothy L. Sayers lacked true happiness, she had at least achieved a measure of personal security; European society as a whole could boast neither. The new dawn that had beckoned peace and promise after November 1918 proved illusory, even self-delusional. The world had seemed malleable then, a vast potential awaiting the devoted commitment of the newly wise and the newly free. Fifteen years later, society was wobbling, careening toward a spectacular and appalling wreck. Potential had turned to poverty, freedom exchanged for fascism. Everywhere, the long weekend showed signs of ending in a very great sorrow. Expending her creative energies in Cloud-Cuckoo Land, Sayers could still see and feel the hopes of her own youth rapidly slipping away. She chose to write about it, spilling England's hopes and afflictions onto the printed page just as she achieved the zenith of her powers as a novelist. Could anyone find something resembling love in a universe slowly driving itself mad?

All during the early 1930s, Sayers had tracked the slow unwinding of modern European society in the interstices of her novels. *Have His Carcase* is especially peppered with references to England's decline, both economic and political. Agricultural conditions were terrible, as no less an expert than Henry Weldon could testify:

"Nothing in farming these days," grumbled Mr. Weldon. "Look at all this Russian wheat they're dumpin' in. As if things weren't bad already, with wages what they are, and taxes, and rates and tithe and insurance. I've got fifty acres of wheat. By the time it's harvested I daresay it'll have cost me £9 an acre. And what shall I get for it? Lucky if I get five. How this damned Government expects the farmer to carry on, I don't know." (154)

Henry Weldon may have been a repulsive and brutal killer, but he was not lying about agricultural conditions. Three years later, Sayers would put much the same words into the mouth of Catherine Freemantle Bendick, farmer's wife and benighted former classmate of Harriet Vane. It was a sad story and altogether too common. In *The Nine Tailors,* William Thoday, anguished victim of the Fenchurch St. Paul tragedy, was already a victim of the agricultural depression when the story began. Once an independent farmer, Thoday had lost his land when the "bad times" came; he was forced to accept work as a tenant for Hilary Thorpe's father. Thoday's brother James was in much the same shape. An officer on a freighter, he was experiencing "an anxious time for men in his line of business, freights being very scarce and hard to come by." It was "all this depression," sure enough (121).

Indeed, the remainder of English society was faring little better. At the inquest into the death of Paul Alexis, Sayers has one of the jurors speak out against the numbers of foreigners who have entered the country since the war. Echoing the real sentiments of many, he demanded that the government do more to keep the riffraff out. An "Empire Free-Trader and member of the Public Health Committee," the juror vehemently argued that with "two million British-born workers unemployed," it was a scandal to allow Russians or any other outsiders to compete for jobs, naturalization papers or no.[1]

Two million represented roughly 16 to 20 percent unemployment, a figure that persisted throughout much of the 1930s. Unemployment peaked at about three million (22.5 percent) in 1932, then fell off all too slowly despite steady growth in industrial production. Leaders in Parliament despairingly came to see persistent 15 percent unemployment as a fact of life.[2]

The sad story of William Bright and the razor in *Have His Carcase* was believable to Lord Peter and the police for precisely this reason. The tale was a familiar one. Bright supposedly had owned a prosperous haircutting establishment in Manchester before the slump; now he wandered from town to town, desperate for any sort of job and drinking to ease the shame. Posing as Bright, Alfred Morecambe laid it on thick:

> "I don't like making this confession. It's very humiliating for a man who once had a flourishing business of his own. I hope you won't think, gentlemen, that I have been accustomed to this kind of thing."
>
> "Of course not," said Wimsey. "Bad things may happen to anybody. Nobody thinks anything of that nowadays." (180)

What finally makes Wimsey and the official police suspicious of Mr. Bright is the fact that he was not on the dole.

In *Murder Must Advertise,* assumptions born of the same prolonged economic crisis actually assist Lord Peter. Passing himself off as an educated man willing to work for four pounds a week, he forgets to dress accordingly, showing up in silk socks and a Saville Row suit. The typists attribute this suspicious circumstance to the cruel effects of the slump; obviously Mr. Death Bredon was a wealthy man who had lost all his money. He would be one more among thousands.

The international depression did not kill the movement for women's rights, though it may have blunted its hopes somewhat. It is difficult to make demands for equal treatment and equal employment, however just, in the face of two million able-bodied unemployed. The villain Henry Weldon spoke for a great many Britishers when he disparaged women's rights as a form of mania. To him and to thousands more, the idea of equality was nonsense. But then, his exposure to women was rather limited. His mother was a sad case, possessing neither brains nor interests. She wandered from one watering hole to the next, vaguely searching for some kind of thrill to occupy her stay on this earth. "I've so often thought that if I could have painted pictures or ridden a motorcycle or something, I should have got more out of life" (67), she lamented. The only other women Henry would know were laboring women, such as his housekeeper, with whom he had little contact, or those he targeted for conquest. Certainly he was not interested in their brains.

Fashion designers fell to believing that the work place was not a woman's place in the early thirties. Whether this was by choice or because societal conditions left them no choice did not matter. Harriet Vane encountered the "return to womanliness" on the dance floor in Wilvercombe, where "long skirts and costumes of the seventies were in evidence—and even ostrich feathers and fans. Even the coyness had its imitators." Harriet was not fooled, nor were very many of the women present:

> If this was the "return to womanliness" hailed by the fashion correspondents, it was to quite a different kind of womanliness— set on a basis of economic independence. Were men really stupid enough to believe that the good old days of submissive woman- hood could be brought back by milliners' fashions? "Hardly," thought Harriet, "when they know perfectly well that one has only to remove the train and the bustle, get into a short skirt and walk off, with a job to do and money in one's pocket." (143–44)

Harriet was perhaps unable to grasp that the situation she described did not match the lot of a great many women in the Britain of the thirties.

For all that hardships obstinately refused to lessen as time crawled slowly from 1929 to 1935, matters could have been worse. They were in fact far worse in nations not far away. Dorothy L. Sayers kept a weather eye on developments in Russia, Italy, and especially Germany. She did not like what she saw.

Russia's experiment in totalitarianism had of course begun during the Great War. The revolution of February 1917 toppled the czar; the Bolshevik Revolution of the following October ruthlessly established the single-party authority of the communists. Widespread civil war, massive confusion, and abject starvation ensued, lasting at least until 1921. The death of Lenin wrought still more disarray at the top; the infighting continued until Josef Stalin emerged as dictator two years later. The Russian economy slowly recovered and modernized under the Stalinist five-year plans, while nominal rights for working men and women improved. The benefits were illusory in the midst of terror; the collectivization of farms was a calculated cruelty, while the highly pub- licized political purges left little doubt as to the character of the dicta- tor. In the west, darker rumors circulated, though Russian secrecy masked the depth of Stalin's brutality.[3]

Italy had been under the one-party rule of Benito Mussolini and the fascists since 1922. On the surface, dictatorship seemed to have some- thing to recommend it, if the example of Italy meant anything. In the midst of worldwide economic chaos, the country seemed to run more or less efficiently. The boggling thought that Mussolini had made the trains run on time became a watchword throughout Europe. That he exercised management and efficiency using the bayonet as persuasion seemed not to matter. And if Italian women were second class citizens, regarded as little more than baby machines, the fascists were not to blame for that. Italian women had been regarded as such for a very long time.[4]

Germany's convulsive leap into totalitarianism in 1933 came as more of a shock. The Lausanne Conference of the previous year had brought an end to Germany's payment of war reparations, but the economic damage was done. Prostrated by the Great Depression, German unemployment reached at least 6.2 million in August 1933. This was merely the official figure and did not include the many who had given up searching for work or those occupying wholly inadequate part-time jobs. The economic disaster naturally produced a political crisis; a majority in the Reichstag advocated one-party rule. Unfortunately, this majority comprised extreme leftists—the communist party—and extreme rightists—the Nazis. Seeking desperately to break the deadlock, Paul von Hindenberg, war hero and president of the Reich since 1925, handed the powers of chancellorship to the leader of the Nazi party, Adolph Hitler.

Hitler's rise to power was entirely constitutional, but it brought an end to the Weimar Republic in all but name. The German people went to the polls in February 1933 for the third time in nine months. This time the Nazis won 45 percent of the seats in the Reichstag. Minor alliances made them the majority party, the first step toward one-party rule. In March, the Nazis adopted a law turning practical legislative power over to the cabinet—fully manned by members of the Nazi party. The Communists, the Nationalists, and the Social Democrats were quickly outlawed. The civil service was purged of all but Nazi loyalists. Dictatorship had come to Germany.[5]

The government moved quickly to consolidate its position. Careful not to trespass on the mostly ceremonial powers of the aged Hindenburg, who still commanded the loyalty and respect of the military, Hitler nonetheless began a radical transformation of German society. To address the economic problems that brought him to power, Hitler quickly outlawed the trade unions and enforced strict managerial control over industry and labor. Fearing the communist alternative, the major industries supported him, as did the average working man. Germany's labor force became a regimented machine, marching to orders issued from the hierarchy. Youth was organized in much the same way. At least there seemed some promise of working again.

Working women, and women generally, were not so fortunate. Nazi ideology dictated that women belonged in the home raising children. To achieve this end, women were forced out of the work place. Political and legal rights were stripped away, leaving women little defense in a country where traditionally many more had worked outside the home than in any other nation in Europe. The Nazis widely publicized the rejoicing women expressed over this turn of fortune. What choice did the women have?[6]

Hitler envisioned a fundamental reshaping of Germany, not simply in its economic and social institutions, but in the essence of its culture. Nazi philosophy was rooted in fantasy, built on a credo of Aryan racial superiority and Teutonic mythology, neither of which had ever existed save in Hitler's own mind. He fed this fantasy to a people flattened by defeat and disaster; too many willingly bought in. He forced the Christian churches into line, planning eventually to displace their function with a Germanic religion emphasizing obedience and racial purity and paying homage to Germanic gods. The persecution of Jews and other "non-Germanic" peoples began immediately. By 1935 the Nuremburg laws excluded all Jews from rights of citizenship.[7]

Hindenburg died in August 1934, removing the last impediment to a complete Nazi takeover. The military, initially cool to Hitler, now pledged their unqualified allegiance. Despite pressures to the contrary, Hitler had done little to alter the composition of the armed forces to this point. Military leaders could not foresee the rise of the SS (*Schutzstaffel*), with its unparalleled array of heinous police powers. Hitler now had all the necessary tools to mold a fully totalitarian state.

England was not entirely immune to the seductive promises of dictatorship. Faced with endemic high unemployment, politicians on the left and the right agitated for stronger one-party rule. Given the strength of Britain's Labour party, the communists appeared to have some advantage, but this proved illusory. Labour stood firm against communist ideology; any member pushing a communist line was unceremoniously booted out. The radical left boasted a membership of sixteen thousand by 1938, but this group exerted little direct political influence. Mainly they confined themselves to antifascist activities, pointing out the dangers to a largely misapprehending public. Radical publishers, including Victor Gollancz, formed the Left Book Club in 1936 to better inform the nation on leftist issues. Membership reached sixty thousand readers.[8]

Massive unemployment inspired the right as well. As Germany lurched toward Naziism in 1932, Sir Oswald Mosely left Ramsey MacDonald's cabinet to form the British Union of Fascists. His ideas for ameliorating the effects of the Depression were rather mild, but his intended means of achieving them were not. Like fascists everywhere, Mosely felt that a multiparty system produced only weakness, confusion, and compromise. Constitutionally, but by force if necessary, he would impose single-party hegemony. Over the next four years, perhaps one hundred thousand Britishers would call themselves fascists at one time or another. Most were of the chronically unemployed classes from traditionally poverty-ridden pockets of major cities. Only six thousand ever actually paid dues to belong to the British Union of Fascists, though the organization claimed one hundred eighty local branches. They held a large rally at London's Olympia Hall in June 1934; demonstrators were savagely attacked and beaten, repelling many. The Union was definitely on the wane by the end of 1936.[9]

Was this, then, what modernism had come to? Did the rejection of tradition, the destruction of conventional social and political order, the denial of history's influence pave the road for the coming dictator? Bereft of stabilizing influences and shorn of their traditional managers, too many European states found themselves turning to the savior, the all-knowing superman who would think for everyone. Freedom from convention in the end perhaps meant no freedom at all. In creating the new, the efficient, the modern state, everything not expressly forbidden became mandatory.

Radical sympathizers from the left and the right populate the later Wimsey novels. Bolshevism was in fact a favorite theme of Dorothy L. Sayers almost from the beginning. Peter's sister almost married the communist organizer George Goyles. The Soviet Club turns up in several novels and short stories; the mysterious but rickety Mr. Perkins of *Have His Carcase* was a member. The suggestion seems to be that all this Soviet business should not be taken too seriously. Mrs. Weldon is convinced that Bolsheviks have done in poor Paul Alexis, but the police are certain that none of the handful of communist agents in England could have been involved.

Sayers takes the fascist threat more seriously. At Pym's Advertising, company photographer Mr. Prout is highly dissatisfied with working conditions. No one is willing to listen when he argues that "What we want in this country is a Mussolini to organize trade conditions." Several weeks later, Prout "created a sensation by coming to the office in a black shirt."[10]

Sayers is sensitive to the anti-Semitic and misogynist tendencies latent in English society, recognizing in these trends the mind-set of the extreme right. In *Murder Must Advertise,* the hysterical woman who witnesses Doctor Herbert Garfield shoving another member of the drug gang beneath a train believes him to be "a prominent member of a gang whose object is to murder all persons of British birth and establish the supremacy of the Jews in England" (265). And, though women occupy important positions at Pym's, they are not treated on exactly the same footing as men. When Brotherhood's, an important client, sends representatives to visit the agency, there are no special directives for the men, but the women must not smoke or expose too much neck and shoulders. None of the men at Pym's are prepared to admit the possibility of women's equality. Even Peter is far more mysogynist than usual, agreeing that women cannot use catapults and generally disparaging their reliability: "'You cannot trust these young women. No fixity of purpose. Except, of course, when you particularly want them to be yielding.' He grinned with a wry mouth" (114).

If such sentiments are suggested by the merest hints in *Murder Must Advertise,* they become essential grist for the plot of *Gaudy Night.* The shadow of totalitarianist threat broods through the entire novel, while antifeminist feelings and questions regarding the proper role of women in society are integral to the entire plot, both in its mystery and in its novel of manners threads.

Sayers began work on *Gaudy Night* immediately after completing *The Nine Tailors.* Having essentially kept the problem of Peter's love for Harriet Vane at arm's length for more than two years, she now at last determined to move matters to their foregone conclusion. Even before completing the novel, she had begun collaborating on a play framing the first few days of the happy couple's marriage—the title: *Busman's Honeymoon.* Still, actually splicing the pair together proved a challenge. She confessed the problem to the co-author of the play, former Oxford schoolmate Muriel St. Clare Byrne: "I think I have got over most of the technical snags in *Gaudy Night* now, but the writing is being horribly difficult. Peter and Harriet are the world's most awkward pair of lovers—both so touchy and afraid to commit themselves to anything but hints and allusions!"[11]

Perhaps the writing would have been less of a trial had Sayers confined herself to writing a straightforward romance. This would not have been worthy of the Wimsey series, however, nor would such a vapid exercise have satisfied Dorothy L. Sayers. *Gaudy Night* was to be a romance, a drawing-room comedy, a detective story of the combined puzzle-thriller variety, a paean to Sayers's beloved Oxford University, and a story examining a serious question while pointing a serious moral. In a letter to Victor Gollancz, Sayers later confessed of *Gaudy Night*:

> [This is] the only book I've written embodying any kind of a "moral" and I do feel rather passionately about this business of the integrity of the mind—but I realize that to make a "detective story" the vehicle for that sort of thing is (as Miss de Vine says of the Peter-Harriet marriage) reckless to the point of insanity. But there it is—it's the book I wanted to write and I've written it— and it is now my privilege to leave you with the baby! Whether you advertise it as a love-story, or as educational propaganda, or as a lunatic freak, I leave to you.[12]

Yes, writing this one had been most difficult.

In no small part, Sayers was driven to writing such a story because the things she so passionately believed in were in mortal danger. The tramp of mindless marching feet could be heard in too many European nations; the pall of anti-intellectual, antithinking totalitarianism loomed ominously large in democratic England. The few and tentative gains accomplished by women stood endangered; the essential human right to choose one's own path could be denied. To be sure of tomorrow's bread, was it necessary that the mass of humanity surrender every freedom they possessed? Was dictatorship desirable, in any form? Dorothy L. Sayers did not think so.

As a counterpoint to the totalitarian potentials of the modern state, Sayers presented the essence of one form of British tradition: Oxford University. Steeped in a heritage of higher learning compassing several centuries, Oxford stood for the uncompromising search for absolute and knowable truth. Each of its colleges, each of its avenues of learning, extended the traditions of the past: true knowledge is the result of honest inquiry constructed on the foundations of past discovery. There can be no break with the past, only a relentless sifting of all that has gone before.

Returning to Oxford for the Gaudy after several years away, Harriet Vane finds herself exhilarated and exalted by the academic atmosphere: "She saw it as a Holy War, and that whole wildly heterogeneous, that even slightly absurd collection of chattering women fused into a corporate unity with one another and with every man and woman to whom integrity of mind meant more than material gain—defenders in the central keep of Man-soul, their personal differences forgotten in face of a common foe" (29).

Gaudy Night is set largely in the university town of Oxford, more specifically within the confines of Shrewsbury College for women, an institution that Sayers has invented and located on Balliol College's "spacious and sacred cricket ground." Although she models much of Shrewsbury life on her own experiences at nearby Somerville, Sayers is careful both to update the quality of the educational experience and to disassociate it from her alma mater. Like Somerville—mentioned enough times in the text to emphasize its separate existence—Shrewsbury's faculty consists entirely of women, roughly twenty dons referred to collectively as the Senior Common Room. They are, of course, resident in the college, assuming responsibility for the education of some one hundred fifty students. Unlike the students of Sayers's generation, the Shrewsbury women of the thirties demonstrate little cooperative enthusiasm and are generally unwilling to participate in any sort of class pageantry. They are more anxious to exercise independence than to promote camaraderie. These students are, in fact, the products of such freedom for women as has been achieved in England by 1935. On the surface, it seems to their elders that they are unappreciative.[13]

For all their ungracious disrespect, their unwillingness to participate in community projects, and their cavalier attitude towards the necessity of the academic gown, the students—the "slack little beasts"—are fiercely loyal to the academic traditions resting at the heart of Oxford. They may be selfish in most ways, but in the face of persecution and adversity they will not betray the college. They are the next generation of warriors in the "Holy War" that Harriet Vane has glimpsed at the Gaudy. "If it ever occurs to people to value the honor of the mind equally with the honor of the body," Peter Wimsey later intones, "we shall get a social revolution of a quite unparalleled sort—and very different from the kind that is being made at the moment" (352)—being made at that moment, in fact, in Germany, in Italy, in Russia, in far-off Japan, and knocking on the door in safe old England.

In *Gaudy Night,* Sayers addresses the question of totalitarianism most obviously in her drawing of the Shrewsbury College porter, Padgett. He is a good man—resourceful, honest, and reliable—a vast improvement over the previous porter. Despite these admirable qualities, Padgett is deeply flawed: he does not think, save in conventions. Carrying out the oddest assignments with his customary acumen, Padgett nonetheless harbors a belief that a women's college is a poor excuse for an institution, that women have no business dabbling in education. His solution to his dilemma is simple, as he reveals in private conversation with a decorating foreman:

> "Young ladies," Padgett was heard to say, "will 'ave their larks, same as young gentlemen."
> "When I was a lad," replied the foreman, "young ladies was young ladies. And young gentlemen was young gentlemen. If you get my meaning."
> "Wot this country wants," said Padgett, "is a 'Itler."
> "That's right," said the foreman. "Keep the girls at 'ome." (120)

Padgett, as it happens, had fought under Major Peter Wimsey in the Great War. Almost twenty years later, he cherished the memories and happily shared them with Harriet Vane. It seems that Padgett and another enlisted man had gotten into a fistfight, arguing whether Wimsey was manly enough to be an officer. Peter had responded by putting both men on extra detail cleaning the encampment. Apparently, "This affair of a mop and a bucket seemed to have made Padgett Peter's slave for life." Harriet could only conclude that "Men were very odd," but the underlying message was more ominous. Too many responsible men like Padgett were only too happy to follow. They did not want to think for themselves (361).

The fascist threat weighs heavily throughout all of *Gaudy Night.* For most of the novel, Peter is abroad performing diplomatic service for the foreign office. Much of his time he spends in Italy, trading cheerful banter while picking the minds of his rivals. Eventually he moves on to Poland before returning home, harrowed by the dangers he has witnessed. War was clearly in the air; it was only a matter of time: "The old bus wobbles one way, and you think, 'That's done it!' and then it wobbles the other way and you think, 'All serene'; and then, one day, it wobbles over too far and you're in the soup and can't remember how you got there" (287).

Harriet Vane, in the meantime, encounters the fascist question all too often, both inside the cloistered walls of Oxford and in the familiar world of writers' London. Harriet had witnessed at first hand the conditions in Hitlerite Berlin during a European tour undertaken in 1933; she is regularly invited to share her knowledge. Among the first dons she interviews at Shrewsbury is Miss Barton, author of a small volume entitled *The Position of Women in the Modern State*. Sayers tells the reader little of the volume's content, but it is easy to infer that Miss Barton has taken it upon herself to defend the rights of women against fascist attacks, especially those in Germany. She is eager to hear Harriet's impressions about the Nazi regime, though she mostly disagrees with them.

Escaping the strange confines of Oxford, Harriet vacations in London between terms, catching up on gossip among the literary set. As a group, they are as narrow and conceited as ever, believing that the recent triumph of a novel entitled *Mock Turtle* should be construed solely as an affront to their collective genius. They can see nothing more than a corrupt bargain between publishers and agents or between publishers and advertisers. No one can take seriously the importance of *Mock Turtle*'s antifascist tone. Harriet hastens back to Oxford.

In a sense, *Gaudy Night* was Dorothy L. Sayers's own version of Miss Barton's *The Position of Women in the Modern State*. Though Sayers vehemently denied any advocacy of feminist views, the moral to which she points in the novel is raised because of the danger posed to women by the rise of totalitarian sentiments. As she describes it, the question she wishes to address is "integrity of the mind"—the necessity of comprehending one's own gifts (whatever they may be) and pursuing a path that will give those gifts the greatest latitude to flower. Every person—man or woman—is different. No one should be slotted into an occupation, a position, or a marriage because of his or her sex, class, or racial background. Everyone has a job to do, and they need to be free, first to discover what that job is and thereafter to do it in peace. It must be up to the individual to decide, not society or the state. This is Dorothy L. Sayers's answer, both to the fascists and to the traditional English who would shove women back onto the Victorian pedestal.[14]

Sayers sketches out the essence of her argument in a long conversation between Harriet Vane and Miss de Vine, the new research fellow in residence at Shrewsbury College. Harriet has taken residence in Shrewsbury to investigate and, she hopes, expose a "poison pen" who has persecuted the college for several months with offensive notes, dirty words written on walls, and malicious pranks. Miss de Vine, a historian specializing in the intricacies of Tudor finance, is a formidable scholar whose "sole allegiance was to the fact," possessing "a mind as hard and immovable as granite" (19). She is a great fan of Harriet Vane's detective stories and is especially pleased to make Harriet's acquaintance. She befriends Harriet in an intensely honest way, expressing a view of life's responsibilities that Harriet finds enlightening and a little frightening:

> "I'm quite sure that one never makes *fundamental* mistakes about the thing one really wants to do. Fundamental mistakes arise out of lack of genuine interest. In my opinion, that is."
>
> "I made a big mistake once," said Harriet, "As I expect you know. I don't think that arose out of lack of interest. It seemed at the time the most important thing in the world."
>
> "And yet you made the mistake. Were you really giving all your mind to it, do you think? Your *mind*? Were you really being as cautious and exacting about it as you would be about writing a passage of fine prose?" (179–80)

After some reflection, Harriet must confess that she had not been as attentive to developing her relationship with Philip Boyes as she was to writing her books. Writing was her job, the one thing to which she devoted undivided attention, the one thing she would never lie about.

The theme of doing one's job ramifies throughout the novel. Peter Wimsey avoids getting shot by a plug-ugly because his mind was "momentarily" on his job. Mrs. Bendick, the Shrewsbury graduate become farmer's wife who so shocked Harriet at the Gaudy, maintains that marriage is "really the most important job," though she admits to reservations. Harriet cannot help but feel "that she had seen a Derby winner making shift with a coal cart" (69, 48–49).

Harriet herself is forced to passionately defend her actions in terms of doing one's proper job. At their first meeting, Miss Barton presses Harriet to explain why she continues to write detective novels after her own near brush with the gallows. Harriet points out that economics played a part in her decision to continue, but adds, more fundamentally: "I know what you're thinking—that anybody with proper sensitive feeling would rather scrub floors for a living. But I should scrub floors very badly, and I write detective stories rather well. I don't see why proper feeling should prevent me from doing my proper job" (31).

She goes on to defend Lord Peter's choice to pursue criminals, whether "as a duty or as an intellectual exercise" (33). It is the legal responsibility of every citizen to enforce the law, and Peter had proven time and again his surpassing ability in detection. Despite whatever reason he gave, and despite his standing as an amateur, catching crooks was Peter Wimsey's job.

To Sayers's mind, there were two difficulties in this business of doing one's job: figuring out what it might be, and then doing it in the face of determined opposition. The world is full of stubborn and conventional people. Most will never trouble to find their own proper job but will instead meekly accept whatever society allots. Italy and Germany were suddenly full of people like that; England had far more than its share.

Early in her stay at Shrewsbury, Harriet Vane rescues Miss Cattermole, an unhappy third-year student who has broken most of the rules in the book without getting much fun out of it. Taxed for the reason, Cattermole confesses that she had never wanted to come up to Oxford at all. She hated it and was there only because her parents wanted her to take advantage of the new opportunities for women. Cattermole wanted to be a cook. Probably she would be a good one, if instinct meant anything. Not every woman was cut out to be an advanced woman: becoming a cook was Cattermole's proper job.

If Miss Cattermole wished to defy the new conventions of her parents to pursue a traditional woman's role, there were many women at Shrewsbury moving in the opposite direction. The struggle to gain acceptance and respect for women's education was within the living memory of every don in the college; the first legitimate degrees for Oxford women graduates were not conferred until 1920. By choosing academe over marriage and family, every one of these women dons defied woman's traditional role. Persecution by the college "poltergeist" inspired an ongoing debate among the dons regarding the wisdom and ethics of their decisions. The college secretary, Mrs. Goodwin, became the focal point for several heated discussions. Had the college given her the position simply because she was a widow with a small child in prep school? Was it right that she be excused from her work every time the child had an illness? Were the bursar and the dean indulging her to assuage their own guilt for not having children of their own? Touchy stuff, certainly. As tempers frayed in the face of failure to identify the poltergeist, such arguments grew more heated.

Another angle on the question of proper jobs and women's roles comes when Harriet Vane, enjoying a spring walk in the park, encounters Annie

Wilson, one of the college scouts, strolling with her two daughters. Annie is conventional in the extreme, fervently determined that her girls will become good wives and mothers. Naturally, she is much distressed when her older daughter announces different designs on life:

> "I want to ride a motor-cycle when I'm bigger," said Beatrice, shaking her curls assertively.
>
> "Oh no, darling. What things they say, don't they, madam?"
>
> "Yes, I do," said Beatrice. "I'm going to have a motor-cycle and keep a garage."
>
> "Nonsense," said her mother, a little sharply. "You mustn't talk so. That's a boy's job."
>
> "But lots of girls do boys' jobs nowadays," said Harriet.
>
> "But they ought not, madam. It isn't fair. The boys have hard enough work to get jobs of their own. Please don't put things into her head, madam. You'll never get a husband, Beatrice, if you mess about in a garage getting all ugly and dirty."
>
> "I don't want one," said Beatrice, firmly. "I'd rather have a motor-cycle."
>
> Annie looked annoyed, but laughed when Harriet laughed.
>
> "She'll find out some day, won't she, madam?"
>
> "Very likely she will," said Harriet. If the woman took the view that any husband was better than none at all, it was useless to argue. (231)

Annie's view went way beyond that. Not only was a woman's—any woman's—sole job to get and serve a husband but also to stand by him, no matter what. In Annie Wilson's understanding, the world belonged exclusively to men. The man's part in the arrangement was to put the family welfare ahead of all other considerations. Lying, stealing, cheating—these matters of personal integrity within the public sphere came a distant second as far as she was concerned. Regrettably, her own husband had shared in this belief and had paid. Exposed as a scholarly liar by a woman, the man had turned to drink and eventually shot himself. This confutation of all she believed was too much for Annie Wilson. Her mind had snapped. She was the campus poltergeist.[15]

Annie's husband was an academic named Arthur Robinson. A promising scholar, he nonetheless failed the most important of intellectual tests: personal integrity. In an obscure archive, Robinson had found a letter that undermined a thesis he had long developed. Rather than owning up to the error and reworking his thesis, he stole the letter to prevent exposure. Unfortunately for him, he ran up against another scholar, one who regarded academic integrity as the measure of all worthwhile. Miss de Vine had no choice but to expose him; the result was disgrace and eventual suicide.

Here is the nexus of the moral problem that Sayers has posed. Arthur Robinson, Miss de Vine, and Annie Wilson have each defined their own jobs according to vastly different sets of values. Robinson stands for what Sayers refers to as the "doctrine of snatch" (180); he will go after what he thinks he wants, paying no heed to consequences or decency. Annie becomes the conventional woman, imprisoning herself and her children in bonds of assumption about women's proper role. Miss de Vine represents the potential of the fulfilled human being; despite her sex, her age, and her health, she is secure in serving the higher morality of collective academe. Miss de Vine is saddened by the consequences of exposing Robinson but knows she had no alternative. She is an honorable human being. Arthur Robinson, on the other hand, was narrow and dishonest; he is dead by his own hand. Annie Wilson, the woman who defined her job and herself in standing by her man, has become a psychopath.

The strength that allows Miss de Vine to carry on her own life in the face of such a tragic affair derives both from the essential rightness of her position and the community of like-minded people surrounding her. She possesses a will of iron; her one allegiance is to the fact, in any circumstance. After hearing what has become of Robinson and Annie, she feels remorse, not because she had done wrong in exposing him, but because she took no steps to see to his welfare afterward. By Sayers's yardstick, morality was clearly on her side, as every one of the Shrewsbury dons understood. That unanimity of commitment to learning, to doing one's job properly, saved them all.

Annie Wilson's long campaign of cruel psychological warfare was intended to undermine the dons' belief in themselves and their calling. To Annie, they were all hypocrites, pretending to a man's place in the world, taking bread from children's mouths. Though they lived through an agony of mutual suspense that spawned bitter personal antagonism, every don remained true to her faith that her proper place was in academe. This was a bond of strength that Annie could not crack. When Lord Peter came as inquisitor to question them, they "tended to avoid one another's eyes; yet they gathered together as though for protection against a common menace" (331). When Peter at last exposes Annie as the poison pen, he pays homage to this sense of community:

> The one thing which frustrated the whole attack from first to last was the remarkable solidarity and public spirit displayed by your college as a body. I think that was the last obstacle that X expected to encounter in a community of women. Nothing but the very great loyalty of the Senior Common Room to the college and the respect of the students for the Senior Common Room stood between you and a most unpleasant publicity. . . . This particular kind of loyalty forms at once the psychological excuse for the attack and the only possible defense against it. (441)

Nothing, no matter how unpleasant, would sway these women from doing what they understood themselves meant to do.

It is Lord Peter Wimsey who solves this case in less than two weeks, after Harriet Vane had struggled with it for months. Peter is the first to point out that he could not have solved it without Harriet's groundwork. She had methodically collected all the documentary evidence; she had maintained a careful chronology of the poison pen's activities. Examining this material, Peter immediately perceives a pattern worth tracing. After conversing with the dons, he quickly runs down the story of Arthur Robinson and his embittered widow. Why did Peter succeed, after Harriet had come so far only to falter in the process of putting two and two together?

The plain fact is that Harriet Vane was experiencing a great deal of trouble determining her proper job. She was a writer first and foremost, a head rather than a heart. Reaching (snatching?) after this self-defined essence of self, she has returned to Oxford, not merely to catch the Shrewsbury poltergeist but to devote herself to endeavors of the intellect. Peter recognizes immediately that she is leaning toward "a spot of celibacy." But she is uncertain. The reason she wants "to get clear of people and feelings and go back to the intellectual side is that that is the only side of life I haven't betrayed and made a mess of" (302–3). The problem is, that kind of life may betray her. Does sheltered residence in college lead to abnormality, to the asylum? Before the investigation is done, Harriet is prepared to believe that any of the dons is capable of being the poison pen. Fear clouds her judgment.

Harriet's writing, normally her refuge from a too-often beastly world, provides no solace this time. Her latest effort, an elaborate puzzle entitled *Twixt Wind and Water,* has bogged down, the characters too symmetrical. As Peter points out, the best solution is to give the characters greater depth, to turn them into real human beings. It will be her first attempt to capture human realities in a detective story, and she is sure it will "hurt like hell" (311).

She is willing to endure this pain, to write the novel she knows she is capable of writing, because she is beginning to grow again. The two-headed misery inflicted by Philip Boyes and the criminal court has at last begun to fade. Harriet can begin to examine herself without reference to that horrid time, to ask whether she is genuinely all head or if she has a heart as well. Can a person possessed of both satisfy the needs of both without betraying one or the other? Can Harriet Vane define a job for herself that allows her to remain true to her intellectual muse without denying her emotions? Does Harriet dare to fall in love?

With so much on her mind, Harriet may be forgiven for not identifying the college poltergeist. In any case, she is a writer, not a detective. It is not her proper job. Peter Wimsey is the true investigator. For Peter, the case is rather simple and straightforward, though not without its uncomfortable moments. The personal will intrude—and at the most troublesome junctures.

Dorothy L. Sayers had more than the usual misgivings about *Gaudy Night*. She thought it a "peculiar book," not really a detective story at all "but a novel with a mild detective interest of an almost entirely psychological kind."[16] She was much relieved when Victor Gollancz telegrammed in September 1935 to assure her that he liked the work. He brought it out immediately and was rewarded with huge sales. Though her books had attracted a steadily growing market for years, *Gaudy Night* was Sayers's first bestseller. Very few of the thousands of readers probably cared much about Dorothy L. Sayers's thoughts on moral integrity and doing one's job. The attraction was in finding out how Peter and Harriet, "the world's most awkward pair of lovers,"[17] could ever find happiness.

By this time, Sayers had strung the thing out over five years. If nothing else, Peter's patience and Harriet's sheer endurance were matchless.

After introducing this most difficult love match in *Strong Poison* (and essentially writing herself into a corner), Sayers approached the problem with great caution. Of her next four novels, only one actually wrestled with Peter and Harriet's difficulties. *Have His Carcase* provided a suggestion of hope for the couple's future, but not much more.

As far as romance is concerned, *Have His Carcase* begins inauspiciously. Harriet pointedly refrains from informing Peter Wimsey of her difficulties; Peter gets the word from a newspaper reporter. Harriet is not altogether pleased when Peter shows up to assist in the investigation. His persistent marriage proposals are more or less a joke, but they are an uncomfortable annoyance. Harriet does not want romance. She wants to be left alone to enjoy her freedom, to write, to heal.

Yet she is maddeningly inconsistent, a reflection of her own confusion. Announcing that she must buy a new frock to carry on investigations at the Resplendent Hotel, Peter suggests she buy a wine-colored one, or claret, more specifically. She does so. Peter cannot help but think "that when a woman takes a man's advice about the purchase of clothes, it is a sign that she is not indifferent to his opinion." They dance together, not without some awkwardness, but ultimately "in silence and harmony" (161, 158).

Peter knows that the ground is treacherous. For a year and a half he had struggled to build up a "delicate structure of confidence" between them (174). The Wilvercombe tragedy dashes it all to pieces. Harriet knows all too well that she is a notorious woman, that the police cannot help but suspect her of murdering Paul Alexis. She can only perceive Peter's presence, ostensibly an innocent expression of his interest in crime as a hobby, as another example of his damnable knight-errantry—Lord Peter to the rescue. She does not want his help; she does not want to be grateful.

Though it is not much help, Peter does not want her to be grateful either. As long as any debt of gratitude stands between them, true love is impossible:

> Do you think it's pleasant for any man who feels about a woman
> as I do you, to have to fight his way along under this detestable
> burden of gratitude? Damn it, do you think I don't know perfect-
> ly well that I'd have a better chance if I was deaf, blind, maimed,
> starving, drunken or dissolute, so that *you* could have the fun of

being magnanimous? Why do you suppose I treat my own sincer-est feelings like something out of a comic opera, if it isn't to save myself the bitter humiliation of seeing you try not to be utterly nauseated by them? Can't you understand that this damned dirty trick of fate has robbed me of the common man's right to be serious about his own passions? Is that a position for any man to be proud of? (175)

The only thing Peter and Harriet can do is try to fight it out as equals. Peter will not give up, and Harriet is just intrigued enough to keep her-self from sending him firmly away. If only they had met as most couples do, without all this extra baggage.

Have His Carcase ends on a note of qualified hope, as Harriet agrees to accompany Peter back to town to escape the horrors of Wilvercombe. There is no promise beyond that, no resolution of their difficulties. Say-ers essentially avoided the problem in her next two Wimsey novels, making only an oblique and veiled reference to Harriet in *Murder Must Advertise*. *Gaudy Night,* therefore, opens essentially at the point where *Have His Carcase* leaves off. Peter and Harriet remain attracted to one another but have found no way past their mutual difficulties.

As Sayers began work on *Gaudy Night,* her own experiment in ro-mantic love was on exceedingly shaky ground. Her marriage to Mac Flem-ing had been rocky almost from the beginning, due in large part to his health problems. Things seemed to grow worse with each passing year. In a letter written to her cousin in August 1934, Sayers gave some hint of the situation:

> The fact is that Mac is getting so queer and unreliable that it is not safe to trust him to do anything at all, and if he is told that he has forgotten anything, he goes into such a frightful fit of rage that one gets really alarmed. The doctors say that he *is* getting definitely queer—but there doesn't seem to be much that one can do about it. . . . It also makes the financial position very awk-ward, as he can't earn any money, and what with his illness and the difficulty of managing his odd fits of temper and so on, it isn't easy for me to get any work done regularly and properly.[18]

At best, life on the home front was a domestic truce. Mac Fleming had become a sick and embittered man, unable to provide his wife the support and respect she needed and deserved. The entirety of *Gaudy Night* was written under this cloud. Desperately unhappy in her own marriage, she chose to explore the ingredients of true romantic happiness in her novel. Peter and Harriet both possessed some understanding of those ingredients after five years. The question was whether she could bring them to a relationship with each other.

As three full years had passed between the awkward dance of *Have His Carcase* and the beginning of *Gaudy Night*, Sayers sets the stage by reviewing Peter's long-suffering progress in wooing Harriet. After the Wilvercombe fiasco, Peter began again the long process of constructing some foundation of mutual confidence and equality. Harriet kept her distance, spending much of her time writing bestsellers and traveling abroad. She tells herself that Wimsey will surely give up if she remains firm, but he is dug in for a long siege. He promises not to make a nuisance of himself but continues to propose at decently spaced intervals:

> " . . . as a birthday treat, and on Guy Fawkes Day and on the Anniversary of the King's Accession. But consider it, if you will, as a pure formality. You need not pay the smallest attention to it."
> "Peter, it's foolish to go on like this."
> "And, of course, on the Feast of All Fools." (63)

The difficulty is that Harriet cannot quite bring herself to put an end to this foolishness. The wounds inflicted by Philip Boyes and the criminal court are slow to heal; she is not capable of honest love. And she is especially incapable of loving Peter Wimsey; the much-cursed debt of gratitude lies between them like a concrete wall. Still, there is just enough there to attract her unwilling attention. Harriet is drawn to Peter, even as she rejects him. She senses that, beneath his blither, he is attempting to atone for something, and she is willing to allow him the opportunity.

So the story of *Gaudy Night* begins. Essentially, the novel is a Harriet Vane story. Her presence in the story is continuous; action is interpreted almost exclusively through her eyes. Peter makes scattered appearances in the early sections of the story, mostly through letters, but does not appear on the scene until the last third of the book. Sayers affords Harriet ample opportunity to explore the conflicts in her own mind. Just what is her proper job? Is she sick of the Bloomsbury crowd? Does she really desire the cloistered life of the Shrewsbury academic? How does she feel about Peter Wimsey, in her heart of hearts? Although Sayers never allows

Harriet to reach any resolution to these issues as the novel progresses, she does provide the reader lavish opportunity to watch Harriet gnaw at them. For Harriet Vane, this is a process of growth or, perhaps more exactly, the shedding of a shell that has become too confining.

Peter Wimsey can only stand by, watch her grow, and hope for the best. He too is in the process of reforming himself, a more deliberate and focused campaign to make up for past errors. It is one thing for him to see that Harriet is the one and only, quite another to make himself worthy of her.

Dorothy L. Sayers had been hard put to bring Peter to this pass. Ever since she had failed to marry him off at the close of *Strong Poison,* she had struggled to humanize her main character. Sayers summarized the process in the essay "Gaudy Night," written in 1937:

> The thing seemed difficult, but not impossible. When I came to examine the patient, he showed the embryonic buds of a character of sorts. Even at the beginning he had not been the complete silly ass: he had only played the silly ass, which was not the same thing. He had had shell-shock and a vaguely embittered love affair; he had a mother and a friend and a sketchy sort of brother and sister; he had literary and musical tastes, and a few well-defined opinions and feelings; and a little tidying-up of dates and places would put his worldly affairs in order. The prognosis seemed fairly favorable; so I laid him out firmly on the operating-table and chipped away at his internal mechanism through three longish books. At the end of the process he was five years older than he was in *Strong Poison,* and twelve years older than he was when he started. If, during the period, he had altered and mellowed a little, I felt I could reasonably point out that most human beings are mellowed by age. One of the first results of the operation was an indignant letter from a female reader of *Gaudy Night* asking, What had happened to Peter? he had lost all his elfin charm. I replied that any man who retained elfin charm at the age of forty-five should be put in a lethal chamber. Indeed, Peter escaped that lethal chamber by inches.[19]

For the most part, Sayers's operation on Peter Wimsey's character resulted in a considerable enhancement of his abilities. By 1935 Peter had acquired both a soul and a host of new physical and mental strengths;

he had become virtually impregnable, the ultimate male animal. It is no surprise that Harriet Vane should suffer from feelings of inferiority.

For Harriet, the uncompromising tradition that is Oxford stands as a refuge from the heady demands of Peter Wimsey's world, "the swift, rattling, chattering, excitable and devilishly upsetting world of strain and uproar" (231). For years, Harriet has understood Peter to be exclusively the man of London, with all the habits and outlook of the numbingly modern town. To choose Peter, she assumes, is to leave behind the beckoning peace of Oxford. However, in *Gaudy Night*, Peter suddenly chooses to expose his own aversions to the modern. Exhausted and frightened by his diplomatic missions abroad, he must explain to Harriet both the fears and the bitterness wrought by the experience. The politicians are nothing but charlatans, full of "haste and violence and all that ghastly, slippery cleverness" (287). How he wishes he could root himself in Oxford's traditions, in its sincere and unstinting quest for knowledge and honest truth. He knows it cannot be done.

Putting off a discussion of the poison pen, Peter next exposes his "one really shameful weakness" when Harriet explains that she had recognized Peter's nephew because of the family resemblance in their hands. This is Peter's most private conceit; he is inordinately proud of possessing the Wimsey hands. In fact, he is proud of the entire Wimsey family tradition and concerned that his nephew will sell it all to Hollywood. For all his embrace of the modern, and for all his fast cars, west-end fashions, lavish international lifestyle, for all his relentless, forward-looking escape in criminology, Peter is in part a traditionalist, wedded as much to Denver and to Oxford as to London. In fact, as he eventually confesses, his life is "a balance of opposing forces." Harriet is stunned. "She had fought him for five years, and found nothing but his strength; now, within half an hour, he had exposed all his weaknesses, one after the other" (289–90).

The process continues. Twice in five minutes, while peaceably punting on the river, Peter is forced to warn Harriet away from matters too personal. She recognizes his affinity for John Donne and his proclivity "to get drunk on words." Next, she surmises correctly that he has "a passion for the unattainable," namely a desire for beauty measured by balance and order. Peter has to keep changing the subject. Just what does he see in Harriet? Ultimately he admits that he loves her for her "devastating talent for keeping to the point and speaking the truth." "I have been running away from myself for twenty years, and it doesn't work," he admits.

Even in the five years or so that she had known him, Harriet had seen him strip off his protections, layer by layer, till there was uncommonly little left but the naked truth.

That, then, was what he wanted her for. For some reason, obscure to herself and probably also to him, she had the power to force him outside his defenses. Perhaps, seeing her struggling in a trap of circumstance, he had walked out deliberately to her assistance. Or perhaps the sight of her struggles had warned him what might happen to him, if he remained in a trap of his own making. (309, 371–72)

Harriet had too long assumed that he saw nothing of her at all, but rather some phantasm of his own imagination, a creature molded by his own inductive triumph: a prize for his magnanimity. By exposing his weaknesses, Peter has allowed her to glimpse her own strengths.

Peter Wimsey is a dashed clever fellow, but he must take care to avoid his most common failing: trying to be too clever. At all costs, he has to learn to accept Harriet as she is and not attempt to force the situation. Any exchange of inner emotions must come naturally. One of the few openings Harriet provides is to include her own half-completed sonnet among the papers recording the work of the poison pen. ("A schoolgirl trick" [370], she berates herself.) Encountering Harriet's octave, Peter cannot resist adding the necessary sestet to complete the sonnet.

Imbibing that sense of surety only an Oxford spring can provide, Harriet's octave, on the surface, is a celebration of a world at peace: "To that still centre where the spinning world / Sleeps on its axis, to the heart of rest." Accidentally discovering this octave some weeks afterward, Peter discerns in the eight lines Harriet's true temperament. For all its acclamation of "the heart of rest," much of the octave registers the turmoil she seeks to leave behind, both in its images and its rhythm. Peter responds with a sestet revealing Harriet's underlying agitation, turning her "peaceful humming top" into a "whip-top" that accepts the necessity of rest only in the sense that tension is at rest in the core of music:

Lay on thy whips, O love, that we upright,
 Poised on the perilous point, in no lax bed
  May sleep, as tension at the verberant core
Of music sleeps . . . (395)

"A very conceited, metaphysical conclusion," Peter writes for Harriet to read. Just as Harriet has demonstrated an uncanny ability to step into Peter's mind, Peter has suggested that he too can perceive her true inward thoughts, at times better than she can herself. This communication through the sonnet inspires Harriet to reflect on Peter's steadfast decency in all his dealings with her; though he possesses the ability, he has avoided trespassing on her personal ground. The truth is that Peter has sacrificed a good deal of himself to build an honest foundation between them. Realizing this, Harriet can only admit that her own conduct over the years has been less than lovely. Sayers closes this reverie with the observation that it "goes to prove that even minor poetry may have its practical uses" (370–73).

There remained two scores to settle, two stumbling blocks that Peter must remove—by not acting. For Harriet, the chief impediment to falling in love with Peter is that infernal debt of gratitude; she owes him her life. Peter must find some way to restore that life to her. Peter's own burden is a deeply felt regret, guilt for his actions in the first days after meeting Harriet. He must also find some way to atone for that.

Strangely, the poltergeist provides him the necessary opportunity. For much of the case, Peter is nowhere in evidence. Hearing that Harriet has embarked on a dangerous investigation, he neither flies to her side nor offers protection or even counsel. He merely wishes her well, observing that "If you have put anything in hand, disagreeableness and danger will not turn you back, and God forbid they should" (222). Peter has learned that Harriet must run her life as she sees fit, no matter the circumstances.[20]

Even when she does send for him, bowing to his superior investigative experience, he is careful both to acknowledge her skill and to give her room to pursue the case in her own fashion. Fully comprehending that the poltergeist is preparing to do violence, he will not offer his protection, hold her hand, or take her away. Instead, he teaches her self defense and buys her a collar to protect her "arum lily" neck from throttling fingers. In the meanwhile, he challenges her to write the true detective novel that she is capable of creating. Harriet finds him "about as protective as a can-opener" (386, 311).

That is the point. He cannot win her love by being protective. To give Harriet her life back, he must stand by and watch as she runs the risks she chooses. When she does end up nearly murdered, he can only thank God it was no worse. Stitched and bandaged, she is her own woman at last, free to marry Peter on equal terms or banish him forever. He has signified for good and all that he will not interfere with her private ground.

Now there remained the matter of apology. Five years before, Peter had begun this strange, intricate dance of the emotions on the wrong foot. Aristocratically accustomed to getting what he wanted, he had pursued Harriet from the day he first set eyes on her—in court, struggling for her life. His own selfishness had inspired him to unforgivable sin; he wished to possess her when she did not possess herself. Now he is deeply ashamed of that behavior: "It has taken me a long time to learn my lesson, Harriet. I have had to pull down, brick by brick, the barriers I had built up by my own selfishness and folly. If, in all these years, I have managed to get back to the point at which I ought to have started, will you tell me so and give me leave to begin again?" (465)

In turn, Harriet offers Peter what she has been most loath to give him: her gratitude, both for saving her life and for giving it back to her. All the scores are settled at last.

Peter then asks, not for her hand in marriage, but for a date. The next evening, after briefly consigning their souls to the magic of Bach, the two stroll by the river. For the first time since coming to Oxford, for the first time seriously in several years, Peter Wimsey asks Harriet Vane to marry him. True to the dream that is Oxford, Harriet signifies in the traditions of assenting, approving academe. Mystery-reading England breathed a collective sigh of relief.

By the time *Gaudy Night* appeared, Dorothy L. Sayers had enmeshed herself in a comfortable and comforting web of friends, fans, and supporters, all of whom shared an enthusiasm for the Wimsey saga. Among the varied participants, the most steady and dependable were longtime friend Muriel St. Clare Byrne, now a successful playwright, Byrne's housemate, Marjorie Barber, and a new acquaintance, novelist Helen Simpson. Sayers also received thoughtful encouragement from her Aunt Maud Leigh, who still shared the home in Witham, serving as a buffer between Sayers and Fleming. Aunt Maud had taken special interest in the predicament of Harriet Vane, offering Sayers invaluable perspective and advice.

In informal meetings and correspondence, Dorothy L. Sayers shared her thoughts on future direction for the series, cheerfully debated bones of contention and character, and encouraged collateral creativity. This slowly evolving "Wimsey industry" compensated for some of the comraderie and warmth denied Sayers by her unfortunate marriage. If her husband could little appreciate the magnitude of her accomplishments, her friends made up for him to some degree.[21]

Perhaps the most important fruit of this informal discussion group was a fleshing out of Peter's history. As part of her effort to "chip away" at his character, Sayers participated in several correspondences speculating on Peter Wimsey's past, including his early family life, his education, his first love affairs, and his service in the war. Apart from the material woven into the later Wimsey novels, Sayers saw fit to summarize some of this material in a "biographical note" appended to new editions of the first four Wimsey novels, re-issued by Gollancz in 1935.[22]

Ostensibly written by Peter's lecherous old Uncle Paul Austin Delagardie (his mother's brother), the "note" explains many of the early experiences that shaped Peter's character and career. The second son of the fifteenth Duke of Denver, Peter was wholly unlike his father, "all nerves and nose," but at least possessed of a brain. His schoolmates at Eton called him "Flimsy" until he emerged as a natural cricketer and became "the fashion." Delagardie assumes credit for teaching Peter a proper taste in wine, food, and clothing; he saw also to his sexual education in Paris. Peter then went up to Oxford "with a scholarship to read History at Balliol," and there became "rather intolerable," affecting a monocle and the air of an aesthete. Romance intervened, for good and bad. Peter fell heavily for Barbara, "a child of seventeen," and was saved from marriage only by her parents' decision that she was too young. He was still waiting when the Great War came. Acquitting himself well as an officer, Peter returned on leave to discover Barbara married to someone else. He returned to the front with the firm intention of getting killed but was instead promoted and decorated for intelligence work. Blown up and buried near Caudry in 1918, he came home with a nervous breakdown. The next two years were touch and go, but with the help of Bunter, Peter pulled himself together. Delagardie recalled the Peter of the immediate postwar period: "I don't mind saying that I was prepared for almost anything. He had lost all his beautiful frankness, he shut everybody out of his confidence, including his mother and me, adopted an impenetrable frivolity of manner and a dilettante pose, and became, in fact, the complete comedian." Then came the theft of the Attenbury emeralds. Joining forces with Charles Parker, Peter applied the skills honed in intelligence to track the thief. A hobby was born—a hobby that became the career Sayers tracked through ten novels and sixteen short stories through 1935.[23]

The "Wimsey industry" acquired a new direction in February 1935, when an authority on heraldry by the name of Wilfrid Scott-Giles wrote to Sayers, inquiring after the Wimsey coat of arms described in her later novels. Utterly mock serious, Scott-Giles speculated that the Wimsey heraldry bore the marks of a great antiquity calling for investigation. Sayers replied in kind, and the two began to spin a history of the Wimsey family stretching back into medieval times. Muriel St. Clare Byrne and Helen Simpson joined in, and a lively game ensued. The group produced a series of pamphlets ("Papers Relating to the Family of Wimsey") for private distribution, and they even delivered lectures on the subject. Some of this material made its way into the novel *Busman's Honeymoon,* while Scott-Giles edited his correspondence with Sayers for eventual publication as *The Wimsey Family.*[24] "Our beautiful game," as Sayers referred to this exercise, was a good deal of fun, but it was a private entertainment, adding little substance to Peter Wimsey, the character solving the popular mysteries.[25]

A far more salient product of the Wimsey industry was a story that became both Sayers's first play and the last completed novel to feature Lord Peter. Even as Sayers struggled to complete *Gaudy Night,* she gave considerable attention to the development of its sequel, *Busman's Honeymoon*—plotting and creating dialogue for Peter and Harriet's honeymoon in the country even as she labored to bring them into one another's arms at Oxford. She kept the materials pertinent to each project in separate rooms at her house in Witham.

The seed that became *Busman's Honeymoon* germinated at a luncheon party in London early in 1935. To amuse Muriel St. Clare Byrne and Marjorie Barber, Sayers recounted an astonishing encounter with a chimney sweep. The sweep, a chubby little man, wore any number of pullovers which he pulled off one by one as the work got hotter. Sayers capped the anecdote by wishing she could put the fellow in a play. "Why don't you?" was St. Clare Byrne's reply. A collaboration was born.[26]

Each of the co-authors brought special skills to the task. Agreeing to build the play around a murder occurring on Peter and Harriet's honeymoon placed Sayers firmly on home ground. Thoroughly familiar both with the traits of the main characters and the fundamentals of good mystery writing, Sayers constructed the essence of the play. Muriel St. Clare Byrne, the experienced playwright, shaped the action to the needs of the stage, honing the dialogue, heightening the drama at the close of each act, and sharpening the visual impact of the murder method. It was a most fruitful cooperation, each allowing full expression of the other's complementary skills.

Sayers felt her way slowly, taking three months to rough out the play's first act. Plotting for the stage was very different from writing a mystery for the printed page; in some ways posing the puzzle proved easier, in others far more difficult. On the stage, the material remains of some murder device are simply a part of the scenery, there for the audience to see should they choose to exercise their detective ability. In the novel, such a device must be described, drawing the reader's attention to its existence. On the other hand, the scope of the setting in the novel is as wide as the author's imagination and ability. Action in virtually all of Sayers's books takes place in an array of geographic locations, each enhancing the impact of the mystery and its resolution in some way. In a play, the action must be confined to a very limited number of settings, readily producible on a very material stage. The action is far more geographically focused.

Originating as a play, *Busman's Honeymoon* was shaped by the conventions of the stage. The number of potential suspects was severely limited (four, really), and much of the investigation had to take place in the form of dialogue, there being little latitude for abstruse scientific analyses, elaborate shadowing of suspects, extended research into legal documents, or other such trappings of the detective novel. Moreover, Sayers and St. Clare Byrne chose to describe their play as "A Detective Comedy in Three Acts." Later, Sayers would subtitle the novel "A Love Story with Detective Interruptions." The emphasis was to be on the lighthearted happiness of the newly married couple, counterpointed by the clumsy investigation necessitated by the discovery of a murdered corpse in their basement. The origin of the entire business, after all, was the comic antics of a chimney sweep who wore too much clothing.[27]

The authors worked on *Busman's Honeymoon* throughout the summer of 1935, completing the play in September, just as Gollancz published *Gaudy Night*. Sayers and St. Clare Byrne immediately began the arduous business of securing a producer. After an initial failure, they found success with Anmer Hall, who located the necessary money. Such things take time; rehearsals did not begin until November 1936, and the first London performance came just before Christmas. The play enjoyed a nine months' run in London.

This rather held matters up, as far as continuation of the Wimsey novels was concerned. After completing the play, Sayers had proceeded directly to work on the novel *Busman's Honeymoon,* which was to embody the play in narrative form while incorporating additional materials. Not wishing to spoil the impact of the play by giving away the solution, Sayers stipulated that the play appear on stage in advance of the novel's release. The theater being what it was, such a course dictated a good deal of waiting. Sayers completed the book in October 1936, but Gollancz did not publish it until the following February.[28]

In some ways, *Busman's Honeymoon* is the oddest of all the Wimsey novels, a beast both satisfying and unfulfilling, neither fish nor fowl. The story's genesis as a play trapped Sayers; it is of necessity a very talky novel, an endless succession of conversations punctuated very seldom by either thought or action. Until the conclusion, the most active moment in the story comes when Peter and Harriet take a ride in the car. It is also the only Wimsey novel to fully hinge on its predecessor—the book is a sequel to *Gaudy Night*. The satisfaction the novel provides derives from seeing Peter and Harriet safely married at last.[29] Certainly it is a Wimsey novel most oriented to the private side of life. Beyond a bare mention early in the book of King George V's Silver Jubilee, there is no reference to current events. Peter has given himself over almost completely to the traditional half of his existence, eschewing the modern as he commences life as a married man. Harriet now understands that the air of security she had perceived in Peter almost from the beginning emanates from allegiance to his traditional British heritage. For all his adaptation to the modern world, Peter "belonged to an ordered society." To her delight, she discovers that she has "married England." In fact, of the two, Harriet now comes closer to embodying a sense of the modern. A woman without family and possessing a means of income entirely her own, it is her sort who "go all sanitary and civilised, and get married in hotels and do their births and deaths in nursing-homes where they give offence to nobody."[30]

The novel begins with a series of vignettes—material purportedly written by persons attending the Wimsey-Vane wedding, including Bunter, Peter's mother and sister-in-law, and the dean of Shrewsbury College. Obviously inspired by the "Wimsey industry," these letters and diary entries provide several perspectives on the marriage. As might be expected, the ceremony has its share of maladroit moments, both in planning and performance. Harriet has fallen head-over-heels in love with Peter, worrying only about negative publicity from her notorious past and her ability to perform the duties incumbent on Lady Peter Wimsey without embarrassing all concerned. Peter is naturally solicitous that the thing be done in loving good taste beyond the glare of reporters' cameras and that Harriet's entrance into noble society be as smooth as possible. The witnesses report a simple, elegant, but private wedding, followed by a successful escape from the newshounds for the honeymoon. Each account has its share of pithy comments, such as this observation, contained in a letter from the dean to Miss de Vine: "I know heaps of couples who are both as stupid as owls and not happy at all—so it doesn't really follow, one way or the other, does it?" (12)

Obviously much smarter than owls, Peter and Harriet have determined on a very private honeymoon in Harriet's childhood hometown of Great Pagford, Hertsfordshire. Both the play and the narrative portion of the novel essentially begin with their arrival at Talboys, a great old Tudor house newly purchased in secret by the Wimseys. Unfortunately, Noakes, the former owner, is not there to meet them, nor is the house prepared for their appearance. All the doors are locked; no key is in evidence. Noakes is in fact dead, lying in the basement with a fractured skull. Thankfully, no one discovers the grisly fact until the following day.

The unscheduled appearance of a murder victim on a honeymoon gives the story two horses to ride, though neither is a terrifically strong one. There is some tension in the romance, as Peter and Harriet must work out their roles as husband and wife and learn how to maintain complementary but separate identities. This is nothing in comparison to the kinds of romantic tensions flowing like kerosene on fire through *Gaudy Night*. There is a murder mystery, of the locked-room variety, but the victim is a close old man no one much liked. There can be just four suspects; no one of them encourages much sympathy either. The limits of the stage have left Sayers with rather a tepid puzzle in comparison with her ten preceding novels.

Sayers seems more interested in exploring the problems of love in marriage than in posing a detective puzzle. Having at long last brought Peter and Harriet to the altar, she is now free to explore her ideal state of wedded bliss—a stark contrast to the reality of her own marriage to Mac Fleming. The reader is made to understand that this couple will succeed, not only because they love each other deeply, but because they respect one another equally as human beings. They have already overcome their most dangerous obstacle: the problem of gratitude. Harriet freely allows Peter to purchase their new home because she knows "he liked giving people things" (18); she in turn expends the proceeds from three short stories to purchase for him a letter of John Donne concerning "Divine and human love." Peter could easily have purchased the letter himself— he had wanted to do so, as a gift for Harriet. The value is not in the letter but in the fact that Harriet has bestowed it. They are free of the mutual burden of necessary gratitude; each can now give to the other freely.[31]

As might be expected, there are awkward moments as they inadvertently test one another. When Harriet discovers information that might incriminate Aggie Twitterton, Noakes's niece (and a hapless human being if ever there was one), Peter automatically assumes that they will share this with the police. Harriet is appalled; the information has come to her in confidence. But Peter's hands are the hangman's hands: catching murderers is his job. Either Harriet must allow him to pursue that job in his usual thorough way, or he must quit. She has the power to make him quit; most women would use it immediately. Harriet will not:

> "If we disagree, we'll fight it out like gentlemen. We won't stand for matrimonial blackmail. . . . You *must* do what you think is right. Promise me that. What I think doesn't matter. I swear it shall never make any difference."
>
> He took her hand and kissed it gravely.
>
> "Thank you, Harriet. That is love with honour." (292)

The difficulty for Peter will be to allow someone to share his most private, self-protected moments. In the face of Barbara and the war, Peter had spent long years constructing mask after mask to protect his emotional fragility; he has been the comedian, the pedant, the clothes-horse, the man about town, the hardworking private detective, and even the harlequin. Harriet's relentless demand for honesty has mostly torn those masks away, but there are still places he keeps hidden, even from her. When Peter comes to understand how the murder was done, he turns more to Bunter than to Harriet. The old habits die hard.

Yet, for the far larger part, this is a story of joy in marriage. Harriet is perfectly thrilled, in every sense, now that all the difficulties and discomfort are behind her. Peter suspects that "If I'd had nothing but a haystack to offer you, you'd have married me years ago." Harriet agrees:

> "I shouldn't be surprised."
>
> "Damnation! think what I've missed."

"Me too. At this moment I could have been tramping at your heels with five babies and a black eye, and saying to a sympathetic bobby, 'You leave 'im be—'e's my man, ain't 'e?—E've a right to knock me abaht.'"

"You seem," said her husband, reprovingly, "to regret the black eye more than the five babies."

"Naturally. You'll never give me the black eye." (37)

Peter too gives himself over to a euphoria verging on giddiness. Holding Harriet in his arms and hearing her sigh "seemed to lift the sealing stone and release some well-spring of laughter deep down within him. It came bubbling and leaping up in the most tremendous hurry to reach the sunlight, so that all his blood danced with it and his lungs were stifled with the rush and surge of this extraordinary fountain of delight. He felt himself at once ridiculous and omnipotent. He was exultant. He wanted to shout" (250). They can only agree that this was "almost like being in love," a faintly ludicrous thought. Peter concludes, mischievously, that "One can't be married *and* in love. Not with the same person, I mean. It isn't done" (272–73). The alert reader can almost hear the lamenting sigh of Dorothy L. Sayers.

Sayers once again demonstrated her choice to be cognizant of the modern without being of the modern in her treatment of sex, that most delicate and delectable of subject matters. True to form, she frankly examined "the interesting revelations of the marriage-bed" (there was little left to reveal for any reader familiar with the works of D. H. Lawrence or Henry Miller), without ever mentioning sexuality in any overt fashion. Only the discerning and lascivious old Paul Delagardie can discern the reason for the "unusual constraint between P. and H." at a dinner party not long before the wedding. Harriet possesses a tiger, not a shabby tiger as Peter feared, but "an entirely new tiger," ready and waiting to pounce. But when, after several misadventures, Harriet and Peter do land in the marriage bed, it is "the end of the journey and the beginning of all delight." This bedroom stuff is supposed to be fun, Sayers reminds the reader. Beyond the fact that Peter and Harriet found it so, there was nothing worthy of report (62, 31).

There is a mystery to be solved in the midst of all this, of course, but it is an infernal nuisance. The news of the body brings an avalanche of reporters to Talboys, along with the official police who carry on their initial inquiries in the Wimsey living room. Meanwhile, creditors have come to demand the furniture—old Noakes was in debt up to his ears. The murder scene is slowly dismantled, first by the happy couple (assisted by Bunter) and subsequently by the movers. As any faithful reader of the Sayers mystery series knows, what is being destroyed is evidence of *how* the murder was done, which is the key to understanding the entire business.

Peter and Harriet talk about the "how" at some length. Comparing memories of the condition of the house upon their arrival, they dwell on possible means of entry, possible times when the murder could have occurred, and possible weapons. Peter is really glad to discuss the case with someone knowing enough to focus on method. All too often, he complains, the official police concentrate largely on motive, a weak indicator at best. Several people may possess a reason for wanting to do someone in (love or money, generally speaking), but that proves nothing. Juries want to look at motive as well, for the same wrong reasons. But if you can trace the method the killer employed, that will point unfailingly to the perpetrator—"When you've got How, you've got Who."

Harriet replies in kind: "I seem to have married my only intelligent reader. That's the way you construct it from the other end, of course. Artistically, it's absolutely correct" (219).

Once again, Dorothy L. Sayers is speaking through Harriet and Peter, coaching her audience on the proper approach to resolving her locked-room mystery. This time the audience includes, not merely armchair readers, but people seated in a theater, eyes on a stage. Somewhere before their eyes there exists the remains of a murder device capable of fracturing a tall man's skull. And that potted cactus hanging by the fireplace near the wireless looks so innocent.

Sayers strews a fair number of red herrings across the investigators' path, but in the end all that matters is the lead-weighted cactus and the memory of a few yards of fishing line. The device is easy enough to reconstruct; once in place it points directly to the murderer: the man who unnecessarily watered the cactus twice in a week's time.

Frank Crutchley is by far the most repulsive of Sayers's murderers, a "pushing" young no-account from London who sticks at nothing. He is a hard worker, serving as a garage mechanic and working part-time as Noakes's gardener. But he works only for the sake of the money and his own ambitions, not for the pride of the job. He is willing to demonstrate the proper respect for Lord and Lady Peter only as long as he thinks there is something to be got out of them—within, he hates the thought of "trucking to a blasted title" (268). He has paid court to poor old Aggie Twitterton solely to get her money (and perhaps her uncle's) for his own garage. In the meantime he has been seeing another woman on the sly, saucy Polly Mason, too modern for Pagford with her silk stockings and motion-picture ways. She is a bit too modern for her own good, ending up carrying the child of a condemned murderer. Crutchley does not care.

Crutchley, in fact, does not care about anything. When Peter reconstructs his death machine and springs the trap, Crutchley knows the game is up. He has but one regret: that he got caught. He would like to escape the strong arms of the police, kill Peter for catching him: "Let me go, blast you! Let me get at him! So you set a trap for me, did you? Well, I killed him. The old brute cheated me. So did you, Aggie Twitterton, blast you! I been done out o' my rights. I killed him, I tell you, and all for nothing" (341).

The play ends at this point, with much the same speech from the murderer. As Crutchley is dragged off stage, Peter seeks Harriet's hand. "This part of the business always gets me down,"[32] he warns. They exchange promises, embracing as the curtain falls. Sayers has paid the necessary debt to her craft, acknowledging that, however repulsive the crime, sending a man to the gallows is a sobering thing.

The book winds through an additional three chapters, providing the reader a full look at Peter's reaction to investigative triumph. Sayers had generally suggested that Peter took it hard when a case came to an end. In *Whose Body?* he suffered a relapse of shell shock after discovering Levy's murderer. *Unnatural Death* left him ready to believe the end of the world had come; exposing *The Unpleasantness at the Bellona Club* as murder led to depression and quarrels with Charles Parker. So it went. In the early chapters of *Gaudy Night*, Sayers hinted that such adverse reactions were typical:

> There had been an evening when he had turned up to keep a pre-viously-made dinner appointment, but had obviously been unfit either to eat or talk. Eventually he had confessed to a splitting headache and a temperature and suffered himself to be personally conducted home. [Harriet] had been sufficiently alarmed not to leave him till he was safely in his own flat and in the capable hands

of Bunter. The latter had been reassuring: the trouble was nothing but reaction—of frequent occurrence at the end of a trying case, but soon over. (64)

In this way, Sayers addressed what was to her a most crucial element in the detective story as human drama: the detective must acknowledge the gravity of his deeds and in some way suffer in consequence.

The last three chapters of *Busman's Honeymoon*—the "Epithalamion"—explore this theme in crucial detail. In the play, it is enough for Harriet to "feel as if the evil spirit has been cast out of this house, and left it clean for you and me."[33] Despite its sudden shock of a climax, the play was intended to be a light comedy. The book, being the eleventh Wimsey novel, demanded much more. Looking at the situation realistically, the Wimseys have spent the first three days of their honeymoon at a crime scene, with policemen, reporters, and total strangers traipsing through at all hours. Even after they expose the murderer, they are left with the haunting echo of his curses. Moreover, they are standing holding hands in a house with no furniture. This is all going to be a little bit depressing, even if all else is equal.

Sayers was now faced with the consequences of entangling murder and romance. Her newly wedded couple must get marriage off on the right foot, but Peter must acknowledge his responsibility for uncovering Frank Crutchley's crime. Love and depression can be a volatile mix; the shadows hang heavy over these last three chapters.

Peter does his best to disguise and dispel the usual reaction. He assumes direct responsibility for Crutchley's predicament and arranges the best legal counsel possible for his defense. For the briefest of moments, the honeymooning Wimseys re-enter the modern world, driving up to London, turning into a movie house to view a "Mickey Mouse and an educational film about the iron and steel industry,"[34] before speaking to Sir Impey Biggs at midnight. That done, Peter and Harriet return to the England of long-standing tradition, driving to Denver, where she is truly initiated into the ancient Wimsey family—ghosts and all. Sayers draws again on the "Wimsey industry" in creating these scenes, filling in considerable detail on the Wimsey family history as well as Peter's personal past. The story of how Bunter came to serve him is for the first time told in full.

Then the return to refurbished Talboys and the trial, the inevitable condemnation. Peter is an emotional wreck. He would like to have Crutchley's forgiveness; he does all he can to ease the prisoner's last hours, even arranging care for Polly Mason and her baby, all to no avail. A bitter and unrepentant Crutchley remains sullen to the end; his only wish is to get the drop over with and see them all in hell.

Peter's anguish is the great final test of his marriage to Harriet. This is a struggle he wants desperately to carry on alone, the last defended place in his own psyche, the part of himself he can share with no one. Harriet can only wait it out. To demand that Peter share this last bit of himself is unthinkable; she can only let him know in subtle but unmistakable ways that she is there if he wants her. He comes at last at four in the morning, shivering, teeth chattering—the exact symptoms exhibited in *Whose Body?* more than thirteen years before. "It's my rotten nerves," he confesses. "I can't help it. I suppose I've never really been right since the War. I hate behaving like this. I tried to stick it out by myself" (378).

This time he turns to Harriet to help him through. She, of course, provides all the rational reasons why he cannot blame himself for the nearing execution, but those reasons do not matter, really, to either of them. Peter must feel what he does; he has a conscience. And now he has a spouse as well; he must share all, even his worst moments. Finally he begins to weep against Harriet's breast. The wounded detective and the romantic lover at last meld into a single person.

Strange to say, Dorothy L. Sayers did not intend to end the Wimsey series with this moment. That is to say, she had plans for further novels, and she did write additional short stories featuring Peter Wimsey. But the "Epithalamion" reads very much like a conclusion, a summing up of a career. Peter is brought full circle, his family explained, the fierce loyalty between Wimsey and Bunter illuminated, and the last stumbling blocks to true love removed. Peter is still the shell-shocked veteran of *Whose Body?;* he is also the detective and the lover triumphant. The triumph is strange and painfully human, characterized not by a crow from the rooftops but by an embarrassed fit of bitter tears. There was very little room left for Peter to grow. As matters turned out, *Busman's Honeymoon* proved to be the last Peter Wimsey novel.

Lord Peter and the Long Week-End

JUST WHAT HAPPENED TO LORD PETER WIMSEY? HE WAS VERY much alive in 1936 and 1937, his marriage celebrated both in the novel and on the stage. Corresponding with Wimsey devotees, his creator outlined ideas for new novels exploring both his hopeful future and his less-than-happy past. The "Wimsey industry" busily continued to fill in the gaps in his heritage, making his family participants in every important event in England's history since William the Conqueror—often on both sides of the issue at hand. New short stories appeared (no better than the old) chronicling minor investigations and the birth of a Wimsey son. The promised twelfth Peter Wimsey novel never appeared. Why did Dorothy L. Sayers abandon this highly popular series at the peak of her success?[1]

Biographers and essayists have offered a variety of explanations, all encompassing at least a grain of truth. Perhaps the intoxicating magic of the stage did Peter in—Sayers thoroughly enjoyed the entire process of staging *Busman's Honeymoon*, a cooperative experience far different from the lonely exercise of wrestling with the novel form. New opportunities to explore her talents as a playwright opened in 1936; she rapidly took advantage of them. Perhaps Lord Peter was simply abandoned as Sayers took to writing plays.[2]

Intimately connected to Sayers's newfound affinity for the stage was a new focus on religious issues. In October 1936—before her plunge into play writing had become public knowledge—the organizers of the annual Canterbury festival invited her to write a play appropriate to the history of the cathedral. Though she was known to the general public almost exclusively as a mystery writer, with no published works bearing seriously on religious issues, she had achieved a reputation for Christian sensitivity in important quarters. She was a minister's daughter, and she had managed to hide her sins quite effectively. And, in *The Nine Tailors,* she had conveyed a heartwarming empathy for the essence of Christian doctrine in a vehicle possessing widespread popular appeal. Presumably she could do as much for the Canterbury festival. Delighted with the invitation, Sayers fell immediately to work, completing *The Zeal of Thy House* in ample time for production in June 1937. Her long-latent interest in religious issues was piqued. It would be difficult to reconcile this new devotion with the career of a detective adamant in his indifference to religion.[3]

There was also the fact that Dorothy L. Sayers had several times confessed to being fed up with Lord Peter and his whimsical ways. His character had become surpassingly difficult to confine to paper; she had harbored a desire to have done with him since at least 1929. Maybe she had quietly decided that enough was enough, that *Busman's Honeymoon* had brought Peter to an artistic conclusion. Though she scribbled a few more things, her heart obviously was not in it—the best course was to let Peter go.[4]

If Sayers was not fed up with Lord Peter, she may well have had her fill of his fans. As the Wimsey stories became increasingly popular, Sayers found herself answering increasingly aggravating letters from readers. A letter to a Miss B. S. Sturgis written in April 1937 finds Sayers patiently explaining that there is no relation "between Mr. Tallboys and Talboys," that "Peter would always have his shirts made for him," and so on. The "infernal nuisance of writing letters to sentimental Wimsey-addicts" eventually wore away her desire to continue, as she admitted in a letter written in 1949.[5]

A fifth explanation examines the direction of the material that Sayers did produce after 1936 detailing the further adventures of Lord Peter. The directions she could take were far from limitless. Before *Gaudy Night,* Sayers was free to place her detective in any situation suited to her imagination—a vacation in Scotland, a layover in Fenchurch St. Paul, or an infiltration of an advertising agency. Now she had saddled Peter with a wife and an abundant supply of happiness; the openings for cases became correspondingly smaller in number. Moreover, when Sayers did take up the pen to turn out another novel, her portrayal of marriage came appallingly close to mirroring the conditions that brought on the great constitutional crisis of 1936. Enough was seemingly enough.[6]

Any and all of these reasons are credible, and there is perhaps one more. Peter Wimsey had sprung to life early in the 1920s, in part the product of the optimism accompanying the birth of the modern age. The prospect had seemed rosy then: a boundless advance into a future of everlasting peace, limitless freedom for men and women of all classes, an embrace of technological wonders, and an end to the malignant stupidities of past leaders, political and social. That future, rather than proving limitless, had lasted for something like eighteen years before the iron door closed once more. There had been no birth of a new civilization from the ashes of the Great War. By 1937 it was obvious that the time that had passed since Armistice Day had been simply a respite, a pause for breath. Europe, having expended nine hundred thousand lives for exactly nothing, was about to go back to war. The "long week-end" was drawing to a close. Peter Wimsey, intimately a product and a figure of that long week-end, was finished as well. An ominous combination of national and international events signalled the end of the era.[7]

The event striking closest to home for the British was the death of King George V on January 10, 1936. The old king had been an enduring and celebrated symbol of government since his accession in 1910 at the age of forty-five. Striking a royal tone suggesting the common touch in an era of increasing democracy, George V became increasingly popular with the English people, as the power of the aristocracy faded. While soldiers and civilians alike lost faith in "the blimps" as the Great War dragged on, George V won hearts with his plain and obvious sympathy for the common enlisted man. He demonstrated a continued wisdom and restraint during the many political and economic crises that punctuated the years following the war. Now he was dead, after suffering bravely through painful illness. Countless thousands listened on the wireless for news of the end. More than a king was passing; a symbol of quiet and steadfast security was giving way before an uncertain future.

The closing of an era might not have had such a dramatic impact had it not been for the sequel. Heir to the throne was the eldest son of

George V, forty-two-year-old Edward Albert, Prince of Wales. Possessed of some good and sensitive qualities, he was nonetheless a weak and ineffectual human being. This did not preclude his accession—one of the paramount characteristics of kingship is that you have filled the entire job description when you are the first male born to the current occupant. There are expectations, however. By the twentieth century, the throne was a cipher in real politics but a critically important symbol of church and state. Above all, the king must prove a fitting symbol.

This, Edward VIII could not do. Scandalous rumors began to circulate almost immediately. Edward had foolishly fallen in love with an American (bad enough) divorcee (still worse) who was in the process of obtaining a second divorce (unthinkable). When Edward VIII made known his intention to marry Wallis Simpson and make her queen, the ministry dug in its heels as one. The head of the Church of England under no circumstances could marry a divorced woman. Stanley Baldwin, prime minister since Ramsey MacDonald's retirement, gave the political performance of his life in guiding England and its wayward king through the crisis. Edward must choose between kingship and love—and do so before his coronation. He chose Mrs. Simpson, which was probably for the best. His younger brother, crowned George VI, proved to be a far more steady and intelligent symbol of leadership.[8]

The distraction could not have come at a worse possible moment. Stanley Baldwin was lionized for his handling of the constitutional crisis of 1936, but the policies of government apart from the crisis were disastrously weak. Fascist aggression throughout Europe was met, not with firm opposition but dithering compromise. Mussolini's government invaded Abyssinia in October 1935, eventually incorporating the ancient kingdom into an Italian fascist empire. The League of Nations imposed pathetically limited economic sanctions, but without visible impact; these were gone within a year. Hitler had already withdrawn from the League, which was pursuing dreams of disarmament while he was imposing military conscription in Germany. Britain, despite criticism from both left and right, began to rearm. In March 1936, Hitler marched troops into the Rhineland, a direct violation of the Treaty of Versailles. Britain made no response, nor did France. German territorial ambitions grew apace— Hitler now aimed to reunite all German-speaking peoples under the Nazi banner.[9]

In July 1936, military aggression found a new outlet, as fascist forces led by Francisco Franco revolted against the newly formed liberal government of Spain. Italy and Germany supplied Franco, while the Soviet Union supplied his opponents. An international brigade of idealists joined the leftist cause and found out just what modern war was all about. The watchword was not valor, it was mechanization or, perhaps, air power.[10]

As peace disintegrated, war assumed an ominous shape. Civilian terror had become an intimate adjunct to military tactics. Feelings ran high in Britain during the Abyssinian crisis, as reports circulated of deliberate bombings of Ethiopian hospitals and schools. In Spain, German planes levelled the defenseless village of Guernica in 1937, massacring most of the inhabitants. The British slowly came to understand that they were not immune. As early as 1932, Stanley Baldwin had warned, "I think it is well for the man in the street to realize that there is no power on earth that can prevent him from being bombed. Whatever people may tell him, the bomber will always get through. . . . The only defense is in offense, which means that you have to kill women and children more quickly than the enemy if you want to save yourselves." By 1934, Baldwin was advising that Britain's military frontier lay not at the Cliffs of Dover but at the Rhine. It was a shame that he did not do more to secure the boundary he so correctly assessed.[11]

Slowly, inexorably, incompetently, Britain chugged toward a war footing. While Baldwin and then his successor, Neville Chamberlain, made concession after infamous concession to Hitler, the military built up and trained its air forces, preparing for the worst. Conscription was introduced in April 1939; by the following September Britain was at war. This time, there was no celebration.[12]

As the atmosphere turned drastic after 1935, the spirit of Dorothy L. Sayers's Wimsey tales could not help but suffer. With few exceptions, Sayers had consistently endeavored to give her books a sense of historical immediacy—as if the events she described had just occurred. In *Murder Must Advertise,* Lord Peter accompanies a royal personage to the theater, while Ginger Joe is asked if he would prefer to meet Ramsey MacDonald rather than Charles Parker. In *The Nine Tailors,* Sayers makes reference to a series of scandalous and headline-grabbing murders and suicides. And, in *Gaudy Night,* she specifically notes that the events take place in the year of King George V's jubilee: 1935.

After turning almost entirely inward to narrate the events of *Busman's Honeymoon,* Sayers planned to return Lord and Lady Peter Wimsey fully to the public arena in her next detective story. The plot of the new novel would be constructed around the most arresting event of the era, the death and funeral of George V.

Dorothy L. Sayers began plotting this novel in the summer of 1936 after completing the novel *Busman's Honeymoon*. She became thoroughly excited as she sketched out her ideas, saying as much in a letter written to Helen Simpson in July 1936: "The scheme looks nice and neat; and is very nearly symmetrical except for the little bulge of PH emotional development, which leads to the solution. I find this scheme so satisfactory that it hardly seems worth while writing the book, does it?"[13]

But write it she did—at least the first one hundred seventy pages. The uncompleted manuscript was found in her attic in Witham after her death in 1957. The title, just as she had advised Helen Simpson, was to be "Thrones, Dominations," derived from a verse discovered in Milton's *Paradise Lost*: "Hear all ye Angels, Progenie of Light, / Thrones, Dominations, Princedoms, Vertues, Powers, / Hear my Decree, which unrevok't shall stand." The theme of the book, "in a nutshell" according to Sayers, was encapsulated in a further verse from *Paradise Lost*. Beelzebub advises his fellow angels, forced from Heaven, that "Thrones and imperial Powers, off-spring of heav'n, / Ethereal Vertues; or these titles now / Must we renounce, and changing stile be call'd / Princes of Hell?" The question Beelzebub poses is a puzzler: should they retain the trappings of heaven in the hope of regaining heaven, or should they cast aside the familiar and start from scratch to create the best hell that they can? A murder mystery built around such a theme would be intriguing indeed.[14]

That there was to be a murder is not in doubt, although no one had died as yet when Sayers stopped writing. The story centered on the interactions between the Wimseys and another married couple, Lawrence and Rosamund Harwell. The Harwells's story parallels that of the Wimseys in certain fundamental ways: Lawrence is wealthy, his wife a former model whom he has rescued from the humiliation of an arrested father. Unlike Peter and Harriet, the Harwells are for the most part unhappy, engaging in bouts of stultifying jealousy. Apparently, Sayers planned to continue the exploration of marriage begun in *Busman's Honeymoon*.

Certainly the story picked up exactly where the previous novel left off. Immediately following Frank Crutchley's execution on January 10, 1936, Peter and Harriet depart for Paris, where they first come across the Harwells. A series of vexing scenes installing Harriet in London society ensue, providing Sayers repeated opportunities to contrast the attitudes of Peter and Harriet with those of Lawrence and Rosamund. All comes to a sudden and crashing halt with the news of the death of King George V.[15]

Dorothy L. Sayers planned to make greater use of an actual historical event in this novel than in any Wimsey story to date. She carefully portrays the variety of reactions to the sad end of a reign, following characters as they move through a London society in mourning. Three days after the king's death, Peter watches the funeral procession to Whitehall in the company of a young French painter. The artist expresses his amazement at the inadequacy of the police and military presence.

> "This is just a village funeral," said Peter. "Nobody would dream of making a disturbance. It is not done. When it comes to a public ceremony, precautions will be taken. But not when we are private."
>
> "It is fantastic," said Gaston Chapparelle. "You think of yourselves as a practical people, yet your empire is held together by nothing but a name and a dream. You laugh at your own traditions and are confident the world will respect them. And it does. That is the astonishing thing about it."
>
> "It may not last."[16]

Two episodes apparently follow the funeral procession, the first involving a series of unhappy confrontations between the Wimseys and the Harwells, the second comprising a rather frank discussion of sexual matters between Peter and Harriet, with Uncle Paul Delagardie joining in. The manuscript breaks off at this maddening point, with no clear indication even of who is about to be murdered.[17]

A sense of loss, of onrushing disaster, pervades the manuscript. At the bottom of this disorganized and uncompleted stack of handwritten pages is a leaf encapsulating a conversation between Peter and his brother, the Duke of Denver. They are trapped at a dinner party ruthlessly organized by Helen, Duchess of Denver, for Harriet's "coming out" in society. Helen finds Harriet impossible to countenance, let alone accept, but Gerald struggles to understand.

> "Well, I say you did dead right," said the Duke. "Good luck to it."
>
> "Thanks, old man."
>
> The Duke hoped something would be forthcoming, but Peter's usually busy tongue was well bridled tonight. A queer business,

thought the Duke. Independence. Silences. Reservations. Modern marriage. Was there any sort of actual confidence? A slippery affair, & he could get no grip on it. He led the way upstairs. At the top of the landing he paused, & said with an odd air of defiance:

"I've been planting oaks in Boulter's Hollow."

Oaks! Peter met his eye firmly, & said without emphasis:

"They should do well there."[18]

An odd air of defiance, indeed. Gerald is planting oaks, those most slow-maturing and forward-looking of trees, while Europe crumbles and his most unsatisfactory son prepares to sell out the family estate. Oaks may well prove a vain gesture, a disdainful sentiment directed toward a reckless and unheeding modern world.

Sayers left no clues to suggest when she stopped writing, or why. Apparently she worked on the manuscript as opportunities arose throughout the latter half of 1936. By early 1937 she had definitely moved on to other projects, meaning that she may have stopped at year's end in 1936. It is not difficult to guess the reason: the abdication took place on December 10. Sayers was in Leeds, working out the bugs in the play, *Busman's Honeymoon,* in advance of the London opening when the constitutional crisis struck.

Dorothy L. Sayers took an avid interest in the abdication and was fully prepared to believe the worst of Edward and Mrs. Simpson.[19] This historic event shed an entirely new, and not altogether complimentary, light on the institution of marriage. Inevitably, this would impact Sayers's own interpretation of the emotions and events she was attempting to portray in "Thrones, Dominations." By unfortunately choosing the highly visible death of George V as a springboard for her fiction, she guaranteed that readers would interpret her ideas with the abdication sequel in mind. Sayers had allowed herself to be trapped by historical events. She quietly put the manuscript away, perhaps hoping to iron out the problem later. In a letter written in November 1938, Sayers confessed, "I have taken a dislike to the story, and have great difficulty doing anything about it."[20]

Crisis followed on crisis after the abdication. International complications rolled menacingly and inexorably on, drowning whatever illusion of peace the Britons may have possessed. Sayers had almost no choice but to leave Peter Wimsey's latest novel in the attic; his world was receding with frightening velocity into a dimly remembered past when hope in some way existed.

Sayers tried to keep Lord Peter alive. In her essay "Gaudy Night," published in 1937, she foresaw "no end to the Wimseys this side the grave" (220). Apparently she had ideas in mind for several more novels, as she suggested in a letter to Sir Donald Tovey, musicologist and devoted Wimsey follower, in April 1936: "What I have got in mind, is the complete history of all Peter's earlier women, leading up to their appearance from time to time in his detective presence. We shall then know what happened to Barbara, to the Viennese singer and also to that unknown lady who was his partner during the Ali Baba period; and may also have some information about those 'trustworthy hands' in which Uncle Paul established him in Paris."[21] Poor Harriet—one can only hope the shock was to be spread over several years' worth of books.

The Wimsey material that Sayers actually produced was far less informative, and paltry besides. In 1936 she published a new anthology of mystery stories, *Tales of Detection,* for Everyman's Library, and she included a new Wimsey story entitled "The Image in the Mirror." A typical Sayers short story, there is much more to be said for the inspiration than for the execution. No better was "The Haunted Policeman," published in *The Strand* and *Harper's Bazaar* in the winter of 1938. This was the next installment in the chronicle of the Wimsey marriage, as the story opens with Harriet giving birth to a son in November 1936. The birth takes place "off"; the puzzle is not worth Peter's time. Two more stories, both featuring Wimsey on his own, appeared in Sayers's last collection of her own mystery fiction, *In the Teeth of the Evidence.* Each is amusing, though adding little to the Wimsey character.[22]

An unfinished short story from this period is suggestive of Dorothy L. Sayers's dilemma. The manuscript, entitled "The Master Key," chronicles a sadly aging and domestic Lord Peter. The story begins with a fistfight in one of Peter's three clubs. He defends a woman's honor against the unseemly insults of the Honorable John Hemlock, a young brute, but comes away second best, his facial features rearranged. Hurrying home, he finds solace in Harriet's sympathy and security in a new household served by a full staff of domestics. Still, he studies his damaged face carefully in the mirror, concerned that he might discover loosened teeth. That John Hemlock comes next morning seeking Peter's aid to clear him of a murder charge apparently did little to sweeten the situation. Sayers dropped the story at this point. Perhaps an aging Wimsey, no longer possessing even the potential to be intrepid, was too much to swallow. Even reviewers had detected the author's problem. Considering the recent publication of *In the Teeth of the Evidence,* the *New Republic* lamented that "The hero of a hundred dangerous escapades is inarticulate in the hands of modern science and, moreover, his teeth are beginning to go."[23]

The Wimseys made their last public appearance in Sayers's lifetime as England fought for its survival in the first months of World War II. In a series of eleven installments appearing in *The Spectator* between November 17, 1939, and January 26, 1940, Sayers presented supposed correspondence among members of the Wimsey family and their acquaintances. Intended as an expression of patriotism and morale booster, "The Wimsey Papers" gave expression to Sayers's views on the war experience and the necessity of looking firmly ahead to a brighter future. Sayers emphasized the need to maintain proper morale. In a supposed letter from Harriet to Helen, she argued that "It isn't fair to expect the ordinary man & woman to struggle unaided against these violent assaults."[24]

The last letter from Peter to Harriet draws on the themes that Sayers had originally examined in *Gaudy Night:* "I have seen the eyes of the men who ask for leadership, and they are the eyes of slaves. The new kind of leaders are not like the old. . . . It's not enough to rouse up the Government to do this and that. You must rouse the people. You must make them understand that their salvation is in themselves and in each separate man and woman among them. . . . They must not look to the State for guidance—they must learn to guide the State."[25] Again, Sayers and Lord Peter drew on the solid traditions of British culture as a weapon to fight modernization in its totalitarian form. Fittingly, this effort was to be the last word from Peter Wimsey, at least in Dorothy L. Sayers's lifetime. The *Papers* convey a sense of finality as far as the Wimseys are concerned. Supposed excerpts from Peter's diary are especially revealing. She lifted the Duke of Denver's announced intention to plant oaks from the "Thrones, Dominations" manuscript, perhaps an indication that she had determined to abandon that final novel. More importantly, she allowed Peter the opportunity to write his own epitaph at the diary's close:

HERE LIES AN ANACHRONISM IN THE VAGUE EXPECTATION
OF ETERNITY

Sayers understood that the forthcoming war would destroy Peter Wimsey's world for all time.[26]

Sayers turned to Lord Peter one last time. After her death in 1957, a short story entitled "Talboys" was discovered among her papers. She had written the story in 1942 but apparently made no attempt to publish it. The story is a paean to wedded bliss; the reader would never guess that the action was set in the middle of World War II. Peter and Harriet have three sons, the youngest still a baby; the mystery involves a theft of prize-winning peaches. Beyond assuring her readers that the Wimseys were all right, there seems to be no good reason why Sayers should write such a tepid story. Certainly she exercised good judgment in quietly putting the work away.[27]

So Peter was done. As much as anything, he was the victim of the onrush of events leading to the war. Sayers decided to wed his story to England's own just as events began to trip one over another. Choosing to anchor a novel in the death of a king, she was unable to complete the writing before the abdication forever colored perceptions of that first event. Things were moving too fast; the England of Peter Wimsey was vanishing, and Peter along with it. He was the product of an era, and the era was gone.

From an end-of the-century perspective, the fictional history of Peter Wimsey has become emblematic of its time. Unlike practically any other of the famous fictional detectives, Lord Peter Wimsey's career was fully defined by a single epoch. He came to life as the long week-end began in the wake of the Great War; he disappeared as World War II sealed the week-end's close. The era shaped and defined Peter Wimsey's character; he in turn reflected its experiences and its values, at least as Dorothy L. Sayers understood them.

Sayers was first and foremost a mystery writer until 1936—a highly successful one in a period that saw the likes of G. K. Chesterton, Agatha Christie, Margerie Allingham, Ngaio Marsh, Ronald Knox, and Arthur Conan Doyle. She began as an educated scholar writing for money and the fun of it and continued because of the initial success and the extra income she came to need desperately. By the end of the twenties, she had established herself, not only as a great mystery writer, but also as an expert on the mystery story. When Dorothy L. Sayers turned her mind to something, she turned all her formidable talents to the task.

She approached the mystery in a conventional way, fashioning a detective in response to Sherlock Holmes, providing a community of support players—a police detective, a forensic analyst, a solicitor, a barrister, a financial expert, a Bohemian artist, several family members, a Bunter, and a Miss Climpson—to help him along. When these grew tiresome, she developed alternative communities, including an artist's colony and an isolated church parish, to assist his endeavors. She read fellow mystery writers intently and voraciously, eventually discerning the flaws in standard practice and defining her own ideals for the proper detective story.

As Sayers grew more conversant with the mystery form, she took to weaving into her stories subtle jabs at the failings and inconsistencies of other writers. Eventually she internalized a mechanism for both expressing her understanding of the mystery's conventions and commenting on the structure of her own novels, by introducing Harriet Vane, the mystery writer as major character. Harriet spoke about plot and procedure with the authoritative voice of Dorothy L. Sayers. Sayers put a great deal of herself into Harriet, but it is possible to make too much of this. Harriet was not the mirror of Sayers; she was different in several respects. Moreover, Sayers placed herself in her books in the person of more than one character: both Hilary Thorpe of *The Nine Tailors* and Miss Meteyard of *Murder Must Advertise* echo memories of Sayers's own experiences. As Sayers herself would be the first to argue, any character in a novel to some extent embodies the character of the author, even if it is no more than a reflection of her worst nightmares. The argument has its counterpart: no character on the printed page is precisely identifiable with its author, even in autobiography. The separation between the words and the self is insurmountable.

Sayers sought to maintain a consistency within the Wimsey series—Peter's characteristics and values remain consonant from one novel to the next—but she endeavored to vary the content as well. She most feared becoming predictable or dull or, worst of all, boring to herself. She explored the range of possibilities for the detective story as she defined them, producing puzzles, thrillers, and several books that embodied elements of both. She was most comfortable with the combined puzzle-thriller. Her most patent puzzle, *The Five Red Herrings*, is, for all its obfuscations, one of her least satisfying novels. She moved twice to the other end of the spectrum, producing something approaching the thriller in *Clouds of Witness* and *Murder Must Advertise*. An intrepid Wimsey, though amusing, is a little difficult to swallow.

If Sayers had a formula, it was constructed around her belief that the truly entertaining mystery challenges the reader to figure not "who done it" but rather how it was done. She began Wimsey's career with a variation on this theme—in *Whose Body?* Sir Julian Freke's villainy is not difficult to spot, but the depths of his hideous scheme are far more difficult to fathom. The idea recurs, in an array of forms, in *Unnatural Death, The Unpleasantness at the Bellona Club, Strong Poison, Have His Carcase,* and, of course, *The Nine Tailors,* where she gives the theme its ultimate twist. By that time, she had begun to subsume the conventional mystery within a larger dimension of creative art; Sayers was not so much devising detective stories as writing literary works in which the mystery points to a larger theme. *The Nine Tailors* is ultimately a redemption story and *Gaudy Night* a novel of manners disrupted by a psychopath. *Busman's Honeymoon* began life as a comedy play.

All of Dorothy L. Sayers's books were far more than simple mystery stories. Despite her later criticisms of the first novels, Sayers from the beginning worked to create an intensely human feel for her stories. Reading the books, one sympathizes—at times empathizes—with a full range of human experiences and human emotions. Sayers's characters were not puppets playing parts in some puzzle intrigue; they were real people, caught up in a drama that would have consequences for all concerned. They were residents of a real world, and their thoughts and actions were shaped by the influences of that larger world.[28]

The most obvious of these influences was the Great War, the defining event of too many lifetimes, lived on into the twenties and thirties. The war in some way affects behaviors in every one of the Sayers novels. At times its effect is on Peter himself, as he displays the aftereffects of shell shock. Other characters display the war's impact as well: Dennis Cathcart's finances were ruined by the war as were George Fentiman's nerves. Campbell and Waters get into a fistfight over whether the Scots or the English displayed the greater bravery—twelve years after the fighting has ended. Jeff Deacon returns to Fenchurch St. Paul a dozen years after accidentally getting sent to the front, one last ghost from the Third Battle of the Marne. In 1935, Peter can still speak of Sergeant Bunter and Private Padgett. And he can still break down and weep, his nerves still unhealed. The postwar years must carry the war along; the weight of the mind-numbing memories intrudes everywhere and at any time. There is no escape.

Whether or not the war spurred the elusive, ill-defined force called modernization, its effects are everywhere visible in the Wimsey stories.

The embrace of technology is the most obvious sign: the fast cars and the crowded omnibus, the ubiquitous telephone and its booth, the yammering wireless, the so convenient airplane, the screaming billboard. England has become a faster, noisier place—or London has, at least, along with a few other places here and there. Wilvercombe is modern enough, with its splashy hotels, jazz music, ballroom dancing, and charming gigolos. Sayers points up the pace of modernization by contrasting the great town of London with any number of truly rural villages, from Stapley to Leahampton to Fenchurch St. Paul. The isolation, the slower pace of life, and the greater sense of community in these villages suggest what has been gained and lost with modern times.

The impact of science and especially medicine held a special fascination for Sayers early in her mystery-writing career. Villains in three of her first four novels prove to be connected to the medical profession; in each case, medical knowledge plays a crucial role in their villainy. Sayers was loathe to lay overmuch reliance on medical theories and therapies, as they seemed altogether divorced from any form of moral consideration. Science created power just as its practice denied the influence of the ethical—empiricism by its nature demanded a moral neutrality. When practitioners claim an ability to cure human deviance through chemical or mechanical means, Sayers's advice is to watch out. The scientist may prove the most deviant of all.

The most consistently elaborated of all Sayers's themes is her concern over the place of women in modern society. She admitted to "a foolish complex against allying myself publicly with anything labelled feminist," arguing that the best course was to take "the feminist position for granted."[29] She was the first to concede, however, that her own career had been made possible by the advance of the feminist cause, which she championed in her own way through her novels. She attacked the problem from two angles—first by drawing strong and independent modern women characters and illustrating their continued difficulties; and second, by pursuing the histories of fierce survivors of the Victorian era.

Loving portraits of Peter's mother, the Dowager Duchess of Denver, along with detailed sketches of Agatha Dawson, Lady Dormer, and Mrs. Wrayburn, provide a clear if repellant picture of women's lives in the nineteenth century. These were successfully independent women, but each was regarded as a social anomaly, in some cases cast out by their own families. By contrast, figures such as Mary Wimsey, Clara Whitaker, Sheila

Fentiman, Marjorie Phelps, and, ultimately, Harriet Vane are accepted as full participants in the public sphere, though each encounters resistance from maledom. An offspring of nobility, a professional, a working wife, a Bohemian artist, and a successful author—these women exhibited the range of potential experiences in modern society. Each is better off than her Victorian counterparts, but each has to struggle upstream in everyday society simply because she is a woman. Perhaps the most suggestive of all Sayers's women is Ann Dorland, with her curious combination of brains, acumen, and utter confusion. She must, on her own, overcome the obstacles to her own freedom and define for herself what she must be. Society, still dominated by selfishly male opinion, will offer no help.

Sayers's novels are increasingly devoted to female characters as the series continues. Most obviously through the capable and fully active presence of Harriet Vane, Sayers emphasizes the talent and potential inherent in the female half of humanity. Miss Climpson, a Victorian relic who flourishes as a sort of private detective when given the chance, perhaps emphasizes the point even more effectively. At the opposite end of the spectrum cowers Mrs. Flora Weldon, a pathetic woman of independent means but lacking the training necessary to make something of herself. She wanders aimlessly, searching for some sort of thrill to enlighten her too-constricted universe. Is this what men really want? If women are denied full access to the public world, this is what happens to them. Comparing Mrs. Weldon to Miss Climpson, the reader glimpses the consequences of potential denied.

While Dorothy L. Sayers revisited such more-or-less continuous themes as the war, the effects of modernization, the changing roles for women, and the impact of science through much of the Wimsey series, she also explored new events and experiences making themselves felt during the period. Historically, such hope as there was early in the postwar era was finally blighted after 1929 by the slump. Sayers reacted sympathetically to the hard times, although her personal fortunes were pretty much the reverse of Britain's as a whole. She became financially secure just as the national economy ground into chronic recession. In her books, she acknowledges the grinding effects of endemic poverty and its influence on popular attitudes. The air of desperation wrought by the slump's insecurities provides an atmospheric backdrop for more than one Wimsey novel. At the same time, Sayers is careful to emphasize that essential English values survive, even in the midst of widespread unemployment.

When the economic downturn brought a measure of desperation to the English people, it served to inspire an array of political solutions. The British tracked events in Europe with a mixture of awe and apprehension. Totalitarianism was on the march: in Russia in 1917, Italy in 1922, Germany in 1933, and Spain in 1936. Politicians at both ends of the political spectrum were prepared to lead Britain down the same path toward a dream of utopian salvation. Sayers grasped the dangers very early in the game, suggesting their pernicious influence in several novels before meeting the issue head-on in *Gaudy Night*. Her answer to totalitarianism was simple and conservative, a celebration of the essential efficacy of Britain's traditions. True, the British people were poorly organized, often divided, often in the way of one another's potential achievements, but there was an unmatched strength to be found in a freedom grounded in traditional values. A rigorous devotion to honest work, coupled with the old-fashioned notion of a sporting ideal and a healthy skepticism of their own history, would see the British through. This was not a terribly original thought, perhaps, but an important expression of opposition to totalitarian assumptions, geared to a popular audience.

While Sayers was well attuned to life in the public sphere, blending into the background of her novels images of both current events and persistent conditions, she was perhaps more vitally interested in the problem of values in English society. What distinguishes Sayers's detective stories is her persistent refusal to paint her fictional world in black-and-white opposites. Every situation, every character, is a realistic blend of good and bad. The persons populating her stories must confront moral ambiguity at every turn. Every action has its consequence; there is no possibility of acting for unremitting good. Even catching the murderer leads to anguished remorse: now another human being must die.

The qualities that Sayers seems to admire most, perhaps because they are so hard to come by, are the elemental virtues of loyalty, honesty, and personal integrity. For all his lighthearted, breezy, devil-may-care pose, these are the attributes most consistently found in Peter Wimsey and in the people he loves most. He falls in love at a distance with Harriet Vane for her honesty; he values his one true friend, Charles Parker, for his cautious integrity. Within his own family, he is closest to his mother and sister, mainly because they have chosen not to behave according to the dictates of their class, but rather to face life plainly.

Sayers became more forthright in her later books, outgrowing the basic dictates of the detective story to investigate the possibilities of a larger world. The values that occupied her attention achieve central importance in the last three novels. The question of doing Christian good in a modern world lies at the heart of *The Nine Tailors,* though Sayers is careful not to proselytize. A minister's daughter, she refrained from taking any religious stand in her novels. Lord Peter remains aloof, while nonconformists look for handles and High Church members become roaming Catholics. Still, the tale of quiet horror in Fenchurch St. Paul has its message: religious questions reflect the very nature of what makes us human.

Gaudy Night, the first story in which Sayers set out to point a moral, raises the riddle of human integrity to a new level. It is a confusing world, Sayers allows, full of contradictory messages and instructions. The only answer is to look into one's own soul and discover what it is that one truly cares about. Doing one's proper job simply means living the life that conscience, ability, and desire dictate. Anyone choosing to place that decision in the hands of another—be it a parent, a lover, a preacher, or a dictator—is a fool. This is Dorothy L. Sayers's essential answer for those who live in a modern world. Memories of the war may weaken the desire to do right, science may threaten traditional moral values, society may wish to deny women the freedom to choose their own lives, and the world may seem a hectic and empty place. Look within, determine your job, and let no obstacle stand in your path.

Both *Gaudy Night* and *Busman's Honeymoon* consider another complex of values and responsibilities, perhaps the questions that concerned Sayers most. Certainly the problems posed by love and marriage plagued her own life most consistently; it is a reflection of her intellectual integrity that she chose to explore them in print. Dorothy L. Sayers was unlucky in love, a victim first of unrequited love, followed by a passionless affair with a prig, then by a short, meaningless affair producing a child whom the father did not want. Then marriage—blissful at first, but turning steadily sour as the years flowed by. The degree of Sayers's success as a writer could be measured by the concomitant unhappiness in her marriage. Given such a history, it is truly amazing that she remained an idealist when it came to romantic love.

The long, painfully awkward courtship of Lord Peter and Harriet Vane would never have occurred had Sayers not believed in true love. It was her strict adherence to a code of love with integrity that forced her to keep Harriet out of Peter's arms at the close of *Strong Poison*. Having then trapped herself, she proceeded to make her main characters—two, now—as human as possible, embodying the capability to love, to distrust, to err, to forgive, and to seek forgiveness. A genuine love, a true love match, must be constructed on a foundation of mutual honesty and respect, an equality of giving and taking.

Dorothy L. Sayers had not reached the end of what she had to say on the subject of love when Peter Wimsey reached the end of his existence. As the long week-end drew to a close with the distant drone of approaching war planes, Sayers bowed to the call of other voices, other demands. She was a popular fiction writer acutely sensitive to the nuances of the real world. Demanding honesty of the characters in her novels, she herself portrayed the England she knew as honestly as she could. When the "great fun" of the detective stories ceased to be appropriate, she stopped writing them. She gave no warning, no explanation, no epitaph. Things were such that she had to make a stop, and she did so. Long afterward, she came to realize that the popular fiction portion of her writing career was done. Purposeful or not, the close of the Peter Wimsey series had the effect of making the stories an identifiable product of a specific historical moment. More than any other popular character, Lord Peter is of that era between the wars; he belongs to no other.

Sayers never killed Wimsey (as much as she at times would have liked to). Never living and never dying, he is oddly immortal. Probably if he had understood his fate, he would have grinned with a wry mouth. He was a responsible, even a serious, detective, but he is remembered best as a lighthearted soul, given to a habit of piffling that Harriet Vane came to share. The last glimpse of the Wimseys comes in the long-unpublished short story, "Talboys"—an utterly forgettable story, but for one line, one last glimpse of Peter at his mischievous best: "Harriet, absolve me now from all my sins of the future, that I may enjoy them without remorse" (451).

Ideal love.

Appendix A:
Coordinated Timeline

1918   ENGLAND   The Armistice (November); Parliamentary Reform Act (women thirty years and older can vote); general election (Lloyd George)

            SAYERS   Publishes *Catholic Tales;* meets Eric Whelpton (May)

            WIMSEY   Intelligence work in Germany; "dreadfully ill"; frontline officer; broke up with girlfriend Barbara

1919   ENGLAND   Treaty of Versailles; IRA organized; Sex Qualification Removal Act; railway strike; Sankey Commission; cenotaph constructed

            SAYERS   Leaves Blackwell's (May); L'Ecole des Roches, Verneuil, Normandy (July); concentrated interest in detective fiction

            WIMSEY   Nursing home, shell shock

1920   ENGLAND   Government of Ireland Act; coal strike; unemployment insurance extended

            SAYERS   Wimsey invented; leaves Normandy (September); official degree from Oxford (October); teaching post, Clapham High School

            WIMSEY   Bunter enters Peter's service (January); Attenbury Emeralds; Mrs. Bilt's Affair; "Copper Fingers"(April)

1921   ENGLAND   Coal miners locked out; Irish Free State; Government of India Act

            SAYERS   Experiments with detective fiction (January); meets John Cournos (March); quits teaching, illness (summer); new teaching post, Acton (autumn); *Whose Body?* completed (November); *Clouds of Witness* begun

WIMSEY   "Footsteps That Ran" (summer)

1922   ENGLAND   Lloyd George resigns; Bonar Law becomes prime minister; Conservatives win general election; BBC formed; economic slump leads to chronic unemployment; Fascists seize power in Italy

SAYERS   Begins work at Benson's (May); relationship with John Cournos ends (late summer); affair with Bill White (December)

WIMSEY   Three months in Italy, two in Paris; "Article in Question" (April); *Whose Body?* (November); "Bone of Contention" (November)

1923   ENGLAND   Stanley Baldwin prime minister; Housing Act subsidizes construction; France occupies Ruhr

SAYERS   Becomes pregnant (spring); affair with White ends (May); work on *Clouds* continues; *Whose Body?* published (May); two months leave from Benson's

WIMSEY   Three months in Corsica; return to Paris; *Clouds of Witness* (October–following January)

1924   ENGLAND   Ramsey MacDonald prime minister; Conservatives win general election (Baldwin prime minister)

SAYERS   John Anthony born (January 3); returns to Benson's (February); discovers Cournos has married; begins correspondence (August)

WIMSEY   "Meleager's Will" (June); "Man With No Face" (August)

1925   ENGLAND   Britain returns to the gold standard; Widows Pension Act; end of subsidization of coal industry

SAYERS   Meets Mac Fleming (latter half of year); last letter to Cournos (October)

WIMSEY   "Practical Joker"; "Dragon's Head" (October)

1926 ENGLAND   General Strike; Electricity Act

      SAYERS   *Clouds of Witness* published (February); marries Fleming
                 (April 13); four short stories done; working on *Unnatural
                 Death*

      WIMSEY   "Stolen Stomach" (May); "Matter of Taste"

1927 ENGLAND   Trade Union Acts make sympathetic strikes illegal;
                 collapse of the Beecham Trust

      SAYERS   *Unnatural Death* published (September)

      WIMSEY   *Unnatural Death* (April–June); "Cat in the Bag"
                 (summer); *Unpleasantness at the Bellona* Club
                 (November–December); "Cave of Ali Baba" begins
                 (December)

1928 ENGLAND   Voting age for women lowered to twenty-one; de-rating
                 brings relief to depressed areas; sound films introduced;
                 BBC comes under government control

      SAYERS   *Unpleasantness at the Bellona Club* published (July);
                 Great Short Stories, First Series (September); father dies
                 (September); *Lord Peter Views the Body* (November);
                 move to Witham, Essex (November)

      WIMSEY   In disguise as ex-footman Rogers to gather evidence for
                 "Ali Baba"

1929 ENGLAND   General election (MacDonald, Labour); Local
                 Government Act; Coal Mines Act; Beaverbrook Crusade
                 for free trade; diplomatic relations with USSR; Hatry
                 Group crashes

      SAYERS   *Tristan* published (July); mother dies (July); leaves
                 Benson's (August)

      WIMSEY   Phillip Boyes murdered (June); "Ali Baba" ends
                 (December); *Strong Poison* begins (December); road
                 accident at Fenchurch St. Paul (New Year's Eve)

1930 ENGLAND   London Naval Conference; colonial secretary opposes
                 Jewish emmigration to Palestine

	SAYERS	*Documents in the Case* (completed February, published July); visits Kircudbright (May and September)
	WIMSEY	*Strong Poison* ends (January); *Nine Tailors* investigation (spring); *Five Red Herrings* (August); vacation with Bunter in Scotland (Kircudbright); returns to Fenchurch St. Paul (Christmas Eve)
1931	ENGLAND	Great Depression begins; gold standard suspended; National Government formed under MacDonald; General Election (MacDonald, National Labour); Statute of Westminster; Japan invades Manchuria
	SAYERS	*Strong Poison* published (January); *Five Red Herrings* published (January); *Great Short Stories*, Second Series; work on Wilkie Collins biography begun
	WIMSEY	*Nine Tailors* ends (mid-January); *Have His Carcase* (June); "Incredible Elopement" (November–following January)
1932	ENGLAND	Mosley forms British Union of Fascists; Import Duties Act; Means Test; Lausanne Conference ends war reparations
	SAYERS	*Have His Carcase* published (April)
	WIMSEY	*Murder Must Advertise* (June–July); "Image in the Mirror" (fall); "Necklace of Pearls" (Christmas); "Queen's Square" (late December)
1933	ENGLAND	Hitler establishes dictatorship
	SAYERS	*Murder Must Advertise* published (February); *Hangman's Holiday* published (May)
	WIMSEY	"Absolutely Elsewhere" (fall); "The Folly" (October)
1934	ENGLAND	Germany withdraws from League of Nations
	SAYERS	*Nine Tailors* published (January); *Great Short Stories*, Third Series
	WIMSEY	"In the Teeth of the Evidence" (February)

1935 ENGLAND General election (Baldwin); Britain begins to rearm; Italy invades Abyssinia; military conscription in Germany; George V Silver Jubilee

SAYERS Work on *Busman's Honeymoon* (play)(February–September); *Gaudy Night* published (September)

WIMSEY *Gaudy Night* (spring); *Busman's Honeymoon* (October–following January)

1936 ENGLAND George V dies; accession of George VI; abdication crisis; Spanish Civil War begins

SAYERS "Thrones, Dominations" begun; *Busman's Honeymoon* opens in London (December); "Gaudy Night" essay written

WIMSEY "Haunted Policeman" (November)

Compiled by the authors, who freely acknowledge the differences between this and other efforts. The dates provided for some of the Wimsey short stories are admittedly guesswork—one guess is as good as another! Our most profound deviation from other chronologies is the dating of "The Cave of Ali Baba"; our justifications may be found in chapter three of the text. For other Wimsey chronologies, see Hodge, "Chronology," *Sayers Review*; Geoffry A. Lee, "The Wimsey Saga: A Chronology," Pamphlet (Witham, Essex: Dorothy L. Sayers Historical and Literary Society, 1977); Stephan P. Clarke, *The Lord Peter Wimsey Companion* (New York: The Mysterious Press, 1985), 522, 524; Terrance Lewis, *Sayers' Wimsey*, 123–27.

Appendix B:
On Sayers and the Sonnet

> Scorn not the Sonnet; Critic, you have frowned,
> Mindless of its just honours.
>
> —Wordsworth

It is of little import to the body of our text, perhaps trenchant only to "some scholar who might some day observe"—as Harriet's imagined academic does of Harriet's imagined *Study of Le Fanu*—that "the authors have handled their subject with insight and accuracy" (*Gaudy Night*, 241). Yet the dexterity with which Sayers puts the sonnet to work in the epigraphs as well as in the text of *Gaudy Night*, her most allusive novel, merits comment.

Harriet and Peter's sonnet recalls a recitation by ("Number there in love was slain"[1]) Romeo and Juliet. To initiate their love, Shakespeare's pair craft a sonnet. Closing on a couplet that the couple shares, the form —British, or in deference dubbed Shakespearean—suits their union perfectly:

ROMEO.	Have not saints lips, and holy palmers too?
JULIET.	Ay, pilgrim, lips that they must use in pray'r.
ROM.	O then, dear saint, let lips do what hands do,
	They pray—grant thou lest faith turn to despair.
JUL.	Saints do not move, though grant for prayers' sake.
ROM.	Then move not while my prayer's effect I take.
	(Romeo and Juliet, I.v.101–5)

Harriet and Peter fashion an Italian, or Petrarchan, sonnet. This form, broken into octave and sestet, affords the more mature couple room to

· 217 ·

meander mentally. Like Romeo, Peter takes the lead part by answering Harriet. As Juliet does, however, so Harriet owns the implicit extra "line" determining rejection or acceptance.

Wimsey's gloss beneath the piece—"A very conceited, metaphysical conclusion!"—points to a device by which ostensible disparities are joined through revelation of their likeness. The effect on the reader may be paraphrased thus: "What?! How could—O yes, of course, I see now." Lodged in lines 9–12, Peter's conceit (Renaissance parlance for ingenious idea) operates just so. A lover's sleep seems not, at first, "tension" fraught; yet on reflection, restive repose limns perfectly the intellectually stimulating, even playfully volatile, interaction of a sophisticated pair.

The image turns the entire sonnet into a conceit, as Harriet and Peter match harmoniously, though her octave and his sestet seem initially opposed. Lord Sestet has in fact discerned Miss Octave's true temperament. For as we have alluded in the text, though she lauds "the heart of rest," Harriet expends considerable creative energy on rendering that turmoil she protests to leave behind. "Wings furled" denotes a bird not flying— but at rest? Her rhythm, too, is agitated by trochees, the stress/light accent pattern that reverses the more soothing iambic unit ("Hére thĕn", "Fóldiňg", "Hére iň clóse pĕrfúme"); and by spondees, units of consecutive stresses, which elongate intensity ("Hére nó tíde rúns"; "wíde zóne"; "stíll cén[tĕr]").

Of course, the sestet does nothing to conceal its agitation, Peter having purposely turned the "peaceful, humming-top [in]to a whip-top . . . sleeping, as it were, on compulsion." Hence, the "drugged, drowsy," monosyllabic final half-line that Harriet laments is a matter of necessity: a finely crafted means of curbing the momentum of a "staggering" (Sir Philip Sidneyan) three-line fall: "For, if thou spare to smite, / Staggering, we stoop, stooping, fall dumb and dead, / And, dying so, sleep our sweet sleep no more."[2] The characters' success coincides with that of their author, for all three have performed a speech-act. Peter (and Sayers) intimate his need for a precarious stability; Harriet (and Sayers) display her corresponding disposition.

We turn now to significant epigraphs. What follows we acknowledge as highly speculative but, like criminal detection, literary criticism oughtn't to overlook the circumstantial.

Prefacing chapter four with Shakespeare's eighty-ninth sonnet neatly foreshadows, with a difference, Harriet and Peter's sonnet:

Thou canst not, Love, disgrace me half so ill,
To set a form upon desired change,
As I'll myself disgrace, knowing thy will:
I will acquaintance strangle and look strange,
Be absent from thy walks, and in my tongue
Thy sweet beloved name no more shall dwell,
Lest I, too much profane, should do it wrong,
And haply of our old acquaintance tell.

By quoting eight lines, Sayers suggestively leaves us a sestet to research. Her inclusion of the middle quatrains should not dissuade us from connecting the first four lines with the last two. (We're dealing, remember, with an inventor of codes, as in the *Have His Carcase* puzzler solved by a schema somewhat similar to the fill-in-the-blank method here endorsed.) The epigraph's relevance (which justifies citation in the first place) goes without saying. Yet the six-line answer rings more relevantly still:

Say that thou dids't forsake me for some fault,
And I will comment upon that offense.
Speak of my lameness, and I straight will halt,
Against thy reasons making no defense. . . .
For thee, against myself I'll vow debate,
For I must ne'er love him whom thou dost hate.
(Sonnet 89, ll. 1–4, 13–14)

Peter is ever "commenting on his own offenses"—and this blither more closely endears him to Harriet and compensates in some respect for the failings that prompt the chatter. The strategy, moreover, is disarming. How chastise one for lameness once the accused party has halted? "For thee, against myself I'll vow," indeed.

Some say thy fault is youth, some wantonness,
Some say thy grace is youth and gentle sport;
Both grace and faults are loved of more and less;
Thou makes faults graces that to thee resort.

The epigraph to chapter ten (209), culled from Shakespeare's ninety-sixth sonnet (ll. 1–4), comments blithely on Saint-George, ransomed over and again by dear Uncle Peter. The final couplet may well articulate (and by its absence from the epigraph, enact) what oft his Lordship thought, though ne'er so well expressed:[3] "But do not so, I love thee in such sort, / As thou being mine, mine is thy good report." (And these lines, incidentally, stand out in Shakespeare's canon because they conclude *two* sonnets, 96 and 36: "Let me confess that we too must be twain, . . ."). Deduction: As incorrigible as the Viscount is his uncle's generosity.

Our whimsy fans us still further—beyond the novel's bounds, though within (we hope) the yard of telling comparison. The publication of Auden's sonnet postdates *Gaudy Night* by one year; even so, the resonance proves difficult to ignore.

"The great man," Harriet reflects, with more than a little cheek intended toward that personage, "could marry where he liked, not being restricted to great women; indeed it was often found sweet and commendable in him to choose a woman of no sort of greatness at all" (53). With similar irreverence, Auden wrote:

> *Who's Who*
> A shilling life will give you all the facts:
> How Father beat him, how he ran away,
> What were the struggles of his youth, what acts
> Made him the greatest figure of his day:
> Of how he fought, fished, hunted, worked all night,
> Though giddy, climbed new mountains, named a sea:
> Some of the last researchers even write
> Love made him weep his pints like you and me.
>
> With all his honours on, he sighed for one
> Who, say astonished critics, lived at home;
> Did little jobs about the house with skill
> And nothing else; could whistle; would sit still
> Or potter round the garden; answered some
> Of his long marvelous letters but kept none.[4]

While consistent with Harriet's sarcasm, this sestet reads antithetically to that in the Vane-Wimsey sonnet. The opposition is semantic and structural. The woman is portrayed in Auden's last half-dozen lines;

conversely, Peter authors their sestet—and he bears no resemblance to the supposed "great man" who, in "Who's Who," is maudlin ("Love made him weep his pints"); and fatuous. (Who—excepting "Who"—runs about naming seas these days? For "figure" one can read "cipher"; "fought, fished, hunted, worked all night" reads like filler in a drugstore "shilling life" biography; and "giddy"ness is prominently featured.) Harriet could never abide such a man, nor could Peter abide being such. He would honor her, rather, by complementing her accomplishment with his own.

Notes

INTRODUCTION

1. Sayers wrote her last Wimsey story, "Talboys," in 1942. This work remained unpublished in her lifetime. See Dorothy L. Sayers, *Lord Peter: A Collection of All the Lord Peter Wimsey Stories,* comp. James Sandoe (New York: Harper and Row, 1972), 431–53.

2. F. Scott Fitzgerald, *The Jazz Age* (New York: New Directions, 1996), 13.

3. Robert Graves and Alan Hodge, *The Long Week-End: A Social History of Great Britain, 1918–1939* (New York: W. W. Norton and Company, 1963).

4. Among the better examinations of Sayers's mystery writings are James Bernard Burleson, "A Study of the Novels of Dorothy L. Sayers" (Ph.D. diss., University of Texas, 1965); Mary Brian Durkin, *Dorothy L. Sayers* (Boston: Twayne Publishers, 1980), 27–100; and Dawson Gaillard, *Dorothy L. Sayers* (New York: Frederick Ungar, 1981).

5. For an angry critique of Sayers's fiction in the context of the postwar era, see Martin Green, "The Detection of a Snob: Martin Green on Lord Peter Wimsey," *The Listener* 69 (Mar. 14, 1963): 461, 464. A broader perspective on the same issue, one that discusses Sayers's work in passing, is Colin Watson, *Snobbery with Violence: Crime Stories and Their Audience* (London: Eyre and Spottiswoode, 1971).

6. The transition from the traditional to the modern is examined in fascinating and challenging detail in Modris Eksteins, *Rites of Spring: The Great War and the Birth of the Modern Age* (New York: Anchor Books, Doubleday, 1989). The historical framework on which this book rests is supplied largely by Eksteins and by Graves and Hodge, *The Long Week-End.* In the pages to follow, we sketch the general political history of Britain and Europe during the era, essentially to remind readers of what was going on in the larger world. We make no claim to original or exhaustive research in these areas. Reference notes should be regarded as little more than suggestions for further reading.

7. One discussion of Sayers's use of real news stories in her works is Sharyn McCrumb, "Where the Bodies are Buried: The Real Murder Cases in the Crime Novels of Dorothy L. Sayers," in *Dorothy L. Sayers: The Centennial Celebration,* ed. Alzina Stone Dale (New York: Walker and Company, 1993), 87–98.

8. For a readily accessible celebration of Sayers's endurance, see Carolyn Heilbrun, "Reappraisals: Sayers, Lord Peter and God," reprinted in Dorothy L. Sayers, *Lord Peter: A Collection of All the Lord Peter Wimsey Stories,* comp. James Sandoe (New York: Harper and Row, 1972), 431–46.

9. Terrance L. Lewis addresses the problem of treating Lord Peter as a real person in his study, *Dorothy L. Sayers' Wimsey and Interwar British Society* (Lewiston, Maine.: Edwin Mellon Press, 1994), v. Lewis's book pioneers the study of Wimsey in historic context. His discussions of Sayers's perspective on the English class system and the effects of "the Slump" are especially enlightening. (See pp. 15–56.)

10. A term for the imaginary which Sayers employs on several occasions. A good example may be found in the "Author's Note" in Dorothy L. Sayers, *Gaudy Night* (1936; reprint, New York: HarperPerennial, 1993), vi. For the sake of consistency, all references to Sayers's fiction will be made to the Harper-Perennial edition, unless otherwise noted.

11. For Terrance L. Lewis on the war, see *Sayers' Wimsey,* 1–14.

12. Terrance L. Lewis treats "The Changing Status of Women" in *Sayers' Wimsey,* 57–74.

13. See Eksteins, *Rites of Spring,* for an elaboration of this argument.

14. Dorothy L. Sayers, *Strong Poison* (1930; reprint, New York: HarperPerennial, 1993), 88.

15. Terrance L. Lewis considers "Politics and the Changing World" in *Sayers' Wimsey,* 89–96.

16. Graves and Hodge, *The Long Week-End,* 291.

1. LORD PETER BEGINS A CAREER

1. In compiling the biographical details of Dorothy L. Sayers for this work, we have made lavish use of seven different biographies, each with its strengths and weaknesses. These are, in order of publication: Janet Hitchman, *Such a Strange Lady: A Biography of Dorothy L. Sayers* (New York: Harper and Row, 1975); Alzina Stone Dale, *Maker and Craftsman: The Story of Dorothy L. Sayers* (Grand Rapids, Mich.: William B. Eerdmans, 1978); Ralph E. Hone, *Dorothy L. Sayers: A Literary Biography* (Kent, Ohio: Kent State University Press, 1979); James Brabazon, *Dorothy L. Sayers: A Biography* (New York: Charles P. Scribner's Sons, 1981); Catherine Kenney, *The Remarkable Case of Dorothy L. Sayers* (Kent, Ohio: Kent State University Press, 1990); David Coomes, *Dorothy L. Sayers: A Careless Rage for Life* (Batavia, Ill.: Lion Publishing, 1992); Barbara Reynolds, *Dorothy L. Sayers: Her Life and Soul* (New York: St. Martin's Press, 1993). It is generally surprising how little space is devoted to the development of the Lord Peter Wimsey novels in any of these. Frankly, we regard Barbara Reynolds's book as far and away the best of the seven, and we will cite her work generally for biographical information. For details of Sayers's early life, consult Reynolds, 1–44.

2. Reynolds, *Sayers: Her Life and Soul,* 45–62. For a personal reminiscence of Sayers from a distant but most perceptive acquaintance, see Vera Brittain, *Testament of Youth* (London: Victor Gollancz, 1933), 106, 482, 508, 510.

3. Ibid., 59–62.

4. An excellent treatment of prewar Europe is Eric Hobsbawm, *The Age of Empire: 1865–1914* (London: Weidenfeld and Nicholson, 1987). See also Oron J. Hale, *The Great Illusion, 1900–1914* (New York: Harper and Row, 1974). An excellent short summary of the subject is provided by Joachim Remak, *The Origins of World War I, 1871–1914,* 2d ed. (New York: Harcourt Brace, 1994).

5. The best work regarding Britain and the approach of the war is Zara S. Steiner, *Britain and the Origins of the First World War* (New York: St. Martin's Press, 1979).

6. Joachim Remak, *Sarajevo: The Story of a Political Murder* (New York: Criterion Books, 1959).

7. Historians generally agree that the most comprehensive and balanced treatment of the Great War is B. Liddell Hart, *History of the First World War* (London: Pan Books, 1970). A less intimidating overview is provided in James L. Stokesbury, *A Short History of World War I* (New York: William Morrow, 1981). Stokesbury's discussion of the impact of new weapons technology may be found on pp. 14–18.

8. Two studies by Martin van Creveld examine von Schlieffen's plan exhaustively: *Supplying War* (Cambridge: Cambridge University Press, 1977) and *Command in Wartime* (Cambridge, Mass.: Harvard University Press, 1977). See also Stokesbury, *World War I,* 32–61.

9. Stokesbury, *World War I,* 36–60.

10. Reynolds, *Sayers: Her Life and Soul,* 72–76. See also Dorothy L. Sayers to Muriel Jaeger, Feb. 6, 1916, *The Letters of Dorothy L. Sayers: 1899 to 1936: The Making of a Detective Novelist,* ed. Barbara Reynolds (New York: St. Martin's Press, 1995), 121–22. Two excellent works examine the impact of trench warfare on the common British soldier: Denis Winter, *Death's Men: Soldiers of the Great War* (London: Penguin Books, 1979); and John Ellis, *Eye-Deep in Hell: Trench Warfare in World War I* (Baltimore: Johns Hopkins University Press, 1976).

11. Stokesbury, *World War I,* 194–307.

12. The best treatment of the peacemaking is Arno Mayer, *The Politics and Diplomacy of Peacemaking* (New York: Random House, 1973).

13. A truly perceptive and captivating study of the grieving necessitated by the war is Jay Winter, *Sites of Memory, Sites of Mourning: The Great War in European Cultural History* (Cambridge: Cambridge University Press, 1995).

14. Graves, *The Long Week-End,* 1–39. For an excellent summary of the recent scholarship on sex and gender relationships during and after the war, see Gail Braybon, "Women and the War," in *The First World War in British History,* ed. Stephen Constantine, Maurice W. Kirby and Mary B. Rose (London: Edward Arnold, 1995), 141–67.

15. Graves, *The Long Week-End,* 1–39; Winter, *Death's Men,* 235–65; Braybon, "Women and the War."

16. Winter, *Sites of Memory,* 1–53.

17. Ibid., 78–116; Dorothy L. Sayers, *Clouds of Witness* (1926; reprint, New York: HarperPerennial, 1993), 189.

18. Winter, *Sites of Memory,* 102–5.

19. Though somewhat dated, the best summary of Britain's postwar troubles is A. J. P. Taylor, *English History, 1914–1945* (Oxford: Oxford University Press, 1965), 120–62.

20. Reynolds, *Sayers: Her Life and Soul,* 63–84.

21. Ibid., 85–106.

22. Ibid., 94–95.

23. A thumbnail sketch of the origins and career of Sexton Blake appears in William L. DeAndrea, *Encyclopedia Mysteriosa* (New York: Prentice Hall, 1994), 29. DeAndrea's work is an excellent source of obscure information on the history and development of detective fiction.

24. Dorothy L. Sayers, "Untitled," unpublished MS, MS 138 (thirteen pages) presumably written in 1920. Sayers Collection of the Marion E. Wade Center, Wheaton College, Wheaton, Illinois (hereafter cited as Sayers Collection, Wade Center). We wish to thank the David Higham Associates on behalf of the Estate of Anthony Fleming for permission to photocopy this manuscript. Barbara Reynolds does an excellent job of describing and analyzing this ragged piece of early Sayers fiction, and she includes this first description of Peter Wimsey, quoted in our subsequent paragraph, in *Sayers: Her Life and Soul,* 171–73.

25. Sayers, "Untitled."

26. Dorothy L. Sayers, "The Mousehole: A Detective Fantasia in Three Flats," unfinished MS, MS 138, *Sayers Collection* (thirteen pages). See also Reynolds, *Sayers: Her Life and Soul,* 174.

27. Dorothy L. Sayers, "How I Came to Invent the Character of Lord Peter," *Harcourt Brace News* 1 (July 15, 1936): 1–2.

28. Sayers to her mother, Jan. 22, 1921, *Letters,* 174.

29. Dorothy L. Sayers, *Whose Body?* (1923; reprint, New York: HarperCollins, 1995), 13, 61.

30. There are, of course, entire libraries of material devoted to Sherlock Holmes. Most, unfortunately, treat him as if he were a real historical figure, seriously compromising the interpretation. A happy exception to this is Rosemary Jann, *The Adventures of Sherlock Holmes: Detecting Social Order* (New York: Twayne Publishers, 1995). There is no substitute for the genuine article however: Arthur Conan Doyle, *The Complete Sherlock Holmes* (New York: Doubleday, 1930).

31. Gordon Phillips, "The Social Impact," in *First World War in British History,* ed. Constantine, Kirby, and Rose, 106–40. Lord Peter explains that Duke's Denver operates at a loss in Dorothy L. Sayers, *Have His Carcase* (1932; reprint,

New York: Harper Perennial, 1993), 154–55. He expresses his fears regarding the future of Duke's Denver in Sayers, *Gaudy Night,* 289.

32. Sayers, *Whose Body?* 165, 177, 186–87. For a perspective on Lord Peter as a "dissenter from the values of Duke's Denver," see Erik Routley, *The Puritan Pleasures of the Detective Story: A Personal Monograph* (London: Victor Gollancz, 1972), 139–41.

33. Sayers, *Whose Body?* 176–77, 186. An excellent discussion of the influence of sport on British society is John Lowerson, *Sport and the English Middle Classes* (Manchester: Manchester University Press, 1993). Perhaps the truest personification of this ethic during the 1920s was the American golfer Bobby Jones. See Peter Dobereiner, "My, But You're a Wonder, Sir," *Bobby Jones: The Greatest of Them All,* ed. Martin Davis (Greenwich, Conn.: The American Golfer, 1996), 38–47. Harriet Vane's thoughts on the subject may be found in Sayers, *Gaudy Night,* 142.

34. Ellis, *Eye-Deep in Hell,* 7–70.

35. Ibid., 161–205; Winter, *Death's Men,* 223–34. Siegfried Sassoon embodied the new attitude in his later war poetry:

> *Base Details*
> If I were fierce, and bald, and short of breath,
> I'd live with scarlet Majors at the Base,
> And speed glum heroes up the line to death.
> You'd see me with my puffy petulant face,
> Guzzling and gulping in the best hotel,
> Reading the Roll of Honour. "Poor young chap,"
> I'd say—"I used to know his father well;
> Yes, we've lost heavily in that last scrap."
> And when the war is done and youth stone dead,
> I'd toddle home and die—in bed.

The Penguin Book of First World War Poetry, ed. Jon Silkin (London: Penguin, 1981), 131.

36. Eksteins, *Rites of Spring,* 139–238; Robert Graves, *Good-Bye to All That* (New York: Doubleday, 1929), 82–244.

37. Ellis, *Eye-Deep in Hell,* 123–59; Eksteins, *Rites of Spring,* 170–91.

38. Dorothy L. Sayers, "Gaudy Night," in *Titles to Fame,* ed. Denys K. Roberts (London: Nelson, 1937). The essay was republished in *The Art of the Mystery Story,* ed. Howard Haycraft (New York: Carroll and Graf, 1992), 208–21. Subsequent citations will refer to the latter source.

39. Sayers to David Higham, Nov. 27, 1936, *Letters,* 405–6.

40. James Brabazon maintains that Dorothy L. Sayers was consciously anti-Semitic, in *Sayers: A Biography,* 216–19, a charge refuted by Carolyn G. Heilbrun in "Dorothy L. Sayers: Biography Between the Lines," in Dale, *Sayers*

Centenary, 1–14. Nancy-Lou Patterson agrees that Sayers's treatment of ethnic stereotypes was ill considered. See "Images of Judaism and Anti-Semitism in the Novels of Dorothy L. Sayers," *Sayers Review* 2, no. 2 (June 1978): 17–24. A most perceptive critique of British anti-Semitism is George Orwell, "Antisemitism in Britain," in *The Collected Essays, Journalism, and Letters of George Orwell,* 4 vols., ed. Sonia Orwell and Ian Angus (New York: Harcourt, Brace and World, 1968), 3: 332–41.

41. Dorothy L. Sayers, ed., "Introduction" to *Great Short Stories of Detection, Mystery, and Horror* (London: Victor Gollancz, 1928). Republished in Haycraft, *Art of the Mystery Story,* as "The Omnibus of Crime," 71–109. Subsequent citations will reference the latter publication.

42. Two excellent books consider the impact of the war on modern literature: Paul Fussell, *The Great War and Modern Memory* (New York: Oxford University Press, 1975); and Samuel Hynes, *A War Imagined: The First World War and English Culture* (London: Bodley Head, 1990).

43. Ezra Pound, *Literary Essays of Ezra Pound* [1935], ed. T. S. Eliot (New York: New Directions, 1968), 4.

44. For examples, see Virginia Woolf, *Mrs. Dalloway* (New York: Harcourt Brace, 1925) and *To the Lighthouse* (New York: Harcourt Brace, 1927); William Faulkner, *The Sound and the Fury* (New York: Random House, 1929) and *As I Lay Dying* (New York: Random House, 1930); James Joyce, *Ulysses* (New York: Random House, 1922). For a discussion of the development of modern narrative form, see James Mellard, *The Exploded Form: The Modernist Novel in America* (Philadelphia: University of Pennsylvania Press, 1980); or Randall Stevenson, *Modernist Fiction: An Introduction* (Lexington: University of Kentucky Press, 1992).

45. Sayers's most unusual experiment came with the publication, with Robert Eustace, of *The Documents in the Case,* an epistolary mystery novel published in 1930 (reprint; New York: HarperPerennial Library, 1987).

46. Sayers to her mother, Nov. 8, 1921, *Letters,* 180.

47. Reynolds, *Sayers: Her Life and Soul,* 225.

2. LORD PETER DISCOVERS THE POSSIBILITIES

1. Mary B. Rose, "Britain and the International Economy," in Constantine, Kirby, and Rose, *First World War in British History,* 231–51; A. J. P. Taylor, *English History, 1914–1945* (Oxford: Oxford University Press, 1965), 134–35, 189, 203–4.

2. Taylor, *English History,* 227–60.

3. Graves and Hodge, *The Long Week-End,* 139–59; Taylor, *English History,* 242–50.

4. Taylor, *English History,* 242–50. For a historical overview of the general strike, see Patrick Renshaw, *Nine Days That Shook Britain: The 1926 General Strike* (Garden City, N.Y.: Anchor Books, Doubleday, 1976).

5. Dorothy L. Sayers, *Unnatural Death* (1927; reprint, New York: Harper-Perennial, 1993), 62.

6. Reynolds, *Sayers: Her Life and Soul,* 107–16.

7. Ibid.; Sayers to John Cournos, Aug. 13, 1925, *Letters,* 237.

8. Reynolds, *Sayers: Her Life and Soul,* 117–70.

9. Sayers to John Cournos, Oct. 27, Dec. 4, 1924, *Letters,* 218, 221.

10. The extant letters from Sayers to Cournos are printed in Sayers, *Letters,* 215–33, 236–41.

11. Reynolds, *Sayers: Her Life and Soul,* 141–70.

12. Sayers to her mother, June 13, 1924, *Letters,* 215.

13. Sayers to her parents, Mar. 3, 1922, *Letters,* 189.

14. Sayers to John Cournos, Jan. 25, 1925, *Letters,* 224.

15. Sayers to John Cournos, Feb. 22, 1925, *Letters,* 230.

16. Sayers to John Cournos, Mar. 28, 1925, *Letters,* 231; Reynolds, *Sayers: Her Life and Soul,* 202–3.

17. Sayers, *Clouds of Witness,* 27–28.

18. Sayers, *Unnatural Death,* 112.

19. Ibid., 217.

20. Ibid.; Sayers to John Cournos, Oct. 18, 1925, *Letters,* 239–41.

21. Sayers, *Unnatural Death,* 21.

22. For further discussion of Sayers's portrayal of women as villains, see Virginia B. Morris, "Arsenic and Blue Lace: Sayers' Criminal Women," *Modern Fiction Studies* 29 (autumn 1983):485–95.

23. Sayers, *Unnatural Death,* 216. For a discussion of Sayers's use of humor, see Catherine Kenney, "The Comedy of Dorothy L. Sayers," in Dale, *Sayers Centenary,* 139–50.

24. Sayers, *Unnatural Death,* 229–30.

25. Peter Laslett, *The World We Have Lost: England Before the Industrial Age,* 3d ed. (New York: Charles Scribner's Sons, 1984).

26. Deborah Valenze, *The First Industrial Woman* (Oxford: Oxford University Press, 1995); Bonnie S. Anderson and Judith P. Zinsser, *A History of Their Own: Women in Europe from Prehistory to the Present,* vol. 2 (New York: Harper and Row, 1988); Genevieve Fraisse and Michelle Perrot, eds., *A History of Women; Emerging Feminism from Revolution to World War,* vol. 4 (Cambridge, Mass.: Belknap of Harvard, 1993).

27. Mary Poovey, *Uneven Developments: The Ideological Work of Gender in Mid-Victorian England* (Chicago: University of Chicago Press, 1988); Judith R. Walkowitz, *Prostitution and Victorian Society: Women, Class, and the State* (New York: Cambridge University Press, 1980). Edward H. Clarke, *Sex in Education: or A Fair Chance for the Girls* (Boston: J. R. Osgood, 1873) provides one of the clearest statements connecting education to physical harm of female reproductive organs.

28. See for instance Nancy Cott, "Passionlessness: An Interpretation of Victorian Sexual Ideology, 1790–1850," *Signs* 4 (1978): 219–36; Carroll Smith-Rosenberg, *Disorderly Conduct: Visions of Gender in Victorian America* (New York: Alfred A. Knopf, 1985).

29. See Cott, "Passionlessness."

30. Deborah Kuhn McGregor, *From Midwives to Medicine: the Birth of American Gynecology* (New Brunswick, N.J.: Rutgers University Press, 1998), 153–55; John Cournos, *The Devil is an English Gentleman* (New York: Liveright, 1932); Reynolds, *Sayers: Her Life and Soul*, 114–16.

31. Judith R. Walkowitz, *City of Dreadful Delight: Narratives of Sexual Danger in Late-Victorian London* (Chicago: University of Chicago Press, 1992); Carl Degler, "What Ought to Be and What Was: Women's Sexuality in the Nineteenth Century," *American Historical Review* 79 (1974): 1467–90.

32. Michael C. C. Adams, *The Great Adventure: Male Desire and the Coming of World War I* (Bloomington: University of Indiana Press, 1990), 9–45.

33. Jann, *Adventures of Sherlock Holmes*, 3–6, 103–26.

34. Adams, *The Great Adventure*, 47–112; Eksteins, *Rites of Spring*, 76–135. For a vivid rendering of what it was for a young woman to grow up amidst the assumptions of the old culture, the reader can do no better than Vera Brittain, *Testament of Youth* (London: Victor Gollancz, 1933).

35. Sayers, *Unnatural Death*, 148.

36. Ibid., 155.

37. Dorothy L. Sayers, *The Unpleasantness at the Bellona Club* (1928; reprint, New York: HarperPerennial, 1993), 14–16.

38. Dorothy L. Sayers, *Strong Poison*, 100–102, 112–14.

39. Reynolds, *Sayers: Her Life and Soul*, 199–211.

40. Sayers, *Unnatural Death*, 37.

41. Reynolds, *Sayers: Her Life and Soul*, 200–201. Reynolds quotes a letter from Sayers to Maurice Reckitt, Nov. 19, 1941.

42. Graves and Hodge, *The Long Week-End*; Sayers, *Clouds of Witness*, 212.

43. Reynolds, *Sayers: Her Life and Soul*, 225–27.

44. Eksteins, *Rites of Spring*, 275–99; Hynes, *A War Imagined*, 425–26.

45. Reynolds, *Sayers: Her Life and Soul*, 35–36; Hone, *Dorothy L. Sayers*, 10.

46. Sayers, *Unpleasantness at the Bellona Club*, 298.

3. Lord Peter Acquires a Soul

1. Taylor, *English History*, 321–49; Graves and Hodge, *The Long Week-End*, 235–53; Charles Kindleberger, *The World in Depression, 1929–1939*, rev. ed. (Berkeley: University of California Press, 1986).

2. Graves and Hodge, *The Long Week-End*, 211–12.

3. Ibid., 212; "Clarence Hatry," *The Banker* 13 (May 1985): 78–79; Thomas Jaffe (ed.), "Clarence Who?" *Forbes* 146 (July 9, 1990): 120.

4. Taylor, *English History*, 321–49.

5. Sayers, *Strong Poison*, 124, 131.

6. Ibid., 136.

7. Reynolds, *Sayers: Her Life and Soul*, 225–26.

8. Sayers to Victor Gollancz, Nov. 25, 1927, *Letters*, 266–67.

9. Reynolds, *Sayers: Her Life and Soul*, 225–26.

10. Sayers to Victor Gollancz, Nov. 28, 1927, *Letters*, 267–68.

11. Sayers to her parents, Aug. 15, 1928, *Letters*, 282.

12. Dorothy L. Sayers, "The Abominable History of the Man with Copper Fingers" and "The Entertaining Episode of the Article in Question," in *Lord Peter Views the Body*, (1928; reprint, New York: HarperPerennial, 1993), 5–40.

13. Sayers, "The Vindictive Story of the Footsteps That Ran," in *Lord Peter Views the Body*, 174.

14. Sayers, "The Undignified Melodrama of the Bone of Contention" and "The Learned Adventure of the Dragon's Head," in *Lord Peter Views the Body*, 93–160, 197–222.

15. For a discussion of the Wimsey short stories, see Durkin, *Sayers*, 84–100.

16. Sayers to Harold Bell, Mar. 12, 1933, *Letters*, 330.

17. Sayers to Harold Bell, Feb. 4, Mar. 12, 1933, *Letters*, 325–34.

18. An anonymous reviewer noted in 1935 that Sayers took meticulous care to maintain an internal consistency in the Wimsey chronology. See "The Exploits of Lord Peter Wimsey," *Times* (London), July 12, 1935, 9.

19. Sayers, "The Cave of Ali Baba," in *Lord Peter Views the Body*, 283–317.

20. Sayers, *Strong Poison*, 126.

21. Three authors have considered aspects of this subject. See Jonathon Hodge, "Chronology," *Sayers Review* 1, no. 4 (July 1977): 10; Geoffrey A. Lee, "The Wimsey Saga," *Proceedings of the Seminar, 1977* (Witham, Essex: Dorothy L. Sayers Historical and Literary Society, Archives), 2–12; Alzina Stone Dale, "Fossils in Cloud-Cuckoo Land," *Sayers Review* 3, no. 2 (Dec. 1978): 1–13.

22. Sayers, "Gaudy Night," in *Titles to Fame*, ed. Dennis K. Roberts (London: Nelson, 1937). Reprinted in Haycraft, *Art of the Mystery Story*, 210.

23. Sayers to Eustace Barton, May 7, 1928, *Letters*, 274.

24. Sayers and Eustace, *Documents in the Case*; Reynolds, *Sayers: Her Life and Soul*, 213–24; Trevor H. Hall, *Dorothy L. Sayers: Ten Literary Studies* (Hamden, Conn.: Archon Books, 1980), 62–103. Sayers's extensive correspondence with Barton is contained in *Letters*, 272–89, 298–99, 302–5, 308, 310–11, 323. Dawson Gaillard maintains that *The Documents in the Case* is Sayers's best crime novel. See Gaillard, *Sayers*, 45–54. H. R. F. Keating also defends *Documents* in "Dorothy L.'s Mickey Finn," in Dale, *Sayers Centenary*, 129–38.

25. Reynolds, *Sayers: Her Life and Soul*, 206–9.

26. Sayers to Ivy Shrimpton, Oct. 18, 1928, *Letters*, 287.

27. Reynolds, *Sayers: Her Life and Soul*, 208–10.

28. Sayers to Ivy Shrimpton, Dec. 10, 1928, *Letters,* 289–90.

29. Reynolds, *Sayers: Her Life and Soul,* 210–11.

30. Sayers to her mother, Apr. 8, July 12, 1926, *Letters,* 245–47, 249–50; Hall, *Ten Literary Studies,* 40–51.

31. Reynolds, *Sayers: Her Life and Soul,* 234–35.

32. Ibid., 231–33.

33. Ibid., 210–11, 225–35; Sayers to Ivy Shrimpton, Nov. 11, 1933, *Letters,* 239.

34. Dorothy L. Sayers, *Tristan in Brittany* (London: Ernest Benn, 1929).

35. Sayers to Donald Tovey, Jan. 18, 1934, *Letters,* 340.

36. Sayers, *Strong Poison,* 45–46.

37. Ibid., 69.

38. Dorothy L. Sayers, *The Nine Tailors: Changes Rung on an Old Theme in Two Short Touches and Two Long Peals* (New York: Harcourt, Brace, and Jovanovich, 1934), 10.

39. For a brief discussion of Sayers's development of Wimsey as a character, see Julian Symons, *The Detective Story in Britain* (Harlow, Essex: Longman, Greens and Company, 1969), 26–28.

40. Sayers, "Gaudy Night," 210.

41. Kevin I. Jones, *Conan Doyle and the Spirits: The Spiritualist Career of Sir Arthur Conan Doyle* (Wellingsborough, England: Aquarium Press, 1989).

42. Ibid., 109–31; Winter, *Sites of Memory, Sites of Mourning,* 58–77.

43. Reynolds, *Sayers: Her Life and Soul,* 112–14.

44. Stephen Spender, *The Struggle of the Modern* (Berkeley: University of California Press, 1963). Virginia Woolf was among a small coterie of Britons who did believe that the nature of art and humanity had really changed: Virginia Woolf, "Mr. Bennett and Mrs. Brown," in *Collected Essays,* vol. 1 (1923; reprint, New York: Harcourt Brace and World, 1966).

45. Eksteins, *Rites of Spring,* 55–135; Malcolm Smith, "The War and British Culture," in Constantine, Kirby, and Rose, *First World War in British History,* 168–83.

46. Wilfred Owen, "Insensibility," in *Penguin Book of First World War Poetry,* 189. John Silkin's introduction provides a thoughtful analysis on the place of the war poets in British literary history.

47. Hynes, *A War Imagined,* 269–463.

48. Smith, "The War and British Culture," 168–83.

49. Sayers, *Strong Poison,* 88.

50. Sayers, "Gaudy Night," 211.

51. For a discussion of Harriet Vane's influence on the direction of the Wimsey stories, see Margaret P. Hanay, "Harriet's Influence on the Characterization of Lord Peter Wimsey," in *As Her Whimsey Took Her,* ed. Margaret P. Hanay (Kent, Ohio: Kent State University Press, 1979), 36–50.

52. Dorothy L. Sayers, *The Five Red Herrings* (previously published as *Suspicious Characters,* 1931; reprint, New York: HarperPerennial, 1993), 176.

53. For a discussion of the novel, see Lionel Basney, "*The Nine Tailors* and the Complexity of Innocence," in Hanay, *As Her Whimsey Took Her,* 23–35.

54. Dorothy L. Sayers, "Notebook: The Nine Tailors," Original Notebook (MS 151), Sayers Collection, Wade Center.

55. Reynolds, *Sayers: Her Life and Soul,* 237–46; Sayers to Victor Gollancz, Sept. 14, 1932, *Letters,* 322–23.

56. Several of Sayers's biographers cite the influence of her religious outlook on the Wimsey stories, though most tend to overdo it, reading backward from her later career as a Christian apologist. This seems especially true of David Coomes, *Sayers: A Careless Rage for Life;* Dale, *Maker and Craftsman;* and to a lesser extent, Hone, *Dorothy L. Sayers;* and Kenney, *Remarkable Case of Dorothy L. Sayers.* See also Stephen Hahn, "Theodocy in Dorothy L. Sayers' *Murder Must Advertise,*" *Renascence* 41 (spring 1989): 169–76.

57. Sayers, *Strong Poison,* 167.

58. For a discussion of Lord Peter's religious development, see Lionel Basney, "God and Peter Wimsey," *Christianity Today* 17 (Sept. 14, 1973): 27–28.

4. LORD PETER DISPLAYS HIS RANGE

1. Among those singing the praises of Sayers's detective stories are "Little 'Tecs' Have Little Crooks," *New Statesman and Nation* 3 (May 7, 1932): 594; and H. R. F. Keating, *Murder Must Appetize* (London: Lemon Tree Press, 1975). For a discussion of Sayers as the Queen of Crime, see "D. L. S.: An Unsteady Throne?" in Dale, *Sayers Centenary,* 23–30.

2. Sayers, introduction to "The Omnibus of Crime," in Haycraft, *The Art of the Mystery Story,* 71.

3. Sayers, "The Omnibus of Crime," 71–83. Quotations, 72.

4. Ibid., 83.

5. Ibid., 89–93; quotation, 89; Reynolds, *Sayers: Her Life and Soul,* 196–97. See also E. R. Gregory, "Wilkie Collins and Dorothy L. Sayers," in Hanay, *As Her Whimsey Took Her,* 51–64.

6. Sayers, "The Omnibus of Crime," 92–97. Sayers later wrote a series of essays on Sherlock Holmes minutiae in which she addressed the mystery of Doctor Watson's given name. See Dorothy L. Sayers, "Studies in Sherlock Holmes," in *Unpopular Opinions* (London: Victor Gollancz, 1946).

7. Sayers, "The Omnibus of Crime," 95–97.

8. Ibid., 97–109. For an intriguing critique of Sayers's critique, see Raymond Chandler, "The Simple Art of Murder," in Haycraft, *Art of the Mystery Story,* 222–37. Two later discussions of Sayers on the mystery story are Catherine Aird, "It Was the Cat!," in Dale, *Sayers Centenary,* 79–86; and Aaron Elkins, "The Art

of Framing Lies: Dorothy L. Sayers on Mystery Fiction," in Dale, *Sayers Centenary,* 99–107.

9. Reynolds, *Sayers: Her Life and Soul,* 173. Sayers enjoyed playing with character names as well. In the short story "The Undignified Melodrama of the Bone of Contention," two brothers named Haviland and Martin fight over their father's unusual will. In the novel *Have His Carcase,* the murderer takes an assumed name while camping out in disguise—the name: Haviland Martin.

10. Sayers, *Whose Body?* 244. For a discussion of Sayers's debt to Bentley, see Barbara Reynolds, "The Origin of Lord Peter Wimsey," *Sayers Review* 2, no. 1 (May 1978): 1–16, 21.

11. Sayers, "The Omnibus of Crime," 104.

12. Dorothy L. Sayers, introduction to E. C. Bentley, *Trent's Last Case* (1930; reprint, New York: Carroll and Graf, 1991), x–xiii; quotation xii.

13. Sayers, *Unnatural Death,* 250; Sayers, "The Omnibus of Crime," 108; DeAndrea, *Encyclopedia Mysteriosa,* 126–27.

14. Sayers, "The Omnibus of Crime," 103.

15. Ibid., 102.

16. Sayers, *Unpleasantness at the Bellona Club,* 304; Willard Huntington Wright, "The Great Detective Stories" in Haycraft, *Art of the Mystery Story,* 58; DeAndrea, *Encyclopedia Mysteriosa,* 367.

17. Sayers to Muriel St. Clare Byrne, Oct. 30, 1930, *Letters,* 310.

18. Sayers to Victor Gollancz, Jan. 22, 1931, *Letters,* 312.

19. Sayers, *Five Red Herrings,* 142; DeAndrea, *Encyclopedia Mysteriosa,* 62; Sayers, "The Omnibus of Crime," 102–3.

20. Two essays considering this issue are R. B. Reaves, "Crime and Punishment in the Detective Fiction of Dorothy L. Sayers," in *As Her Whimsey Took Her,* 1–13; and R. D. Stock and Barbara Stock, "The Agents of Evil and Justice in the Novels of Dorothy L. Sayers," in Hanay, *As Her Whimsey Took Her,* 14–22.

21. Sayers, *Five Red Herrings,* 194–95; Sayers to Victor Gollancz, Sept. 20, 1930, *Letters,* 309–10; Freeman Wills Crofts, *Sir John McGill's Last Journey* (Catchogue, N.Y.: Buccaneer Books, 1930).

22. Sayers, "The Omnibus of Crime," 108; DeAndrea, *Encyclopedia Mysteriosa,* 79.

23. Sayers, *Five Red Herrings,* 272; Sayers, "The Omnibus of Crime," 79.

24. Sayers, "The Omnibus of Crime," 89.

25. For a comparison of Sayers's use of railways to that of Freeman Wills Crofts, see P. L. Scowcroft, "Railways and the Detective Fiction of Dorothy L. Sayers," *Proceedings of the Seminar, 1980* (Witham, Essex: Dorothy L. Sayers Historical and Literary Society, Archives, 1980).

26. Sayers to Victor Gollancz, Jan. 22, 1931, *Letters,* 311–12.

27. *Have His Carcase,* 14, 61.

28. Ibid., 187.

29. Ibid., 290.

30. Ibid., 112.

31. Sayers to Victor Gollancz, Sept.14, 1932, *Letters*, 322–23.

32. Sayers to Harold Bell, Mar. 12, 1933, *Letters*, 330.

33. Sayers, "Gaudy Night," 209–10. For a discussion of Sayers's plotting, focusing on *Murder Must Advertise*, see Stephen Hahn, "'Where Do Plots Come From?' Dorothy L. Sayers on Literary Invention," *Columbia Library Columns* 37 (Feb. 1988): 3–12.

34. Dorothy L. Sayers, *Murder Must Advertise* (New York: HarperPerennial, 1993), 118.

35. For a brief description of Sayers's most successful campaign, see "Do You Remember the Mustard Club?," pamphlet (Witham, Essex: Dorothy L. Sayers Historical and Literary Society, 1976).

36. Terrance L. Lewis, *A Climate for Appeasement* (New York: Peter Lang, 1991), 109–25.

37. Sayers, *Strong Poison*, 229.

5. LORD PETER ACHIEVES A BALANCE

1. Sayers, *Have His Carcase*, 278–79.

2. Taylor, *English History*, 262–97, 321–50; Graves and Hodge, *The Long Week-End*, 235–53.

3. Robert C. Tucker, *Stalin in Power: The Revolution from Above, 1928–1941* (New York: Norton, 1990); Sheila Fitzpatrick, *The Russian Revolution, 1917–1932*, 2d ed. (New York: Oxford University Press, 1994).

4. Victoria De Grazia, *How Fascism Ruled Women: Italy, 1922–1945* (Berkeley: University of California Press, 1992).

5. David Schoenbaum, *Hitler's Social Revolution: Class and Status in Nazi Germany, 1933–1939* (New York: Norton, 1997); Alan Bullock, *Hitler: A Study in Tyranny* (New York: Harper and Row, 1962).

6. Henry A. Turner, *German Big Business and the Rise of Hitler* (New York: Oxford University Press, 1985); Detlev J. K. Peukert, *Inside Nazi Germany: Conformity, Opposition, and Racism in Everyday Life* (London: Batsford, 1987).

7. Eksteins, *Rites of Spring*, 300–331; Raul Hilberg, *Perpetrators, Victims, Bystanders: The Jewish Catastrophe, 1933–1945* (New York: Aaron Asher Books, 1992).

8. Graves and Hodge, *The Long Week-End*, 312–45; Taylor, *English History*, 396–97.

9. Taylor, *English History*, 284–86, 374, 418–19.

10. Sayers, *Murder Must Advertise*, 19, 277.

11. Sayers to Muriel St. Clare Byrne, June 24, 1935, *Letters*, 350.

12. Sayers to Victor Gollancz, Sept. 26, 1935, *Letters,* 357.

13. Ibid., author's note, vii; Pauline Adams, *Somerville for Women: An Oxford College, 1879–1993* (Oxford: Oxford University Press, 1996); S. L. Clark, "Harriet Vane Goes to Oxford: *Gaudy Night* and the Academic Woman," *Sayers Review* 2, no. 3 (Aug. 1978): 22–43.

14. Sayers to Victor Gollancz, Sept. 26, 1935, *Letters,* 357; Dorothy L. Sayers, "Are Women Human?" in *Unpopular Opinions* (London: Victor Gollancz, 1946). Two discussions of Sayers and feminism are Laura Krugman Ray, "The Mysteries of *Gaudy Night*: Feminism, Faith, and the Depths of Character," *Mystery and Detection Annual* (Beverly Hills: D. Adams, 1973), 272–85; and Kathleen L. Maio, *Unnatural Women: A Feminist Study of Dorothy L. Sayers,* Women and Literature Ovular, Goddard/Cambridge Graduate Center (Oct. 1975).

15. For a discussion of Annie Wilson, see S. L. Clark, "The Female Felon in Dorothy L. Sayers' *Gaudy Night*," *Publication of the Arkansas Philological Association* 3 (1977): 59–67.

16. Sayers to Muriel St. Clare Byrne, Sept. 8, 1935, *Letters,* 354.

17. Sayers to Muriel St. Clare Byrne, July 16, 1935, *Letters,* 350.

18. Sayers to Ivy Shrimpton, Aug. 21, 1934, *Letters,* 341–42.

19. Sayers, "Gaudy Night," 211–12.

20. A persuasive discussion of this aspect of the story is Carolyn G. Hart, "*Gaudy Night*: Quintessential Sayers," *Sayers Centenary,* 45–50.

21. Reynolds, *Sayers: Her Life and Soul,* 265–67.

22. In 1935, Gollancz acquired the rights to the first four Wimsey novels from the original British publishers, reissuing each with the "Biographical Note" appended.

23. Sayers, "Biographical Note," in *Whose Body?* vii–xv.

24. Wilfred Scott-Giles, *The Wimsey Family* (London: Victor Gollancz, 1977).

25. Reynolds, *Sayers: Her Life and Soul,* 265–67; Sayers to C. W. Scott-Giles, Feb. 26, 28, Mar. 25, Apr. 10, 15, Aug. 5, 1936, *Letters,* 368–74, 381–85, 397–98.

26. Reynolds, *Sayers: Her Life and Soul,* 263–75.

27. Dorothy L. Sayers and Muriel St. Clare Byrne, *Busman's Honeymoon: A Detective Comedy,* published with Dorothy L. Sayers, *Love All: A Comedy of Manners* (Kent, Ohio: Kent State University Press, 1984).

28. Reynolds, *Sayers: Her Life and Soul,* 261–72.

29. For a brief discussion of marriage and the detective story, see P. D. James, "Ought Adam to Marry Cordelia?" *Murder Ink,* ed. Dilys Winn (New York: Workman Press, 1977), 68–69.

30. Dorothy L. Sayers, *Busman's Honeymoon: A Love Story With Detective Interruptions* (New York: HarperPerennial, 1993), 92, 115.

31. For a discussion of the marriage, see B. J. Rahn, "The Marriage of True Minds, in Dale, *Sayers Centenary,* 51–65.

32. Sayers and St. Clare Byrne, *Busman's Honeymoon* (play), 120.

33. Sayers and St. Clare Byrne, *Busman's Honeymoon* (play), 120.

34. Sayers, *Busman's Honeymoon* (novel), 349.

6. LORD PETER AND THE LONG WEEK-END

1. In a general review of mysteries published by *Time* in 1938, the author noted that "the erudite Dorothy Sayers is now one of the most popular of mystery writers; her successful *Murder Must Advertise* sold only 9,000 copies, her audience growing slowly with each book until her most recent. *Busman's Honeymoon* reached a high of 20,000." "Murder Market," *Time* 31 (Feb. 28, 1938): 67.

2. Alzina Stone Dale argues this position in *Maker and Craftsman,* 99–100; as does Brabazon, *Dorothy L. Sayers: A Biography,* 158; Hitchman, *Such a Strange Lady,* 112–13; and Durkin, *Dorothy L. Sayers,* 81.

3. Barbara Reynolds seems to lean toward new-found religious inspiration in *Sayers: Her Life and Soul,* 240; Catherine Kenney makes a stronger argument in *The Remarkable Case of Dorothy L. Sayers,* 215–16. Details on the composition of *Zeal of Thy House* may be found in Reynolds, 273ff.

4. Ralph E. Hone emphasizes this explanation, *Dorothy L. Sayers: A Literary Biography,* 82; David Coomes favors this as well, *Dorothy L. Sayers: A Careless Rage for Life,* 119.

5. Sayers to B. S. Sturgis, Apr. 9, 1937, *Letters,* 20–21; Sayers to Sir Henry Aubrey-Fletcher, Oct. 24, 1949, quoted in Reynolds, *Sayers: Her Life and Soul,* 339.

6. See Alzina Stone Dale, "Wimsey: Lost and Found," *The Armchair Detective* (Spring 1990): 142–51, esp. 145–46.

7. Janet Hitchman, *Such a Strange Lady,* 112; and Ralph E. Hone, *Dorothy L. Sayers,* 82, mention this possibility, though neither explores it.

8. Graves and Hodge, *The Long Week-End,* 346–65; Taylor, *English History,* 398–405.

9. Joachim Remak, *The Origins of the Second World War* (Englewood Cliffs, N.J.: Prentice-Hall, 1976).

10. Hugh Thomas, *The Spanish Civil War,* rev. ed. (New York: Harper and Row, 1977); George Orwell, *Homage to Catalonia* (New York: Harcourt Brace, 1938).

11. Graves and Hodge, *The Long Week-End,* 312–26; quotation, 315.

12. Taylor, *English History,* 389–437.

13. Sayers to Helen Simpson, July 2, 1936, *Letters,* 395.

14. Ibid., 396; Reynolds, *Sayers: Her Life and Soul,* 339–40.

15. The original manuscript of "Thrones, Dominations" is among the holdings in the Sayers Collection, Wade Center. Alzina Stone Dale provides a synopsis of the manuscript in "Wimsey: Lost and Found," 147–51; reprinted in *Sayers Centenary,* 67–78. The manuscript has now been completed and published: Dorothy L. Sayers and Jill Paton Walsh, *Thrones, Dominations* (New York: St. Martin's Press, 1998).

16. Dorothy L. Sayers, "Thrones, Dominations," Unpublished MS, MS 219, Sayers Collection, Wade Center, 92. The selection is misquoted in Dale, "Wimsey: Lost and Found," 150. Jill Paton Walsh renders this conversation correctly in Sayers and Walsh, *Thrones, Dominations*, 74.

17. Sayers, "Thrones, Dominations," MS 219, Sayers Collection, Wade Center. Jill Paton Walsh omitted the discussion of Peter's sexuality from her completed version of the novel. Apart from this omission, Walsh followed Sayers's storyline quite faithfully, reorganizing the pages in a sensible fashion but retaining Sayers's words almost verbatim. Roughly the first one-third of the completed version of *Thrones, Dominations* is Sayers; the remainder is the creation of Walsh.

18. Sayers, "Thrones, Dominations," 171; Sayers and Walsh, *Thrones, Dominations*, 31.

19. Sayers to L. C. Kempson, Dec. 20, 1936, *Letters*, 409–10.

20. Sayers to Nancy Pearn, Nov. 5, 1938, *Letters*, 94.

21. Sayers to Sir Donald Tovey, Apr. 18, 1936, *Letters*, 388–89.

22. Dorothy L. Sayers, *In the Teeth of the Evidence* (New York: Harper Perennial, 1993). All of the Wimsey short stories are gathered in Dorothy L. Sayers, *Lord Peter: A Collection of All the Lord Peter Wimsey Stories*, ed. James Sandoe (New York: Harper and Row, 1972).

23. Dorothy L. Sayers, "The Master Key," Unfinished MS, MS 133, Sayers Collection, Wade Center; Janet Thom, "Lord Peter Passes His Prime," *New Republic* 102 (Feb. 19, 1940): 253.

24. Dorothy L. Sayers, "The Wimsey Papers: Number 14, Harriet Vane to the Duchess of Denver," MS 242, Sayers Collection, Wade Center.

25. Dorothy L. Sayers, "Wimsey Papers," *The Spectator* (Nov. 1939 to Jan. 1940). Eleven "papers" appeared in all.

26. Sayers, "Wimsey Papers: Number 7, Extracts from the Private Diary of Lord Peter Wimsey," MS 242, Sayers Collection, Wade Center.

27. Sayers, "Talboys," *Lord Peter: Collection*, 431–53.

28. For an analysis of the moral themes in Sayers's detective fiction, see Janice Brown, *The Seven Deadly Sins in the Work of Dorothy L. Sayers* (Kent, Ohio: Kent State University Press, 1998), 53–214.

29. Sayers, "Are Women Human?" 106–13.

APPENDIX B: ON SAYERS AND THE SONNET

This epigraph is taken from Wordsworth's "Scorn not the Sonnet; Critic, you have frowned," *The Complete Poetical Works of Wordsworth*, ed. Andrew J. George (Boston: Houghton Mifflin, 1932), 4.

1. Cf. "The Phoenix and the Turtle," l. 28. *The Riverside Shakespeare*, ed. G. Blakemore Evans, et al. (Boston: Houghton Mifflin, 1997), 1891.

2. With which compare: "Pleasure might cause her reade, reading might make her know, / Knowledge might pitie winne, and pittie grace obtaine" (Sir Philip Sidney, "Astrophel and Stella," 1.3–4). The sonnet closes on the dictum,

"looke in thy heart and write." His "conceited . . . conclusion" notwithstanding, Wimsey doubtless followed Sidney's advice.

3. Cf. Alexander Pope's definition of wit, from "An Essay on Criticism," in *The Poems of Alexander Pope,* ed. John Butt (New Haven: Yale University Press, 1963), ll. 297–98.

4. *Complete Poems of W. H. Auden,* ed. Edward Mendelson (New York: Vintage, 1991), 126.

Bibliography

PRIMARY SOURCES

Auden, W[ystan] H[ugh]. *Complete Poems of W. H. Auden*. Edited by Edward Mendelson. New York: Vintage, 1991.

Brittain, Vera. *Testament of Youth*. London: Victor Gollancz, 1933.

Cournos, John. *The Devil is an English Gentleman*. New York: Liveright, 1932.

Crofts, Freeman Wills. *Sir John McGill's Last Journey*. Catchogue, N.Y.: Buccaneer Books, 1930.

Doyle, Arthur Conan. *The Complete Sherlock Holmes*. New York: Doubleday, 1930.

Faulkner, William. *As I Lay Dying*. New York: Random House, 1930.

——. *The Sound and the Fury*. New York: Random House, 1929.

Fitzgerald, F. Scott. *The Jazz Age*. New York: New Directions, 1996.

Joyce, James. *Ulysses*. 1922. Reprint, New York: Modern Library, 1961.

Orwell, George. "Antisemitism in Britain." In *The Collected Essays, Journalism, and Letters of George Orwell,* vol. 3. Edited by Sonia Orwell and Ian Angus. New York: Harcourt, Brace and World, 1968, 332–41.

Orwell, George. *Homage to Catalonia*. New York: Harcourt Brace, 1938.

Pound, Ezra. *Literary Essays of Ezra Pound*. 1935. Edited by T. S. Eliot. Reprint, New York: New Directions, 1968.

Pope, Alexander. *The Poems of Alexander Pope*. Edited by John Butt. New Haven: Yale University Press, 1963.

Remarque, Erich Maria. *Ian Westen Nichts Neues*. [1928]. *All Quiet on the Western Front*. Trans. A. W. Wheen. Boston: Little, Brown, 1929.

Sayers, Dorothy Leigh. "Are Women Human?" In *Unpopular Opinions*, 106–16.

——. *Busman's Honeymoon: A Love Story with Detective Interruptions*. 1935. Reprint, New York: HarperPerennial. 1993.

——. *Clouds of Witness*. 1926. Reprint, New York: HarperPerennial, 1993.

——. Eleven "Wimsey Papers." *The Spectator*. Nov. 1939–Jan. 1940.

——. *The Five Red Herrings*. (Previously published as *Suspicious Characters*. London: Victor Gollancz, 1931.) New York: HarperPerennial, 1993.

——. "Gaudy Night." In *Titles to Fame*. Edited by Dennis K. Roberts. London: Nelson, 1937. Reprinted in Haycraft, *Art of the Mystery Story*, 208–21.

——. *Gaudy Night*. 1935. Reprint, New York: HarperPerennial. 1993.

——, ed. *Great Short Stories of Detection, Mystery, and Horror,* First Series. London: Victor Gollancz, 1928.

——, ed. *Great Short Stories of Detection, Mystery, and Horror,* Second Series. London: Victor Gollancz, 1931.

——, ed. *Great Short Stories of Detection, Mystery, and Horror,* Third Series. London: Victor Gollancz, 1934.

——. *Hangman's Holiday.* London: Victor Gollancz, 1933.

——. *Have His Carcase.* 1932. Reprint, New York: HarperPerennial, 1993.

——. "How I Came to Invent the Character of Lord Peter." *Harcourt Brace News* 1 (July 15, 1936): 1–2.

——. *"In the Teeth of the Evidence," and Other Stories.* 1940. Reprint, New York: HarperPerennial, 1993.

——. Introduction to E. C. Bentley, *Trent's Last Case.* 1930. Reprint, New York: Carroll and Graf, 1991, x–xiii.

——. Introduction to *Great Short Stories of Detection, Mystery, and Horror,* First Series. Edited by Dorothy L. Sayers. London: Victor Gollancz, 1928. Reprinted as "The Omnibus of Crime," in Haycraft, *Art of the Mystery Story,* 71–109.

——. *The Letters of Dorothy L. Sayers, Volume I, 1899 to 1936: The Making of a Detective Novelist.* Edited by Barbara Reynolds. New York: St. Martin's Press, 1995.

——. *The Letters of Dorothy L. Sayers, Volume II, 1937 to 1943: From Novelist to Playwright.* Edited by Barbara Reynolds. New York: St. Martin's Press, 1997.

——. *Lord Peter Views the Body.* 1928. Reprint, New York: HarperPerennial, 1993.

——. *Lord Peter: A Collection of All the Lord Peter Wimsey Stories,* comp. James Sandoe. New York: Harper and Row, 1972.

——. "The Master Key." MS 133. Sayers Collection, Wade Center.

——. "The Mousehole: A Detective Fantasia in Three Flats." MS 138 (1921). Sayers Collection, Wade Center.

——. *Murder Must Advertise.* 1933. Reprint, New York: HarperPerennial, 1993.

——. *The Nine Tailors: Changes Rung on an Old Theme in Two Short Touches and Two Long Peals.* New York: Harcourt, Brace and Jovanovich, 1934.

——. "Notebook: The Nine Tailors." MS 151. Sayers Collection of the Marion E. Wade Center, Wheaton College, Wheaton, Illinois (cited as Sayers Collection, Wade Center).

——. "The Omnibus of Crime," in Haycraft, *Art of the Mystery Story.* New York: Carroll and Graf, 1992, 71–109.

——. *Strong Poison.* 1931. Reprint, New York: HarperPerennial, 1993.

——. "Studies in Sherlock Holmes." In *Unpopular Opinions,* 134–90.

——. "Thrones, Dominations." MS 219. Sayers Collection, Wade Center.

——. *Tristan in Brittany.* London: Ernest Benn, 1929.

——. *Unnatural Death.* 1927. Reprint, New York: HarperCollins, 1993.

——. *The Unpleasantness at the Bellona Club.* 1928. Reprint, New York: Harper-Perennial, 1993.

——. *Unpopular Opinions.* London: Victor Gollancz, 1946.

——. "Untitled." 1920. Sayers Collection, Wade Center.

——. "The Wimsey Papers: Numbers 7, 14"; "Extracts from the Private Diary of Lord Peter Wimsey"; "Harriet Vane to the Duchess of Denver." MS 242. Sayers Collection, Wade Center.

——. *The Zeal of Thy House.* New York: Harcourt Brace, 1937.

——. *Whose Body?* 1923. Reprint, New York: HarperCollins, 1995.

Sayers, Dorothy L., and Muriel St. Clare Byrne. *Busman's Honeymoon: A Detective Comedy/Love All: A Comedy of Manners.* (Second play solely by Sayers.) Kent, Ohio: Kent State University Press, 1984.

Sayers, Dorothy L., with Robert Eustace. *The Documents of the Case.* 1930. Reprint, New York: HarperPerennial Library, 1987.

Sayers, Dorothy L., and Jill Paton Walsh. *Thrones, Dominations.* New York: St. Martin's Press, 1998.

Shakespeare, William. *The Riverside Shakespeare,* 2d. ed. Gen ed. G. Blakemore Evans. Boston: Houghton Mifflin, 1997.

Silken, Jon, ed. *The Penguin Book of First World War Poetry.* London: Penguin, 1981.

Sylvester, Richard S., ed. *English Sixteenth-Century Verse: An Anthology.* New York: W. W. Norton, 1984.

Woolf, Virginia. "Mr. Bennett and Mrs. Brown." In *Collected Essays,* vol. 1. New York: Harcourt Brace, 1923, 319–37.

——. *Mrs. Dalloway.* New York: Harcourt Brace, 1925.

——. *To the Lighthouse.* New York: Harcourt Brace, 1927.

Wordsworth, William. *The Complete Poetical Works of Wordsworth.* Cambridge ed. Edited by Andrew J. George. Boston: Houghton Mifflin, 1932.

Secondary Sources

Adams, Michael C. C. *The Great Adventure: Male Desire and the Coming of World War I.* Bloomington: University of Indiana Press, 1990.

Adams, Pauline. *Somerville for Women: An Oxford College, 1879–1993.* Oxford: Oxford University Press, 1996.

Aird, Catherine. "It Was the Cat!" In Dale, *Sayers Centenary,* 79–86.

Anderson, Bonnie S. and Judith P. Zinsser. *A History of Their Own: Women in Europe from Prehistory to the Present,* vol. 2. New York: Harper and Row, 1988.

Basney, Lionel. "God and Peter Wimsey." *Christianity Today* 14 (Sept. 1973): 27–28.

——. "*The Nine Tailors* and the Complexity of Innocence." In Hanay, *As Her Whimsey Took Her,* 23–35.

Brabazon, James. *Dorothy L. Sayers: A Biography.* New York: Charles Scribner's Sons, 1981.

Braybon, Gail. "Women and the War." In Constantine, Kirby, and Rose, *The First World War in British History*, 141–67.

Brown, Janice. *The Seven Deadly Sins in the Work of Dorothy L. Sayers*. Kent, Ohio: Kent State University Press, 1998.

Bullock, Alan. *Hitler: A Study in Tyranny*. New York: Harper and Row, 1962.

Burleson, Bernard. "A Study of the Novels of Dorothy L. Sayers." Ph.D. diss., University of Texas, 1965.

Chandler, Raymond. "The Simple Art of Murder." *Atlantic Monthly* (Dec. 1944). Reprinted in Haycraft, *Art of the Mystery Story*, 222–37.

"Clarence Hatry." *The Banker* 13 (May 1985): 78–79.

Clark, S. L. "Harriet Vane Goes to Oxford: *Gaudy Night* and the Academic Woman." *Sayers Review* 2, no. 3 (Aug. 1978): 22–43.

———. "The Female Felon in Dorothy L. Sayers' *Gaudy Night*." *Publication of the Arkansas Philological Association* 3 (1977):59–67.

Clarke, Edward H. *Sex in Education: or, A Fair Chance for the Girls*. Boston: J. R. Osgood, 1873.

Clarke, Stephen P. *The Lord Peter Wimsey Companion*. New York: The Mysterious Press, 1985.

Constantine, Stephen, Maurice W. Kirby, and Mary B. Rose, eds. *The First World War in British History*. London: Edward Arnold, 1995.

Coomes, David. *Dorothy L. Sayers: A Careless Rage for Life*. Batavia, Ill.: Lion Publishing, 1992.

Cott, Nancy. "Passionlessness: An Interpretation of Victorian Sexual Ideology, 1790–1850." *Signs* 4 (1978): 219–36.

Dale, Alzina Stone, ed. *Dorothy L. Sayers: The Centenary Celebration*. New York: Walker and Company, 1993.

———. "Fossils in Cloud-Cuckoo Land." *Sayers Review* 3, no. 2 (Dec. 1978): 1–13.

———. *Maker and Craftsman: The Story of Dorothy L. Sayers*. Grand Rapids, Mich.: William B. Eerdmans, 1978.

———. "Wimsey: Lost and Found." *The Armchair Detective* (Spring 1990): 142–51.

De Grazia, Victoria. *How Fascism Ruled Women: Italy, 1922–1945*. Berkeley: University of California Press, 1992.

DeAndrea, William L. *Encyclopedia Mysteriosa*. New York: Prentice Hall, 1994.

Degler, Carl. "What Ought to Be and What Was: Women's Sexuality in the Nineteenth Century." *American Historical Review* 79(1974): 1467–90.

"Do You Remember the Mustard Club?" Pamphlet. Witham, Essex: Dorothy L. Sayers Historical and Literary Society, 1976.

Dobereiner, Peter. "My, But You're a Wonder, Sir." In Martin Davis, ed. *Bobby Jones: The Greatest of Them All*. Greenwich, Conn.: The American Golfer, 1996, 38–47.

Durkin, Mary Brian. *Dorothy L. Sayers*. Boston: Twayne Publishers, 1980.

Eksteins, Modris. *Rites of Spring: The Great War and the Birth of the Modern Age*. New York: Anchor Books, Doubleday, 1989.

Elkins, Aaron. "The Art of Framing Lies: Dorothy L. Sayers on Mystery Fiction." In Dale, *Sayers Centenary*, 99–107.

Ellis, John. *Eye-Deep in Hell: Trench Warfare in World War I*. Baltimore: Johns Hopkins University Press, 1976.

"The Exploits of Lord Peter Wimsey." *Times* (London), July 12, 1935, 9.

Fitzpatrick, Sheila. *The Russian Revolution, 1917–1932*, 2d ed. New York: Oxford University Press, 1994.

Fraisse, Genevieve and Michelle Perrot, eds. *A History of Women: Emerging Feminism from Revolution to World War*, vol. 4. Cambridge, Mass.: Belknap of Harvard, 1993.

Fussell, Paul. *The Great War and Modern Memory*. New York: Oxford University Press, 1975.

Gaillard, Dawson. *Dorothy L. Sayers*. New York: Frederick Ungar, 1981.

Gilbert, Colleen B. *Bibliography of the Works of Dorothy L. Sayers*. Hamden, Conn.: Archon Books, 1978.

Graves, Robert. *Good-Bye to All That*. New York: Doubleday, 1929.

—— and Alan Hodge. *The Long Week-End: A Social History of Great Britain, 1918–1939*. New York: W. W. Norton, 1963.

Green, Martin. "The Detection of a Snob: Martin Green on Lord Peter Wimsey." *The Listener* 69 (Mar. 14, 1963): 461.

Gregory, E. R. "Wilkie Collins and Dorothy L. Sayers." In Hanay, *As Her Whimsey Took Her*, 51–64.

Hahn, Stephen. "Theodocy in Dorothy L. Sayers' *Murder Must Advertise*." *Renascence* 41 (Spring 1989): 169–76.

——. "'Where Do Plots Come From?' Dorothy L. Sayers on Literary Invention." *Columbia Library Columns* 37 (Feb. 1988): 3–12.

Hale, Oron J. *The Great Illusion, 1900–1914*. 1st Torchbook ed. New York: Harper and Row, 1974.

Hall, Trevor H. *Dorothy L. Sayers: Ten Literary Studies*. Hamden, Conn.: Archon Books, 1980.

Hanay, Margaret P., ed. *As Her Whimsey Took Her*. Kent, Ohio: Kent State University Press, 1979.

——. "Harriet's Influence on the Characterization of Lord Peter Wimsey." In Hanay, *As Her Whimsey Took Her*, 36–50.

Harmon, Robert B., and Margaret A. Burger. *An Annotated Guide to the Works of Dorothy L. Sayers*. New York: Garland, 1977.

Hart, B. Liddell. *History of the First World War*. London: Pan Books, 1970.

Hart, Carolyn G. "*Gaudy Night*: Quintessential Sayers." In Dale, *Sayers Centenary*, 45–50.

Haycraft, Howard, ed. *The Art of the Mystery Story*. New York: Carroll and Graf, 1992.

Heilbrun, Carolyn. "Dorothy L. Sayers: Biography Between the Lines." In Dale, *Sayers Centenary*, 1–14.

——. "Reappraisals: Sayers, Lord Peter and God." Reprinted in Sayers, *Lord Peter*, 431–46.

Hilberg, Raul. *Perpetrators, Victims, Bystanders: The Jewish Catastrophe, 1933–1945*. New York: Aaron Asher Books, 1992.

Hitchman, Janet. *Such a Strange Lady: A Biography of Dorothy L. Sayers*. New York: Harper and Row, 1975.

Hobsbawm, Eric. *The Age of Empire: 1865–1914*. London: Weidenfeld and Nicholson, 1987.

Hodge, Jonathon. "Chronology." *Sayers Review* 1, no. 4 (July 1977): 10.

Hone, Ralph E. *Dorothy L. Sayers: A Literary Biography*. Kent, Ohio: Kent State University Press, 1979.

Hynes, Samuel. *A War Imagined: The First World War and English Culture*. London: Bodley Head, 1990.

Jaffe, Thomas, ed. "Clarence Who?" *Forbes* 146 (July 9, 1990): 120.

James, P. D. "Ought Adam to Marry Cordelia?" *Murder Ink*. Edited by Dilys Winn. New York: Workman Press, 1977, 68–69.

Jann, Rosemary. *The Adventures of Sherlock Holmes: Detecting Social Order*. New York: Twayne Publishers, 1995.

Jones, Kevin I. *Conan Doyle and the Spirits: the Spiritualist Career of Sir Arthur Conan Doyle*. Wellingsborough, England: Aquarium Press, 1989.

Keating, H. R. F. "Dorothy L.'s Mickey Finn." In Dale, *Sayers Centenary*, 129–38.

——. *Murder Must Appetize*. London: Lemon Tree Press, 1975.

Kenney, Catherine. "The Comedy of Dorothy L. Sayers." In Dale, *Sayers Centenary*, 139–50.

——. *The Remarkable Case of Dorothy L. Sayers*. Kent, Ohio: Kent State University Press, 1990.

Kindleberger, Charles. *The World in Depression, 1929–1939*. Rev. ed. Berkeley: University of California Press, 1986.

Laslett, Peter. *The World We Have Lost: England Before the Industrial Age*. 3rd ed. New York: Charles Scribner's Sons, 1984.

Lee, Geoffrey A. "The Wimsey Saga." *Proceedings of the Seminar, 1977*. Witham, Essex: Dorothy L. Sayers Historical and Literary Society, Archives, 2–12.

Lewis, Terrance L. *A Climate for Appeasement*. New York: Peter Lang, 1991.

——. *Dorothy L. Sayers' Wimsey and Interwar British Society*. Lewiston, Maine: Edwin Mellon Press, 1994.

"Little 'Tecs' Have Little Crooks." *New Statesman and Nation* 7 (May 1932): 594.

Lowerson, John. *Sport and the English Middle Classes*. Manchester: Manchester University Press, 1993.

Maio, Kathleen L. *Unnatural Women: A Feminist Study of Dorothy L. Sayers.* Women and Literature Ovular. New York: Goddard/Cambridge Graduate Center, October 1975.

Mayer, Arno. *The Politics and Diplomacy of Peacemaking.* New York: Random House, 1973.

McCrumb, Sharyn. "Where the Bodies are Buried: The Real Murder Cases in the Crime Novels of Dorothy L. Sayers." In Dale, *Sayers Centenary,* 87–98.

McGregor, Deborah Kuhn. *From Midwives to Medicine: the Birth of American Gynecology.* New Brunswick, N.J.: Rutgers University Press, 1998.

——. *Sexual Surgery and the Origins of Gynecology: J. Marion Sims, His Hospital, and His Patients.* New York: Garland Press, 1989.

Mellard, James. *The Exploded Form: The Modernist Novel in America.* Philadelphia: University of Pennsylvania Press, 1980.

Morris, Virginia B. "Arsenic and Blue Lace: Sayers' Criminal Women." *Modern Fiction Studies* 29 (Autumn 1983): 485–95.

"Murder Market." *Time,* Feb. 28, 1938, 67.

Patterson, Nancy-Lou. "Images of Judaism and Anti-Semitism in the Novels of Dorothy L. Sayers." *Sayers Review* 2, no. 2 (June 1978): 17–24.

Peukert, Detlev J. K. *Inside Nazi Germany: Conformity, Opposition, and Racism in Everyday Life.* London: Batsford, 1987.

Phillips, Gordon. "The Social Impact." In Constantine, Kirby, and Rose, *The First World War in British History,* 106–40.

Poovey, Mary. *Uneven Developments: The Ideological Work of Gender in Mid-Victorian England.* Chicago: University of Chicago Press, 1988.

Rahn, B. J. "The Marriage of True Minds." In Dale, *Sayers Centenary,* 51–65.

Ray, Laura Krugman. "The Mysteries of *Gaudy Night*: Feminism, Faith, and the Depths of Character." *Mystery and Detection Annual.* Beverly Hills: D. Adams, 1973, 272–85.

Reaves, R. B. "Crime and Punishment in the Detective Fiction of Dorothy L. Sayers." In Hanay, *As Her Whimsey Took Her,* 1–13.

Remak, Joachim. *The Origins of the Second World War.* Englewood Cliffs, N.J.: Prentice-Hall, 1976.

——. *The Origins of World War I, 1871–1914,* 2nd ed. New York: Harcourt Brace, 1974.

——. *Sarajevo: The Story of a Political Murder.* New York: Criterion Books, 1959.

Renshaw, Patrick. *Nine Days That Shook Britain: The 1926 General Strike.* Garden City, N.Y.: Anchor Books, Doubleday, 1976.

Reynolds, Barbara. *Dorothy L. Sayers: Her Life and Soul.* New York: St. Martin's Press, 1993.

——. "The Origin of Lord Peter Wimsey." *Sayers Review* 2, no. 1 (May 1978): 1–16, 21.

Rose, Mary B. "Britain and the International Economy." In Constantine, Kirby, and Rose, *The First World War,* 231–51.

Routley, Erik. *The Puritan Pleasures of the Detective Story: A Personal Monograph.* London: Victor Gollancz, 1972.

Schoenbaum, David. *Hitler's Social Revolution: Class and Status in Nazi Germany, 1933–1939.* New York: Norton, 1997.

Scott-Giles, Wilfred. *The Wimsey Family.* London: Victor Gollancz, 1977.

Scowcroft, P. L. "Railways and the Detective Fiction of Dorothy L. Sayers." *Proceedings of the Seminar, 1980.* Witham, Essex: Dorothy L. Sayers Historical and Literary Society, Archives, 1980.

Smith, Malcolm. "The War and British Culture," in Constantine, Kirby, and Rose, *First World War in British History,* 168–83.

Smith-Rosenberg, Carroll. *Disorderly Conduct: Visions of Gender in Victorian America.* New York: Alfred A. Knopf, 1985.

Spender, Stephen. *The Struggle of the Modern.* Berkeley: University of California Press, 1963.

Steiner, Zara S. *Britain and the Origins of the First World War.* New York: St. Martin's Press, 1979.

Stevenson, Randall. *Modernist Fiction: An Introduction.* Lexington: University of Kentucky Press, 1992.

Stock, R. D., and Barbara Stock. "The Agents of Evil and Justice in the Novels of Dorothy L. Sayers." In Hanay, *As Her Whimsey Took Her,* 14–22.

Stokesbury, James L. *A Short History of World War I.* New York: William Morrow and Company, 1981.

Stuart, Ian. "D. L. S.: An Unsteady Throne?" In Dale, *Sayers Centenary,* 23–30.

Symons, Julian. *The Detective Story in Britain.* Harlow, Essex: Longman, Greens and Company, 1969.

Taylor, A. J. P. *English History, 1914–1945.* Oxford: Oxford University Press, 1965.

"The Exploits of Lord Peter Wimsey." *Times* (London), July 12, 1935, 9.

Thom, Janet. "Lord Peter Passes His Prime." *New Republic* 19 (Feb. 1940): 253.

Thomas, Hugh. *The Spanish Civil War.* Rev. ed. New York: Harper and Row, 1977.

Tucker, Robert C. *Stalin in Power: The Revolution from Above, 1928–1941.* New York: Norton, 1990.

Turner, Henry A. *German Big Business and the Rise of Hitler.* New York: Oxford University Press, 1985.

Valenze, Deborah. *The First Industrial Woman.* Oxford: Oxford University Press, 1995.

Van Creveld, Martin. *Command in Wartime.* Cambridge, Mass.: Harvard University Press, 1977.

——. *Supplying War.* Cambridge: Cambridge University Press, 1977.

Walkowitz, Judith R. *City of Dreadful Delight: Narratives of Sexual Danger in Late-Victorian London*. Chicago: University of Chicago Press, 1992.

——. *Prostitution and Victorian Society: Women, Class, and the State*. New York: Cambridge University Press, 1980.

Watson, Colin. *Snobbery with Violence: Crime Stories and Their Audience*. London: Eyre and Spottiswoode, 1971.

"The Exploits of Lord Peter Wimsey." *Times* (London), July 12, 1935, 9.

Winter, Denis. *Death's Men: Soldiers of the Great War*. London: Penguin Books, 1979.

Winter, Jay. *Sites of Memory, Sites of Mourning: The Great War in European Cultural History*. Cambridge: Cambridge University Press, 1995.

Wright, Willard Huntington. Introduction to *The Great Detective Stories*. Edited by Willard Huntington Wright. New York: Charles Scribner's Sons, 1927. Reprinted as "The Great Detective Stories," in Haycraft, *Art of the Mystery Story*, 33–70.

Youngberg, Ruth Tanis. *Dorothy L. Sayers: A Reference Guide*. Boston: G. K. Hall, 1982.

Index

Conundrums for the Long Week-End
was designed by Christine Brooks;
composed in 10/13.5 Sabon Roman Old Style
with display type in Parisian
on a Macintosh G4 using PageMaker 6.5;
printed by sheet-fed offset lithography
on 50# Turin Book stock,
Smyth sewn and bound over binder's boards in Arrestox cloth,
and wrapped with dust jackets printed in three colors
by Thomson-Shore, Inc., of Dexter, Michigan;
and published by
The Kent State University Press
Kent, Ohio 44242